Brian J. Robb is the *New York Times* and *Sunday Times* best-selling biographer of Leonardo DiCaprio, Johnny Depp, and Brad Pitt. He's also written acclaimed pop culture books on silent cinema, the films of Philip K. Dick, Wes Craven, Laurel and Hardy, and the TV series *Doctor Who* and *Star Trek*. He is co-editor of the popular website Sci-Fi Bulletin and lives in Edinburgh.

A BRIEF HISTORY OF

SUPERHEROES

Brian J. Robb

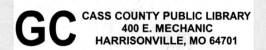

ROBINSON

RUNNING PRESS
PHILADELPHIA · LONDON

For Jerry and Joe and Stan and Jack
The true superheroes of comic book history

Constable & Robinson Ltd
55–56 Russell Square
London WC1B 4HP
www.constablerobinson.com

First published in the UK by Robinson,
An imprint of Constable & Robinson, 2014

A copy of the British Library Cataloguing in
Publication data is available from the British Library

ISBN 978-1-47211-055-8 (paperback)
ISBN 978-1-47211-070-1 (ebook)

1 3 5 7 9 10 8 6 4 2

First published in the United States in 2014 by Running Press Book Publishers,
A Member of the Perseus Books Group

Books published by Running Press are available at special discounts for bulk purchases
in the United States by corporations, institutions, and other organizations. For more
information, please contact the Special Markets Department at the Perseus Books
Group, 2300 Chestnut Street, Suite 200, Philadelphia, PA 19103, or call (800) 810-4145,
ext. 5000, or email special.markets@perseusbooks.com.

US ISBN: 978-0-7624-5231-6
US Library of Congress Control Number: 2013954852

9 8 7 6 5 4 3 2 1
Digit on the right indicates the number of this printing

Running Press Book Publishers
2300 Chestnut Street
Philadelphia, PA 19103-4371

Visit us on the web!
www.runningpress.com

Typeset by TW Typesetting, Plymouth, Devon

Printed and bound in the UK

CONTENTS

PART 1: ORIGINS!

I

COMIC BOOKS TO BLOCKBUSTERS: THE RISE OF THE SUPERHERO

Imagine a young American boy, ten or twelve years old, picking up a new comic book at the local drug store or newsstand, pestering their parents for a dime to buy it. It's April 1938, and the comic the kid has in his hands is something new, something called *Action Comics*. He's never seen it before, and it says '#1', right there on the cover. And, boy, what a cover . . .

Under the sizeable Action Comics logo and the 10¢ price slug, there's a picture the kid just can't believe. There's a guy dressed like a circus strongman (blue bodysuit, red trunks, red cape waving in the wind), and he's lifting a car above his head and smashing it into a rock face. There's a cowering man on the ground beneath the car, and two others, one running away in the background, the other coming straight out of the cover towards the reader, his head gripped in his hands in terror. What is all this about?

The introduction of Superman (the guy in the cape) was a seismic moment in American pop culture. It's unlikely that hypothetical young comic book reader knew that at the time – the guys at DC Comics who'd published the book certainly didn't. Only Jerry Siegel and Joe Shuster, a pair of creative Cleveland teenagers who dreamed up Superman, had any idea he might catch on. Years before they'd even been professionally published, original sketches of an action hero who would later become Superman were adorned with scribbled notes patterned after the kind of hype Jerry and Joe saw on American news-stands in the Thirties: 'The smash hit strip of 1936' and 'The strip destined to sweep the nation!' They were modest young men, but these guys had big dreams.

Even more astonishing, not only to Siegel and Shuster, but also to the kids who bought, read, and (more often than not) tossed away *Action Comics* #1 is what those comics would one day be worth. Today, it is estimated that fewer than 100 copies of that first issue remain in existence. *Action Comics* #1 (graded 8/10 on the accepted quality measurement) was the first-ever comic book to sell for $1 million, in 2010. That same year a second copy (graded 8.5) sold for $1.5 million. Actor Nicolas Cage (once cast as Superman for an unmade movie) had his copy of *Action Comics* #1 stolen in 2000, only for it to be recovered in 2011, and then sold for $2.16 million. That's a lot of dimes . . .

That same kid from 1938, a couple of years older, might have been in a movie house to see the first instalment of the 1941 Captain Marvel serial, the first comic book superhero to make it to the movies. He probably also saw *The Phantom* (1943), based on a newspaper strip hero; *Batman* (1943), the dark knight of the comics; and *Captain America* (1944), the wartime superhero who punched out Hitler. He definitely listened to the Forties Superman radio serial, three times a week after school, and maybe his younger brother or sister saw the *Superman* serial when that character finally made his movie debut in 1948. Little could they have imagined the sights and sounds of twenty-first-century superhero cinema, a period where summer movie blockbusters are dominated by characters first created in the four-colour comics of the Thirties and Forties, and dramatically developed in the Sixties.

The two companies that drove the superhero revolution in pop culture are now huge commercial enterprises whose productions dominate summer movie screens. *The Avengers* (2012), based on a superhero team created in the Sixties for Marvel Comics, is the third-highest-grossing film of all time having taken $1.5 billion worldwide. DC Entertainment is teaming up its top two superheroes, Superman and Batman, in one highly anticipated movie in 2015. It took until the twenty-first century for digital effects to reach a stage where what had long played on the comic book page could truly be brought to the screen. Now, the biggest audiences for superheroes are in cinemas and on DVD, not reading the comics that first gave birth to them.

From their secret origins in myth and legend, as well as in the adventurers of nineteenth-century pulp fiction heroes, the first comic book superheroes, Superman and Batman, gave rise to an all-conquering genre. Most superheroes fall somewhere on the scale between those two, who are in so many ways natural opposites. Superman stands in the light, a figure of action who wears no mask; his alter ego Clark Kent is from a rural background. Batman is a creature of the night, a figure of mystery, who hides behind a mask better to instil fear in his criminal prey in the urban jungle of Gotham.

What are the core ingredients that made up the American comic book superhero as first established by Superman in *Action Comics* #1 in 1938? Most superhero figures have an unusual start in life, often requiring them to leave their homes to avoid a terrible fate. Superman's life-saving escape from Krypton as a baby is the urtext for this superhero trope. Similarly, a vague history in youth helps – growing up on a nondescript Kansas farm – as it allows future writers to fill in the blanks or reinvent the specifics. Parents are often removed, as with Superman and Batman, as it makes the hero more vulnerable. Becoming an orphan seems to be important to making many superheroes self-reliant from an early age.

The key attribute of many, if not most, superheroes is some kind of super-power. Superman can travel at great speed, has super strength and can fly. Some superheroes simply rely on perfecting their unique human skills or attributes, as in the case of Batman, Iron Man, or Green Arrow. Other regularly seen attributes include a fatal weakness or a defect to be overcome, including Superman's aversion to Kryptonite, Daredevil's blindness, or the Hulk's inability to control his wrath-driven transformations. Superheroes sport almost magical weaponry, including Thor's hammer and Green Lantern's power ring.

Superheroes exhibit a strong moral code and a selfless dedication to the public good: they're usually out to do the right thing regardless of any possible rewards and often at the expense of their own personal lives. The motivation for this crime-fighting life is often deeply personal: the death of Spider-Man's Uncle Ben at the hands of a mugger, or the killing of Bruce Wayne's parents. For Superman his humanitarian service is core to his being, while for someone like Wonder Woman it is a formal calling, a selfless role to be fulfilled willingly. Such figures often adopt a secret identity, both to conceal their unusual powers and abilities, but also to allow them to operate in the world as a near-normal figure, so Superman's alter ego is *Daily Planet* reporter Clark Kent, while Batman is the philanthropist millionaire Bruce Wayne. Both these key figures, and many others have troubled romantic lives, usually as a result of their complex secret lives. Many adopt specific costumes with distinctive insignia or themes, such as Superman's shield-encased S-symbol, Batman's identification as a bat-like figure, or Spider-Man's web symbolism woven across his outfit.

The stories featuring these superheroes often include a supporting cast of assistants, recurring characters who are the hero's friends, co-workers, or potential romantic partners. There's also a rogues' gallery of villains (super- or otherwise) who function as the heroes' antagonists, including such classic foes as Lex Luthor (opposite Superman), the Joker (Batman), and the Green Goblin (Spider-Man). Often the superhero's mirror image, the super-villain may also adopt an outlandish costume, use a variety of super-weapons, and enact a myriad of evil plans. They are always defeated, but they always return to wreak havoc once again . . .

For superheroes, being independently wealthy (like Bruce Wayne, the X-Men's Professor Xavier, or Green Arrow's Oliver Queen) can come in handy, as it then affords the hero a secret base or hidden headquarters (such as Batman's Batcave), and a way to pay for all the vehicles, weapons and supplies a hero might need.

Many of these characteristics were established by the first comic book superheroes – Superman, Batman, Captain Marvel and the Flash – while their successors, rivals, and equals would often be born out of a need by their creators to react against these original superhero models. As comic book superheroes matured, through the propaganda of the war years of the Forties, into the censorious Fifties, where they were under attack, and through the counterculture of the Sixties that gave birth to many new superheroes, they developed and diversified in all sorts of imaginative and fascinating ways. After a period of relative stagnation and decline in the Seventies, the superhero was reinvented in the Eighties and Nineties, as darker, more serious figures, often revived in creator-owned independently published comic books and graphic novels. After several false starts, the twenty-first century saw the domination of the movies by superhero franchises, including Batman, Superman, The X-Men and Spider-Man.

The concept of the superhero is a uniquely American creation, born of troubled economic times, and forever changing to better fit with new audiences and new challenges. This is the story of the rise of the American superhero, from mass appeal in lowly Depression-era comic books to their blockbuster success in the twenty-first century's most popular movie franchises.

A note on comic book cover dates . . . Most comic books were on sale at news-stands up to two months before the date stated on the cover. Published cover dates are used throughout, and only when relevant is the actual month of publication highlighted. Comic book history is generally divided up into several widely recognized 'ages': the Golden Age is from 1938 to the mid-Fifties; the Silver Age from the mid-Fifties to 1970; the Bronze Age from 1970 to the mid-Eighties; and the Modern Age from the mid-Eighties to the twenty-first century. These divisions have been used in the text.

2

SECRET ORIGINS: THE PRE-HISTORY OF THE SUPERHERO

The classic American comic book superhero didn't emerge fully formed. Ancient myths and legends are littered with 'supermen', gifted by the gods with extraordinary powers. Folkloric heroes grew from figures like Robin Hood, while literature gave birth to masked avengers like the Scarlet Pimpernel. 'Penny Dreadfuls', dime novels, radio dramas, and movie serials all featured masked crime fighters, such as the Green Hornet and the Phantom. These mythological influences and myriad pulp magazine heroes would feed into the birth of the modern superhero, culminating in the creation of Superman in 1938.

The superhero template made popular through American comic books during the Depression originated in antiquity, in stories ancient cultures retold across centuries, forming the basis for today's myths and legends. Many told of a pantheon of gods and goddesses who boasted of superhuman prowess. Not all supernatural heroes were gods, far removed from everyday humanity. In some tales, humans might encounter gods and be endowed with superhuman powers. Others might be descended from the congress between gods and humans, and so inherit their abilities.

These stories told ancient peoples where they had come from, looking back to the remote past and offering a 'creation myth' account of their origins. The world in which these early peoples lived appeared to them to have been created, so required a creator, usually some 'thing' with greater powers than them – a god. These myths and legends were also ways of prolonging the power of an elite or the status quo of those in powerful positions within a tribe or society. They offered explanations of why things were as they were, explaining the roots of tribal customs, of their civilization's institutions, and the origins of their specific taboos.

Whether these myths and legends were distorted accounts of real world events, in which the gods were involved in human affairs; or allegorical stories representing natural forces and the tides of time; or simply an attempt to encapsulate a frightening world in human terms, they have come down to us as a set of tales that underlie our own popular storytelling. The mythological heroes of these ancient tales served as intermediaries between the human and the divine, with some active in both worlds.

Among the most common are the Greek legends: the word 'hero' is of Greek derivation, describing a warrior who is also a protector. The oldest surviving sources are the works of Homer, the *Iliad* and the *Odyssey*, focusing on the Trojan War (believed by the Greeks to have taken place in the twelfth or thirteenth century BC). The Greek pantheon of the Twelve Olympians – the Greek gods inhabiting Mount Olympus – consists of Zeus, Hera, Poseidon, Demeter, Athena, Hestia, Apollo, Artemis, Ares, Aphrodite,

Hephaestus, and Hermes. Many of their attributes would be applied to modern-day comic book superheroes (they might be the first superhero team). With a heritage traced back centuries, the canonical twelve secured their rule in a war with the Titans, an even older race of super-powered gods. Similar stories of a 'war in heaven', concerning the overthrow of an older generation or power base, were told across Europe and into the near east, with echoes in Scandinavian, Babylonian, and Judaic mythologies.

Zeus (descended from the Titans) and Hera were the King and Queen of the gods. Poseidon represented the seas, earthquakes, and tidal waves. Demeter was the god of fertility and the seasons, with Athena the goddess of wisdom, defence, and strategy. Hestia was a domestic goddess, while Apollo was the god of truth and prophecy. The huntress Artemis was the god of animals and the wild, Ares the god of war, and Aphrodite the goddess of love. Hephaestus was the god of metal and fire, while Hermes – with winged sandals – represented speed. Beyond these core twelve there were many more minor gods or demigods closely tied to the Olympians.

Direct comparisons can be drawn between the most famous comic book superheroes and these Greek forebears. Superman has roots in the divine hero Hercules (better known by this Roman name, he was Heracles to the Greeks). He was the greatest of Greek heroes, a paragon of masculinity with extraordinary strength. Superman co-creator Jerry Siegel admitted his superhero was '. . . a character like Samson, Hercules, and all the strongmen I ever heard of rolled into one, only more so . . .' Similarly, Wonder Woman is a variation on Athena, from the Greek legends of the Amazons, a nation of all-female warriors. The Hulk is an Earthbound version of Ares, an angry god always ready for a fight. While none are a simple one-to-one match, they share enough core elements for it to be possible to pair up Greeks gods and superheroes such as

Poseidon with Aquaman, or Hermes with the Flash. The Greek tales of heroes and their deeds provided a ready-made template for superheroes. Marvel Comics writer and editor Stan Lee once referred to superheroes as '. . . a twentieth century mythology' featuring '. . . an entire contemporary mythos, a family of legends that might be handed down to future generations'.

Their adventures sound like the tales of comic book superheroes. Perhaps the first legendary Greek superhero was Perseus, whose defeat of the monstrous Titans informed the founding myths of the Olympians. A demigod, Perseus killed the Gorgon Medusa before rescuing Andromeda from a sea monster unleashed by Poseidon. Perseus was enacting the prophecy of the Oracle, fulfilling his heroic destiny. Another classic tale chronicles the Labours of Hercules. These twelve tasks were performed by strongman Hercules as a penance for killing his sons during a spell of madness. These Greek legends, alongside others about Achilles, Jason and the Argonauts, or Theseus and the Minotaur, were a rich source of story and characters for the most successful superheroes. The creators of DC Comics and Marvel Comics drew freely upon these tales and legends for their modern fantasy epics.

The existence of these god-like heroes is not enough on their own to explain the mythic roots of the modern comic book superhero. Also required is the notion of the 'heroic quest', a mono-myth found in similar forms across many cultures, usually in the shape of epic tales or legends. It is best summed up in scholar Joseph Campbell's idea of the 'hero's journey'. Campbell describes the essentials: 'A hero ventures forth from the world of the common day into a world of supernatural wonder: fabulous forces are there encountered and a decisive victory is won: the hero comes back from this mysterious adventure with the power to bestow boons on his fellow men.'

For example, the Mesopotamian epic of Gilgamesh, whose Old Babylonian variation dates back to the eighteenth century BC, recounts the story of the semi-divine but mortal King of Uruk, Gilgamesh, who battles and defeats his opposite, the wild man Enkidu. Together (like a superhero and his sidekick) they embark on a heroic journey to the Cedar Mountains to defeat the monstrous guardian, Humbaba. Further adventures see the pair battle the Bull of Heaven, after Gilgamesh spurns the advances of the goddess Ishtar. After Enkidu's death, brought about by Ishtar, Gilgamesh embarks on a quest for immortality. Marvel Comics used Gilgamesh directly as one of the Eternals, immortals who have long been mistaken for gods.

As well as establishing the sidekick (also seen in Iolaus with Hercules, and Patroclus with Achilles), the Gilgamesh tale sees the hero renounce sexual temptation, as do many comic book heroes. Gilgamesh is also a figure who seeks transcendent power, a way to overcome the limits of the normal physical world (in his case, the power to live forever). Most superheroes (not all, Batman is merely a physically exceptional, gadget-aided man) exhibit an attribute that allows them to overcome Earthly limitations, whether it is unpowered flight, super strength, or super speed.

Similarly, Homer's Greek epics provided the outline for many a hero's journey, the 'epic tale' chronicling the heroic deeds and major events that impact upon history. From the Epic of Gilgamesh, through the Indian Sanskrit *Mahabharata*, to Homer's *Iliad* and *Odyssey*, right up to the Roman *Aeneid* by Virgil, the epic tale took shape and proved to be a major influence on the creation and evolution of later superhero stories.

Another example is the Old English epic *Beowulf*, dating from some point between the eighth and the early eleventh century, that tells of a Scandinavian adventurer who comes to the aid of the King of the Danes, Hroögar, whose kingdom is under attack by the monster Grendel. Beowulf slays

both the monster and its mother, returning to his home-
land a hero, and becomes king of his people. Around fifty
years later, the older Beowulf kills a dragon, but is himself
fatally wounded in the fight.

Beowulf and other ancient epics shaped a template that
is applicable to many superhero origin stories, such as that
of Captain Marvel. Youthful radio reporter Billy Batson
hears Campbell's 'call to adventure' when he is chosen to
become the champion of the wizard Shazam. He travels
underground via a mysterious subway system, encounters
Shazam and is reborn into the world changed. Whenever he
utters the wizard's name, he is struck by a magic lightning
bolt and transformed into an adult superhero, the world's
mightiest mortal: Captain Marvel. Throughout the Forties,
Captain Marvel comic books outsold even those featuring
Superman.

Alongside myths and legends, characters from folklore
helped shape superhero archetypes. Superheroes often
follow a code, a set of rules of behaviour that obliges them
to fight on behalf of the poor, the downtrodden, and the
oppressed, and against the criminal and the wrong-doer.
The basis of this may come from the English folk hero
Robin Hood, who famously robbed from the rich and gave
to the poor. The most popular retelling of the Robin Hood
legend has him as a late-twelfth-century outlaw. He is a
supporter of King Richard the Lionheart, whose absence
on the Third Crusade has enabled the misrule of the kingdom by his brother, John. Various retellings play with
Hood's social status – in some versions he's a commoner,
in others an aristocrat – but the core has him battling on
behalf of the common people against their oppression.

Robin Hood is an influential precursor of the superhero.
He wears a 'costume', that serves to both hide him in the
forest (it is traditionally Lincoln green) and to disguise his
true identity. Both Superman and Batman, among many
others, use costumes to alternately stand out or blend in

with their environments and to disguise their alternative identities as Clark Kent and Bruce Wayne. Robin Hood invariably fights for right, against imposed might, and that's also the mission statement of most modern super-heroes. Both Robin Hood and many superheroes are out-laws, in the sense that they place the delivery of justice over and above strict adherence to the law, especially if they are fighting against a corrupt establishment. Robin Hood seeks both to alleviate the suffering of the poor, and – just as importantly – to punish oppressors: he's an inspiration to such overtly vigilante characters as Batman.

Stories of super-men, those among humanity endowed with powers beyond mere mortals, are as old as human his-tory, as is the making of pictures. Cave drawings in France and Spain from between 10,000 and 25,000 years ago record everyday events and heroic feats. From Egyptian tomb paintings and hieroglyphics from around 1300 BC, to surviving examples of medieval sequential art such as the Bayeux Tapestry (a seventy-metre length of embroidered cloth depicting the Norman conquest of England, circa AD 1100), and Mexican codices, an early form of bound book circa AD 1500, men and women have created images that told stories, often of adventure or amazing achieve-ments. The earliest surviving examples of illustrated nar-rative – a story told through sequential images and words – include Greek friezes and the Roman Trajan's Column from AD 113. Since illustrated manuscripts and picture-based versions of Bible stories were used to spread the 'Word' to the illiterate (such as the Biblia pauperum, or Paupers' Bible), the urge to communicate through stories told in pictures has been irresistible.

For most of these examples, the viewer or reader had to go to the story, as it was often in a fixed geographi-cal location, either painted directly onto or hung upon a wall. It was only with the invention of mechanical printing techniques in the fifteenth century and the later development of publishing as a mass medium in the West that graphic storytelling came to the reader. Moveable type was developed in China early in the second millennium AD, but it would take several centuries for the techniques to spread to Europe. The first printing press in Europe appeared around 1450, introduced by Johannes Gutenberg in Germany, followed by William Caxton in Britain.

The mass-market printing revolution in the sixteenth century resulted in the spread of printed books, and among the most popular (and the most numerous) were the works of Dutch Renaissance theologian Erasmus and the religious tracts of Martin Luther, German professor of theology. By the seventeenth and eighteenth centuries the first newspapers – regular printed illustrated broadsheets of information and current affairs – began appearing across Europe, initially in Germany. The first successful British daily newspaper – the *Daily Courant* – appeared in 1702. The earliest American newspaper appeared in the colonial period, with Benjamin Franklin's older brother James producing the *New England Courant* in 1721.

Much early printed material was religious, but by the eighteenth century, artists such as painter and printmaker William Hogarth, and caricaturists James Gillray and Thomas Rowlandson, were combining words and pictures to comment on politics, fashion, and social mores. Hogarth augmented satirical images with textual captions (anticipating comic book speech balloons). Comics historian Maurice Horn claims that Hogarth's works 'can be acknowledged as the first direct forerunners of the comic strip'. Prior to Hogarth and his contemporaries there had been an artistic convention of using 'speech scrolls' in the Medieval and Renaissance periods and in some older Mesoamerican art – literally a scroll unfurling from the mouth with text indicating what they were thinking or saying. Hogarth combined the attribution of speech with a sequential series of images to make a point or tell a story.

By the 1730s Hogarth was producing his 'moralizing art' in the form of the six-scene *A Harlot's Progress* (1732) and the eight-scene follow-up *A Rake's Progress* (1735). The first told of the desperate life of a poor country girl who becomes a prostitute upon moving to London. The final images depict her death due to venereal disease and her funeral. Despite (or because of) its sensationalist subject matter, *A Harlot's Progress* was a huge success. More than 1,200 sets of engravings were sold to collectors for a guinea each, and pirated copies of Hogarth's work soon followed, before the artist obtained an Act of Parliament – the Engraving Copyright Act 1734 – that protected the producers of original works from others selling unauthorized copies. The eight frames of sequel *A Rake's Progress* depicted the dissolute life of Tom Rakewell, the son of a rich merchant who indulges in luxurious living, visiting brothels and gambling, only to end his life in the madhouse.

Early in the nineteenth century, Swiss artist Rodolphe Töpffer's sequential stories were told as pictures with extended captions running below (following Hogarth) and were available across Europe and throughout the United States, often in pirated editions. His innovation was to put the emphasis on entertainment, rather than 'moral improvement'. His *littérature en estampes* (picture stories) were published as albums, often over 100 pages in extent. In 1845, Töpffer outlined his approach to the 'picture story' in his *Essay on Physiognomy* noting that '. . . to construct a picture-story . . . you must invent some kind of play where the parts . . . form a satisfactory whole. You make a book: good or bad, sober or silly, crazy or sound in sense.'

Although he regarded his work as having a potentially powerful impact, Töpffer was aware of the negative critical reaction surrounding such 'comic books' even at this early stage in their evolution: '. . . the picture story, which critics disregard and scholars scarcely notice, has greater influence at all times, perhaps even more than written literature'. He recognized the power of the combination of images with text in sequence, as one without the other would not contain the same meanings readers would ascribe to them combined in interaction. Töpffer's work inspired imitators, especially Gustave Doré whose picture story album *The Labours of Hercules* (1847) followed Töpffer's example, although he told the tale of this ancient 'superman' through more accomplished art than Töpffer.

Newspapers and magazines, such as *Punch* (from 1841), often carried caricatures after the style of Hogarth, commenting on current news events and prominent society personalities, which by then were becoming known as 'cartoons'. In Germany in 1865, caricaturist William Busch developed one of the earliest comic strips, *Max and Moritz*. This followed the misadventures of two youthful troublemakers and featured moralistic stories told through illustration and rhyming couplets. In the United States, a newspaper war between Joseph Pulitzer's *New York World* and William Randolph Hearst's *New York Journal* was partly fought through the use of comic strips to attract readers. Pulitzer debuted *The Yellow Kid* in 1895, chronicling the life of the shaven-headed title character in a New York slum area called Hogan's Alley. Created by artist Richard Felton Outcault, *The Yellow Kid* presented '. . . a turn-of-the-century theater of the city, in which class and racial tensions of the new urban, consumerist environment were acted out by a mischievous group of New York City kids from the wrong side of the tracks.' Outcault innovated in the use of speech text to indicate direct character dialogue, although it was often written on the nightshirt of the 'yellow kid' (where a new yellow ink was tested by the printer, hence the nickname). The term 'comic book' was first used in 1897 to describe Outcault's 'McFadden's Row of Flats' supplement in the *New York Journal*.

Busch's work on *Max and Moritz* was a direct inspiration to a German immigrant to the United States, Rudolph Dirks, who created *The Katzenjammer Kids*, a comic strip about a pair of rebellious twins that ran in Hearst's *New York Journal* from 1897 for thirty-seven years. The strip was drawn by Harold H. Knerr, following Dirks's stories. As well as further developing the use of speech balloons after Outcault, Dirks innovated by introducing 'thought balloons' indicated by a series of broken bubbles leading to the word balloon, as well as by using such graphic symbols as a log being sawed through for loud snoring and sparkling stars to indicate pain.

The Pulitzer-Hearst newspaper war from 1887 saw the development of several popular comic strips. Among them were *The Little Bears* (1893–96), the first American strip to use recurring characters, with the first use of colour printing for comic strips appearing in 1897. By 1912, Hearst had introduced an entire page of his *New York Daily Journal* devoted solely to comic strips, thereafter colloquially known as the 'funny pages' or 'funny papers'. By 1922, magazine-style collections of reprinted daily newspaper comic strips were a regular feature on US news-stands. The stage was set for the rise of the four-colour comic books (after the four inks – cyan, magenta, yellow and black – used to produce full colour) and the arrival of the distinctive American superhero.

The silent movies of Douglas Fairbanks cemented the visual image of the masked avenger in the popular imagination in the early twentieth century, paving the way for comic book superheroes. Fairbanks played several swashbuckling characters in movies packed with derring-do and the righting of wrongs. Key among them were *The Mark of Zorro* (1920), *Robin Hood* (1922) and *The Black Pirate* (1926, the first full-length Technicolor film). These costumed heroes – Zorro wears a face mask and leaves his 'Z' mark behind to signify his presence – and pirate figures were central to the success of early swashbuckler movies, and Fairbanks's easy athleticism led to him embodying several of these characters.

Many of the early movie heroes drew upon characters from Victorian literature, several of whom owed an equal debt to the legends and stories of Robin Hood. Initially presented in a play in 1903, and then a novel from 1905, Baroness Orczy's Scarlet Pimpernel established the notion of the hero with a secret identity in the popular imagination (although not a hero, Robert Louis Stevenson's tale of *The Strange Case of Dr Jekyll and Mr Hyde*, 1886, prefigured the idea of a character with a dual identity). The Pimpernel is English aristocrat Sir Percy Blakeney who rescues French aristocrats from their fate as guests of Madame Guillotine during the French Revolution. The Scarlet Pimpernel exhibits several attributes that would later become standard superhero conventions, including a penchant for disguise, a wicked way with a signature weapon (a sword), and the ability to out-think and outwit his adversaries. He creates a popular image for himself by leaving behind a calling card depicting a scarlet pimpernel flower at each of his interventions. By drawing attention to his alter ego Blakeney creates a public furore and hides behind his public face as a slow-thinking, foppish playboy (like Bruce Wayne). While the French revolutionary authorities hunt for the masked man, Sir Percy establishes a network of supporters, the League of the Scarlet Pimpernel, that aid his endeavours – an inspiration for later superhero teams, such as the Justice League. Perhaps unsurprisingly, given her title of 'Baroness', Orczy was writing from the point of view of the nobility. The Scarlet Pimpernel fails as a proto-superhero as his fight is for the privileged rather than the ordinary.

The next step was Zorro, Johnston McCulley's black-masked outlaw who defended the poor of early California against tyrannical officials and other villains. Starting in

1919, McCulley's pulp hero appeared in *All Story Weekly*, one of many pulp magazines that ran serialized stories between the late 1800s and the Fifties. Zorro first appeared in the five-episode adventure *The Curse of Capistrano*, the alter ego of nobleman Don Diego de la Vega. Wearing a black cloak and a wide-brimmed sombrero, as well as a black cowl mask, Zorro uses a rapier sword to carve his distinctive 'Z' symbol in three swift strokes. As with the Scarlet Pimpernel, Don Diego plays the role of a dandy, wearing lace and avoiding violence as he's (supposedly) useless with a sword. Impoverished noblewoman Lolita Pulido has no time for the passionless Diego, but she is intrigued by the outlaw Zorro (just as Lois Lane spurns Clark Kent, but is fascinated by Superman). By night, Zorro strikes, avenging the helpless, punishing cruel politicians, and aiding the oppressed (his superhero code).

The first story concluded with Zorro publicly exposed, his secret identity revealed (a similar fate befell *Iron Man*'s Tony Stark). The unexpected success of the debut tale – which resulted in the Fairbanks movies – led to Zorro's secret identity being quickly re-established and more than sixty further stories from McCulley, up to the author's death in 1958 (the same year that Disney launched a popular *Zorro* television serial). Zorro would feature in over forty films, ranging from the Fairbanks silent movie to two films starring Antonio Banderas, *The Mask of Zorro* (1998) and *The Legend of Zorro* (2005).

Pulp fiction – whether in the form of the Victorian 'penny dreadfuls', the American short-story magazines, or the 'dime' novels of the early twentieth century, not to mention radio serials of the Twenties and Thirties – produced a variety of heroic and villainous characters that would influence the comic book superheroes of the late-Thirties and early-Forties. The British 'penny dreadfuls' – lurid serial magazines that cost one penny (or less), printed on cheap pulp paper, and aimed at working-class young readers – provided cheap escapism for a newly literate population. Charles Dickens' first works appeared in serial form, but the genre is best remembered for gothic and adventure tales, and introduced characters such as Sweeney Todd in *The Demon Barber of Fleet Street* (running 1846–7), real-life eighteenth-century highwayman Dick Turpin (whose exploits followed the Robin Hood model in the 254-instalment *Black Bess* serial, 1867–8), and the detective Sexton Blake (1893), heavily influenced by Arthur Conan Doyle's Sherlock Holmes (1887–1927). Holmes's 'deductive reasoning' might be a superpower (with the trademark deerstalker and pipe as a 'costume'), while the rarely seen Professor Moriarty provides a template for the super-villain, as did the pulp fiction embodiment of the 'yellow peril' in Sax Rohmer's Fu Manchu (1913–59, in works by Arthur Henry Sarsfield Ward, the true 'Sax Rohmer'). Equally, Holmes's chronicler Dr John Watson might be thought of as an archetypal superhero sidekick.

Other British fictional heroes, such as W. E. Johns' Biggles (pilot and adventurer James Bigglesworth, whose adventures ran from 1932 until Johns' death in 1968), John Buchan's Richard Hannay (in five novels, starting with *The Thirty-Nine Steps*, 1915), and Herman Cyril McNeile's Bulldog Drummond (1920–54), provided a kind of 'stiff upper lip' heroism of a duty-bound kind that saw selfless men (almost never women) embark upon uncertain adventures often simply for the thrill of it all.

Beyond these reckless Imperial adventurers, the American pulp magazines gave rise to the dedicated, altruistic crime fighter. Following in the masked exploits of Zorro were mesmerist the Shadow (1930), 'peak human' Doc Savage (1933), and the Spider (1933). Starting on magazine publisher Street & Smith's radio show *The Detective Hour* in July 1930, the Shadow introduced Lamont Cranston (although the character was initially anonymous, simply narrating stories), a crime-fighting vigilante who used psychic powers (primarily 'the power to cloud men's minds') to defeat his enemies. Writer Walter B. Gibson (under the nom de plume of 'Maxwell Grant') developed the character in print as an ambiguous figure, initially neither hero nor villain. Operating after dark, the Shadow had no compunction in breaking into properties and using fear to dissuade ne'er-do-wells from their nefarious activities. Various writers developed the character, initially an adventurer and crime fighter named Kent Allard (who later takes on the better-known Lamont Cranston identity), through countless short stories and numerous novels. The Shadow employs various helpers who might be thought of as sidekicks, such as his driver 'Moc' Shrevnitz, Harry Vincent, a man he saves from suicide, and newspaper reporter Clyde Burke. He even has his own film noir 'moll', in the shapely form of socialite Margo Lane. The Shadow's mixed approach to crime fighting means he both aids and is wanted by the police (a fate that later befell both Batman and Spider-Man). His enemies include mad scientists, international plotters, spies, and criminal kingpins, including recurring foes Shiwan Khan, the Voodoo Master, the Prince of Evil, and the Wasp. The best-recalled radio version of *The Shadow* had a young (only twenty-two) Orson Welles as Lamont Cranston between 1937 and 1938. *The Whistler* (1942–55) was a similar radio drama (later a B-movie series) knock-off of the Shadow.

There were echoes in the Shadow of Leslie Charteris's pulp novel hero the Saint, who first appeared in *Meet the Tiger* in 1928. Like the Shadow, Simon Templar was feared by the criminal underworld as he failed to play by the 'rules'. Templar battled what he referred to as 'the Ungodly', donating the proceeds of their crimes to charity (minus his 10 per cent 'finders' fee'). This 'Robin Hood of modern crime' was pursued internationally by the forces of law and order, and was occasionally helped out by a gang known as the Five Kings. Appearing in magazines and books from

1928 until 1983, the Saint featured in a series of B movies
and a long-running radio series with Vincent Price (among
others), before finding a home on television in the Sixties
and Seventies.

Other significant pulp fiction crime fighters who laid the
foundations for the age of the superhero included Doc Savage
and the Spider (both 1933). Savage was a heroic adventurer
created in-house for Street and Smith Publications, with
Lester Dent as the series' main contributor. Known as the
Man of Bronze (a superhero appellation, after the title of the
first adventure), Doc Savage featured in 181 editions of his
eponymous magazine between 1933 and 1949, before going
on to appear across other media (comics, radio, novels,
movies). Created following the success of the Shadow for
Street & Smith, Clark 'Doc' Savage had no superpowers,
but he had been raised from birth under 'scientific' supervision to be a perfect specimen of humankind, exhibiting
the best masculine attributes in intelligence, strength, and
physical prowess. Doc Savage was intended to be 'the best
a man could be', for the mid-Thirties, and the publisher's
ads for the novels billed him as a 'superman'. Among his
superior abilities were his photographic recall, great physical strength, wide knowledge of science, and mastery of
disguise and impersonation. Dent described the character
as a combination of the mind of Sherlock Holmes with the
physicality of Tarzan and the kindliness of Abraham Lincoln. From his base (a precursor of the Fantastic Four's HQ)
on the eighty-sixth floor of a skyscraper resembling the
Empire State Building, Savage fought evil with the aid of the
'fabulous five': a chemist, a lawyer, a builder, an electrical
engineer, and an archaeologist/geologist. A fleet of vehicles,
from cars and trucks to aircraft and boats were available to
him from a secret hangar on the Hudson River – financed
by gold donated from a Central American mine once held
by Mayans. Savage also had an assortment of useful gadgets and weapons at his disposal. He would retreat to his

'Fortress of Solitude' in the Arctic (pre-dating Superman's iconic icy base by several years). Rational science was the hallmark of the Doc Savage series, so no matter how outlandish a villain or device appeared to be, it would always have a fairly plausible scientific explanation, even if more than a few stretched the scientific reality of the time.

The Spider was developed by a rival pulp publisher, Popular Publications, in 1933 as a direct competitor for Street & Smith's the Shadow. Yet another millionaire playboy, Richard Wentworth passed his time fighting crime in New York wearing a black cape and a slouch hat – later he'd affect make-up or a face mask to create a figure more frightening to underworld villains (Batman's later motivation for his disguise). As with so many pulp detectives, the Spider was a master of disguise, often masquerading as small-time crook Blinky McQuade to gain intelligence from criminals. The often violent stories saw the Spider – known as 'the Master of Men' – engage villains involved in nationwide criminal enterprises, sometimes leading to the deaths of hundreds of people. Surrounded by the usual array of helpers and antagonists, the Spider would leave a red ink drop of blood upon the heads of criminals he'd executed as a warning to others. The original ran for a decade, while two cliffhanger movie serials – in 1938 and 1941 – turned him into a more traditional superhero, complete with spider graphic cape.

Created for radio in 1936, the Green Hornet was another crime-fighting masked vigilante. Actually related to the Lone Ranger (as his great-nephew), the Green Hornet was rich kid newspaper publisher Britt Reid, who (according to the original narration) 'hunts the biggest game of all: public enemies that even the G-Men [FBI agents] cannot reach!' His sidekick, Kato, was of Japanese origin (until after Pearl Harbor, when he became 'Filipino'), and fulfilled the roles of chauffeur, bodyguard, and enforcer – the muscle to Reid's brains.

Beyond the pulps and radio serials, proto-superheroes appeared in newspaper comic strips. The super-strength of Popeye came from magical spinach (Popeye himself was a riff on the much earlier strongman Hugo Hercules strip featured in the *Chicago Tribune* in 1902–3). *The Phantom* (1936), created by Lee Falk, featured in a daily syndicated newspaper strip and wore a skin-tight purple bodysuit and 'domino' eye mask (standard for many superheroes). The look came from Robin Hood (often depicted in tights), while the mask without pupils came from Greek busts. Falk had form, having already created villain-battling hypnotist Mandrake the Magician two years before.

The first masked crime-fighter (without superpowers) published exclusively as a comic book character (having not previously appeared on radio or in newspaper strips) was the Clock, created by George Brenner for the Comic Magazine Company. The character is the missing link between the radio and pulp magazine heroes and the popular superheroes that originated in comic books. Former District Attorney Brian O'Brien styled himself 'the Clock', leaving behind a calling card of a clock face with the slogan 'the Clock has struck!' His sole concession to the developing field of superhero costuming was an eye mask, otherwise he wore a standard suit. The character may have been an influence on Will Eisner's more successful Forties vigilante superhero the Spirit.

The final pieces of the superhero puzzle were the science fiction and fantasy pulp heroes of the early twentieth century, including Edgar Rice Burroughs' *John Carter of Mars* (1912) and *Tarzan* (1912), Philip Francis Nowlan's pulp space hero *Buck Rogers* (1928), Robert E. Howard's *Conan the Barbarian* (1932) and Alex Raymond's newspaper-strip hero *Flash Gordon* (1934). These were prototypes of later characters, with Tarzan's athleticism, strength, and mystical abilities with the animal kingdom, Conan's warrior ways, and the future gadgets and technology of Buck and

Flash (as well as their costuming choices – each regularly sported a cape) all contributing elements to the iconic
figure of the American comic book superhero.

An unsung figure is pulp science fiction writer Philip
Gordon Wylie. He created several influential characters,
such as Hugo Danner in the 1930 novel *Gladiator*, who
has superhuman strength and bulletproof skin, a clear
forerunner of Superman. Similarly, Wylie's novel *The
Savage Gentleman* (1932) sees a man hide his son away on
an isolated island where he trains him as an ideal physical specimen, an influence on Doc Savage. Wylie's *When
Worlds Collide* (1933, co-written with Edwin Balmer and
filmed in 1951) prefigured some of Alex Raymond's Flash
Gordon stories and could have influenced Jerry Siegel
and Joe Shuster in developing Superman's escape from the
doomed planet Krypton. Wylie had a strong interest in
the future, not only in mankind's survival of a possible
nuclear war, but as a species. His philosophical thoughts,
expressed in novels and essays were the backdrop against
which the first comic book superheroes were created.

Prior to the launch of Superman in 1938, comics had been
consigned largely to the 'funny pages' of newspapers and
magazines where characters like Frederick Burr Opper's
Happy Hooligan (from 1900) thrived. The misadventures
of these characters and others – such as *The Katzenjammer Kids* – were collected in reprint compilations between
1902 and 1905. As the medium began to define itself, a
host of soon-to-be classic characters appeared in American publications. Windsor McKay explored the world of
dreams through *Little Nemo in Slumberland* (from 1905),
Mutt and Jeff made their debuts in 1907, with prominent
characters *Krazy Kat* (1913) and *Popeye* (1929) following.
The science fiction strips featuring Buck Rogers and Flash
Gordon showed that the medium could be used to tell serious serialized stories.

It wasn't until 1933 that the modern comic book format was established. Previously collected newspaper strip reprints appeared in a variety of shapes and sizes. Charged with creating a publication as an incentive to be given away with retail goods, Eastern Color Printing Company salesman Max C. Gaines devised a full-colour newsprint comic book format, familiar to millions of regular purchasers today. This led to the creation of the 64-page comic book *Famous Funnies*, a 10¢ news-stand publication that carried a variety of full-colour reprinted Sunday newspaper strips. Gaines would become co-publisher of All-American Publications (home of superhero characters Green Lantern, Wonder Woman and Hawkman, and absorbed by DC Comics), and founder of Educational Comics (later EC Comics, notorious publisher of Fifties horror comics). A host of new 'picture story magazines' followed *Famous Funnies*, including *New Comics* (1935), the first to carry wholly original material, and whose publisher National Allied Publications would soon become National Periodical Publications and, finally, DC Comics.

These larger-than-life pulp heroes and villains were draft versions of the classic American comic book superheroes. In the final years of the Thirties everything was in place for the birth of the definitive American superhero. It would take the creative endeavours of two young men – Jerry Siegel and Joe Shuster – and one iconic figure, Superman, to launch an enduring entertainment industry.

3

SUPERMAN ARRIVES: THE FIRST COMIC BOOK SUPERHERO

The world of superhero comics began in the late-Thirties and early-Forties. It was the often-inadvertent creation of a diverse bunch of men, from ex-bootleggers and gangster wannabes, pulp magazine publishers and pornographers, to the creative sons of Jewish immigrants trying to be more American than their neighbours. Out of this soup of conflicting interests and unlikely inspirations emerged a new art form that would take the rest of twentieth-century entertainment by storm.

The multi-million dollar industry built around super-heroes that dominates the annual summer blockbuster movie season started with just two men, one extraordinary character, and one comic book: *Action Comics* #1, published in April 1938 (cover dated June). The two men were Jerome (known as Jerry) Siegel and Joe Shuster, and the character was Superman, from whom virtually all other superheroes

derived, either in imitation of or in direct reaction to the
Man of Steel who fell to Earth from the planet Krypton.

Most extraordinarily, the culturally important and lasting figure of Superman was created by two socially awk-
ward teenagers from Cleveland in the middle of America's
Great Depression. He was not a corporate creation, nor
the work of a pulp fiction writer or a newspaper strip veteran: Superman and the mythos established in the first run
of appearances in *Action Comics*, newspaper strips and a
long-running radio series, came from the imagination of a
couple of downtrodden kids who dreamt big dreams.

Siegel and Shuster were both born in 1914, Shuster
in July and Siegel in October. Shuster had been born in
Toronto, Canada, to Jewish immigrants, moving to Cleveland, Ohio, in 1924. He attended Glenville High School,
becoming friends with Siegel in 1931. Siegel had grown up
in Cleveland, and was also the son of Jewish immigrants.
The pair struck up a fast friendship, sharing a love of science fiction in movie serials, pulp magazines, and newspaper comic strips. They were avid readers of *Amazing
Stories* and *Weird Tales*, pulps that offered them regular
doses of strangeness and imagination. They loved to catch
the latest Douglas Fairbanks swashbuckler at the movies.
Most importantly of all, they devoured the daily and
Sunday newspaper comic strips, especially the space opera
adventures of Buck Rogers or Edgar Rice Burroughs'
jungle adventures of Tarzan. Siegel once said: 'When Joe
and I first met, it was like the right chemicals coming
together.' The pair dared to hope their interests might
offer them a way out of their impoverished circumstances.
Siegel and Shuster wanted to not only read about imaginary worlds, they wanted to create them.

Both were shy young men – Shuster being the image of
the bespectacled non-sporting youth – and they didn't have
a wide circle of friends. Like Clark Kent, Siegel worked for
a newspaper: *The Torch*, based at Glenville High School.

He brought Shuster in as a contributor, and the pair produced short comic strips and humorous stories to entertain fellow students. In the pages of *The Torch* Siegel wrote and Shuster illustrated a comic parody of their favourite hero, Tarzan, called Goober the Mighty.

The pair had little luck in selling their original stories to the pulps they loved, so self-publishing – following the model of the newsletter *Science Fiction Digest* to which Siegel subscribed (edited by fan Julius Schwartz, later to be a key figure at DC Comics) – seemed like the way to go. Siegel had already published one of the earliest science fiction fanzines called *Cosmic Stories* by the time he met Shuster, so the pair happily collaborated on another fanzine called *Science Fiction*, subtitled 'The Advance Guard of Future Civilization'.

Only five issues of *Science Fiction* were ever produced, using the duplicator machine at Glenville High School. In the second issue Siegel published his own review of Philip Wylie's two-year-old novel *Gladiator*. It was in the pages of issue #3, published in January 1933, that the earliest version of Superman made his unsung appearance. In a story entitled 'The Reign of the Superman', Siegel and Shuster invented a bald, telepathic villain named 'the Superman'. This nascent version of their later superhero was not a physically powerful hero interested in doing the right thing. Instead, he was more like the eventual form of Superman's antagonist Lex Luthor. Siegel picked the name Superman from Friedrich Nietzsche's 1883 philosophical work *Also Sprach Zarathustra*, in which the philosopher had introduced the concept of the Übermensch – translated as the 'overman' or 'superhuman'. The phrase had recurred in the title of the 1903 George Bernard Shaw play *Man and Superman*. Siegel wrote the story and Shuster provided the strong, simple illustrations, beginning a creative partnership that would bring them great fame, but little fortune.

In the story a mad scientist (beloved of the pulps)

experiments on a vagrant, Bill Dunn, enticing him with
the offer of 'a real meal and a new suit'. The experiment
results in Dunn developing telepathic powers and becoming obsessed with his own superiority. Dunn decides he
should rule the world as the first of a new race of 'supermen'. Having killed the scientist, seeing him as a potential
rival, Dunn is shocked to discover that his powers were
temporary and without the scientist he cannot recreate the
experiment. The would-be 'superman' is forced to return
once more to his life on the breadline.

'The Reign of the Superman' was a rather simple moral-
ity tale, but within it were the seeds of a more important
character and a world-conquering mythos. The chemical that turned Bill Dunn into a superhuman came from
a meteor from outer space. While testing his new-found
mental powers, Dunn casts his mind far into the void
where he witnesses a battle between strange creatures. The
extraterrestrial origins of the later Superman, Kal-El from
the planet Krypton, start here. The story also sees Dunn's
'superman' team up briefly with a newspaper reporter
(named 'Forrest Ackerman' after the well-known fan who
would later edit *Famous Monsters of Filmland* magazine)
who is not as helpless as he first appears – the origins of
Superman's alter ego of Clark Kent. 'As a science fiction
fan, I knew of the various themes in the field,' said Siegel.
'The superhuman theme had been one of the themes ever
since Samson and Hercules . . . I just sat down and wrote
a story of that type – only in this story the superman was
a villain.'

Although their fanzine was little seen, with as few as
fifty copies printed (sought-after collectors' items today),
Siegel and Shuster continued to pursue their creative ambitions. They next turned to newspaper strips. They came
up with their own Buck Rogers-style strip called *Interplanetary* Police, but the idea was rejected by United Features Syndicate, the Cleveland-based news and features

distributor that supplied many newspapers. Their next idea was about a pair of friends (like themselves) who invent a device allowing them to see through anything and view distant events – a precursor of Superman's X-ray vision.

Picking up a copy of Chicago-based Consolidated Book Publishers' title *Detective Dan, Secret Operative Number 48*, the pair noticed the magazine was running original strips, not just Sunday newspaper reprints. They promptly revived their 'Superman' and put together a sample comic book, sending it to Consolidated. As Siegel recalled: 'It occurred to me that Superman as a hero rather than a villain might make a great comic strip character in the vein of Tarzan, only more super and sensational . . . Joe and I drew it up as a comic book – this was in early 1933. We interested a publisher in putting it out, but then he changed his mind, and that was the end of that particular version of "The Superman".'

Consolidated had responded to 'The Superman' positively, but decided to discontinue *Detective Dan* after just one issue. Upset by the rejection, Shuster burnt every page of 'The Superman', except for the cover Siegel rescued from the flames. This second incarnation of Superman was on the side of right, but he had no superpowers beyond superior strength. Nor did the character have a special outfit – there was no cape, simply a man in a T-shirt and trousers who physically set about evil-doers. It was, however, one more important step in the evolution of the classic Superman.

Although they'd only been trying for a few months, the efforts of Siegel and Shuster to turn professional had gone nowhere and their high school graduation loomed. Time was running out for them to make their mark and escape their fates as further jobless statistics of the Great Depression. Siegel had an after-school delivery job earning four dollars a week, while Shuster had recently become a street vendor of ice cream. Deep down both believed these were not the jobs they were intended for: they had greater ambitions, if only they could figure out a way to have their voices heard.

In 1934 a successful version of Superman finally coalesced. Lying awake one night, Siegel dreamt a new form for his superhero. The next morning he hurried to see Shuster so the pair could draft the new-look Superman. 'We talked about the character a great deal and I made sketches,' said Shuster, recalling Siegel's excited visit. The new character had superpowers, but instead of being purely mental, they would be physical, giving the character a stronger visual image. He would be a great hero, battling tyranny and evil. He would have a distinctive look. 'Let's put him in this kind of costume,' Shuster remembered suggesting. 'Let's give him a big 'S' on his chest, and a cape – make him as colourful as we can and as distinctive as we can.' Shuster was intent on making the costume as brightly coloured as possible, using primary colours to take advantage of the new colour printing used in comics. He wanted the cape so he could suggest movement, speed, and action in his art.

The look had partly come from their thoughts of Superman as the ultimate athlete, like a circus strongman and acrobat combined. The distinctive costume, comprising a tights-and-cape combination, came from circus performers. Perhaps either Siegel or Shuster had Jewish strongman Siegmund (or Zishe) Breitbart in mind, a Polish-born vaudevillian of the Twenties who bent iron bars and tore apart metal chains. It was also a look they'd seen in a new comic strip favourite. Alex Raymond's *Flash Gordon* daily newspaper strip had begun early in 1934 and featured outer-space denizens who wore high-collared robes and wafting capes.

Shuster had another source of inspiration for the physical look of their new Superman. Despite his lack of interest in athletics, he was rather taken with the new fad for body-building. Charles Atlas – real name Angelo Siciliano

– had emerged as the face and the body of the new fitness movement during the Twenties. He'd appeared in a series of health and fitness magazines published by Bernarr Macfadden, but subsequently set out on his own to promote weightlifting as the way to better health. For his part, Shuster had regularly practised weightlifting for a time, and his awareness of the culture of 'physical perfection' and the magazine articles featuring Charles Atlas may have played a large part in the way he decided to draw Siegel's Superman.

Their final masterstroke was to make this new embodiment of Superman an immigrant, like their families. He would come from outer space, an alien sent to Earth as a baby when his father discovers that a cosmic cataclysm is about to destroy their home planet (this may have been influenced by Ming's attacks on Earth with fiery meteors in the early *Flash Gordon* strips). Their hero would not be human, so would not be susceptible to human weaknesses.

This new Superman drew on many mythic archetypes [see chapter 2], but most obvious are the tales of Moses and Jesus, two Biblical figures destined to 'save the world'. This would be the mission for Superman, to keep mankind (essentially America, as became clear during the Second World War) safe from evil. However, this hero would be a stranger in a strange land, never truly at home no matter how hard he tried to fit in. Like Siegel and Shuster themselves, Superman would be an eternal outsider.

With Douglas Fairbank's Zorro fresh in their minds, and years of reading about pulp adventurers and criminals with dual identities, the pair opted to give their secular American messiah a truly human face. This alter ego would not be that of a spoiled aristocrat as so many of the pulp and radio heroes were. Given how extraordinary the character of Superman was, his creators opted to make his human face as ordinary as possible. Clark Kent would be like them: shy, shortsighted, bumbling, working class, and socially inept. Like his creators, he'd work on a newspaper. His look and character was modelled after another movie hero – bespectacled silent comedian Harold Lloyd – while his name came from Clark Gable, a big star in the mid-Thirties. The real name of pulp hero Doc Savage was Clark Savage Jr, only one of many similarities with Superman. The name 'Kent' also featured as one of the identities of the Shadow, Kent Allard (note the surname of his sidekick, Margo Lane). Nonetheless, it was the perfect shell within which to hide a superhero.

Jerry Siegel may have had an altogether more personal reason for wishing to create a 'superman' who would fight on the side of right, one rooted in family tragedy. Siegel's father Mitchell (his original name was Michel, but he'd adopted the American name Michael – as on his death certificate – and was known as Mitchell to his family) was a Jewish immigrant from Lithuania who ran a second-hand clothes store in Cleveland. On the night of 2 June 1932 there was a robbery at the store and Siegel's father died. Although the police report suggested gunshots were fired, sixty-year-old Mitchell Siegel actually died of a heart attack. Some in the Siegel family believed Mitchell's death was murder, despite the coroner's report indicating there were 'no wounds'. Jerry Siegel's first thoughts about Super-man came in the weeks immediately following his father's death: it is little wonder that the then-seventeen-year-old youth dreamt up a fantasy hero figure who could repel bul-lets, and who would fight for truth and justice against the criminal underworld. While the figure of the 'strongman' in myth and legend was a factor, it is perhaps all the more poignant that this mythically resonant superhero should have his origins on the night a lonely boy lost his father.

In writing his 2010 thriller *The Book of Lies*, comic book writer (DC Comics' *Identity Crisis*, among others) Brad Meltzer exhaustively researched the 1932 death of Mitchell Siegel. Meltzer was amazed to discover a letter published in the 3 June 1932 edition of the *Cleveland Plain Dealer* newspaper – the day after the death of Mitchell Siegel – calling for vigilante action against increasing crime. The writer of the letter was one 'A. L. Luther' – possibly the origin of Superman's arch nemesis Lex Luthor. Meltzer noted: 'Why did the world get Superman? Because a little boy named Jerry Siegel heard his father was murdered and, in grief, created a bulletproof man.'

Siegel and Shuster gave their Superman Christ-like attributes (an only son sent to Earth to help mankind), but there's much of Hebrew hero Samson in the mix. Although Jewish, the boys were appealing to the widest audience, and that meant Christian America. They needed to invent a witness (or disciple) for Superman, someone who could observe and comment upon him from a purely human perspective, providing a point of view for the reader. The result was Lois Lane, ace reporter on the *Daily Star* (it would be another two years before it became the more familiar *Daily Planet*). If Siegel couldn't be a journalist, the next best thing was to put his characters into that world. It also had the added advantage that the newspaper setting could be a useful driver of stories. It gave Clark Kent, and so Superman, a vantage point to observe humanity.

Lane got her first name and aspects of her personality from an adolescent crush of Siegel's, a student named Lois Amster – something he admitted in later life. While the character of Lois Lane had ambition, independence, and courage, she would be much criticized as a fantasy figure created by an adolescent male. The question often arises: how could Lois not tell that Clark Kent and Superman were one and the same? How could she spend her time wistfully dreaming of a relationship with one (Superman), while dismissing the other (Clark)? It was a topic various interpretations of the Superman mythos would tackle over many years. The simplicity of the concept allowed for endless reinvention and elaboration, yet at his core Superman always remained the ultimate immigrant, and Lois would be his human connection.

A second source for Lois Lane was an artists' model used by Shuster for figure work: Joanne Carter, who would later marry Siegel. As Superman had been rejected several times, Shuster blamed his art even though Siegel was also rethinking and reinventing the core concepts of who their Superman was. His advertisement for a figure model in the *Cleveland Plain Dealer* brought Carter to his door. She had no modelling experience, and he was barely an adolescent, but the pair hit it off. Shuster told Carter all about Superman, so by the time she met Siegel she was already enthusing about the ideas the youthful pair had for their potential comic strip.

Another inspiration for the spirited 'girl reporter' came from the movies. Both Siegel and Shuster were keen moviegoers, so saw many of the films and film series of the Thirties, possibly including the ongoing Torchy Blane newspaper-set comedy-dramas. Glenda Farrell initially starred as the fast-talking reporter Torchy Blane, always finding herself in trouble in pursuit of the big story. Warner Bros. released nine films in the B-movie series (each barely an hour) between 1936 and 1939 (concluding the year after Superman debuted). Later instalments saw actress Lola Lane (note the name and the initial alliteration, also 'Blane' is one letter away from 'Lane') take on the role in *Torchy Blane in Panama* (1938), followed by Jane Wyman in the final film *Torchy Blane . . . Playing with Dynamite* (1939).

Despite their burst of invention, Siegel and Shuster had no luck in selling Superman. In desperation, Siegel had sent their latest sample material to the reprint-only *Famous Funnies* but the package was rapidly returned to them unopened. Although the coincidentally appropriately named Super Magazines, Inc. had shown some interest, nothing was to come of that either. Finally, the pair had some much-needed success in the world of comics in 1935, but not with Superman.

Siegel and Shuster's first professional sale was to minor publisher Major Malcolm Wheeler-Nicholson's comic book *New Fun*, a just-launched anthology. National Allied Publications (later DC Comics) was running original material in New Fun, not reprinted newspaper strips. Wheeler-Nicholson was a forty-five-year-old pulp writer, the son of a suffragette, who was now pioneering the new American comic book form. The son of a journalist father and magazine publisher mother, he attended a military academy and joined the US Cavalry in 1917. A colourful and eventful military career followed (according to a self-penned and perhaps fanciful autobiography), and although he was court-martialled and resigned his commission as a result of public criticisms of the army, he continued to bill himself as 'Major'. His work for the pulps had a strong military background and was packed with incidents of derring-do and adventure, many supposedly drawn from his own (possibly exaggerated) exploits. Having established National Allied Publications (hereafter referred to as National) to produce a comic book rival to *Famous Funnies*, he had to create original material as all the well-known strips were tied up with major publishers. It was a fortuitous necessity that was eventually to give rise to one of popular entertainment's enduring corporate giants.

Wheeler-Nicholson saw the potential in Siegel and Shuster. He had little investment behind his business, so was more disposed than most to take a gamble on untested talent. For their part, Siegel and Shuster were less inclined to offer their long-in-development Superman to a new publisher who might not go the distance – recent history was littered with the remnants of many fly-by-night pulp publishers. That summer they sent sample work to National, and were quickly commissioned to produce a single-page strip entitled *Henri Duval of France, Famed Soldier of Fortune*. The swashbuckler strip appeared in *New Fun* #6 (October 1935) and it was right up Wheeler-Nicholson's street. The strip ran for four instalments.

That same issue contained another Siegel and Shuster strip, *Doctor Occult: The Ghost Detective*, published under their pseudonyms of Leger and Reuths (they were advised to use other names if they had more than one piece in an issue). The first instalment of their supernatural crime-fighter series saw the Sam Spade-like Dr Occult tackle a vampire, assisted by his girlfriend, Rose Psychic. The character would go on to have a chequered history, but he is still occasionally used in the wider DC Comics Universe. Having achieved these two successes, Siegel and Shuster decided to offer Superman to Wheeler-Nicholson and National, keen for it to finally see publication.

The publisher was impressed with Superman, but felt that to do the concept justice it should be published in colour and that each instalment should run across several pages, which *New Fun* was not doing at the time. The company was also unstable financially, with Wheeler-Nicholson finding it difficult to sell comics built around original – so unknown – characters. Siegel and Shuster continued to work for National, providing the strip *Federal Men* for the January 1936 debut issue of the company's newest publication, *New Comics*. This strip – featuring government agent Steve Carson, based upon the then-new FBI – became the central strip in *New Comics*, with the comic book changing its name several times first to *New Adventure Comics* (from #12), then simply to *Adventure Comics* (from #32). These crime strips allowed Siegel and Shuster to refine their respective writing and illustrative skills, but their love of science fiction and fantasy was never far away. The following year, in January 1937, they ran the story 'Federal Men of the Future' that included a character called 'Jor-L'. Late in 1936, Siegel and Shuster used the Dr Occult strip to try out some of their unused ideas for Superman, giving the character super-strength, the ability to fly, and a blue costume with a red cape.

Facing financial ruin, Wheeler-Nicholson took one last gamble and launched a third comic book called *Detective Comics* early in 1937 (later the home of Batman from 1939, after Wheeler-Nicholson sold his interest in publishing company Detective Comics, Inc. to his partners – or had the company stolen from him, depending on who's telling the story). Siegel and Shuster contributed a strip called *Slam Bradley* to the debut issue of *Detective Comics*, using the concept of Superman from their abandoned 'The Superman' draft. Bradley was styled an 'ace freelance sleuth, fighter and adventurer' who appeared in his first splash page battling four nefarious villains at once.

A fourth title – *Action Comics* – was added to the National roster, with former magazine distributors Harry Donenfeld and Jack Liebowitz now running the company. In 1932 they had formed publisher and distributor Independent News from the ruins of a couple of indebted companies. Wheeler-Nicholson distributed his titles through them, a decision he would come to regret. The Major had fallen heavily into debt, which led to him owing Independent News a significant sum. Perhaps he hadn't realized the kind of people he was now in business with . . .

Donenfeld had reputedly been a bootlegger during Prohibition, with strong connections to gangster Frank Costello – it was said he had moved alcohol across the border alongside legitimate shipments of Canadian pulp paper used in his print enterprises. Through his underworld connections, Donenfeld had secured a lucrative contract to print millions of subscription leaflets for the Hearst magazine empire, including titles *Good Housekeeping* and *Cosmopolitan*. He also had a hand in the publishing of pornography, with a series of racy pulps with titillating titles like *Pep*, *Bedtime Stories*, and *Spicy Detective*. His regular run-ins with the censors saw him on the lookout for a new publishing field: the world of four-colour comic books seemed tempting.

Donenfeld's partner was accountant Jack Liebowitz, someone who could efficiently run the business side of the operation while Donenfeld struck the deals and schmoozed the clients (legitimate and illegitimate alike). Liebowitz was left wing and idealistic, heavily involved with the International Ladies' Garment Workers Union. He became involved with Donenfeld's myriad companies following the Wall Street Crash of 1929, offering the maverick businessman a steady hand at the financial tiller. Despite their chalk and cheese personalities, Donenfeld, the would-be gangster and playboy, and Liebowitz, the dull accountant, were complementary in business.

In launching *Detective Comics* during 1937, Wheeler-Nicholson had been forced to take Donenfeld and Liebowitz on as partners in lieu of settling his debts. By 1938 the pair had pushed Wheeler-Nicholson out and taken over the company's assets, including National (although the company did not officially become DC Comics until 1977, it will hereafter be referred to as DC, taking its name from the initials of *Detective Comics* and featuring the distinctive DC logo from the Forties). Donenfeld and Liebowitz now owned a growing comic book publisher with significant potential, if they could find the right people to manage it.

Vincent 'Vin' Sullivan and Sheldon 'Shelly' Mayer had come to DC Comics as part of the takeover by Donenfeld and Liebowitz. They'd worked under Wheeler-Nicholson, but had little regard for the comic book innovator. 'He wasn't a very good businessman,' recalled Sullivan. 'It was a new industry and we were struggling all the time.' Looking for a strong cover feature for *Action Comics*, Sullivan and Mayer dipped into the company 'slush pile' (unsolicited manuscripts and strips sent in, hopeful of publication) where they found the long-neglected Superman pitch.

For a while Siegel and Shuster had tried to sell their idea as a newspaper strip with some interest from the United Features Syndicate in 1937. Now Vin Sullivan was offering them the thirteen-page lead strip in *Action Comics*, so they rapidly reformatted the intended daily Superman strips into a form suitable for the by-now standardized comic book page. Although asked for a strict eight panels per page, Shuster experimented with the developing art form, producing pages with large splash illustrations and others with as few as five panels. Siegel even suggested the image of Superman lifting a gangster's car for the cover of *Action Comics* #1.

For over five years, Siegel and Shuster had been refining their concept of Superman, from bald-headed telepathic villain to red-caped superhero from space, defender of mankind. 'All this time we really felt that we had something that was very different,' said Siegel. 'Something that the public really would take to its heart.' With the arrival of *Action Comics* #1 on US news-stands in April 1938, the Golden Age of American comic books had truly begun.

The first great surge of popularity for superheroes, many inspired by Siegel and Shuster's Superman, is called the 'Golden Age', from the late-Thirties to the early-Fifties. Comic books were never more popular as mass entertainment than during this period (although it is arguable that the comic book-inspired superhero movies of the early twenty-first century are even more popular than the original comic books).

The archetype of the superhero was defined and refined, with many of the best-known and longest-lasting heroes making their debuts, including the non-super-powered vigilante Batman, the wartime patriotic figure Captain America, the feminist icon Wonder Woman, and the adolescent fantasy figure Captain Marvel (a superhero that, even more than Superman, appealed directly to the downtrodden teen's wish to be superior in physical strength to bullies and tormentors). Comic books became a major industry with a host of talented writers and artists dedicating themselves to exploring the artistic and storytelling possibilities of the colourful new medium.

As several new and long-established magazine publishers moved into the lucrative comic book field, a range of independent artists' studios sprang up around New York to produce content for these material-hungry companies. This 'shop system' would become a breeding ground for many writers and artists who would contribute much to the Golden Age.

One of the most successful and innovative was the Eisner & Iger shop (also known as the Universal Phoenix Syndicate), run by the partnership of cartoonists Will Eisner and S. M. Iger. Struggling for work the pair had set up in business with just $15 in capital, before attracting contracts from several comic book publishers and pulp houses such as Fiction House and Everett M. Arnold. An artists' shop worked like an assembly line, with artists in rows at art tables in often dingy, low-rent buildings in the cheaper areas of New York City, one doing pencils (rough artwork), another inking (finished artwork), someone colouring (the colourist), and someone else adding the speech-bubble lettering (the letterer). Each page would move along this production line, added to and developing closer to the finished item at each stage. 'We made comic book features pretty much the way Ford made cars,' said Eisner. He and Iger would employ freelancers to produce the comic art, selling them to publishers at around $5 per page.

The shops were a great clearing house, mixing on-the-job training for young up-and-coming artists with providing a home for older journeymen illustrators or those who'd lost jobs elsewhere thanks to the economic situation. These shops' work-for-hire systems, which also resulted in a lack of credit for individuals, would be adopted wholesale by comic book publishers leading to a variety of disputes over creative credits and recompense for unexpectedly successful characters. From the early days of the comic book shop system many of the creative talents – writers, artists, editors, and managers – would emerge who gave birth to the superheroes that would dominate the medium.

For Siegel and Shuster, in the immediate aftermath of the publication of *Action Comics* #1 little had changed from the days before Superman existed in the public arena. One of the more unpleasant legacies of their unexpected success were the repeated battles between them and their heirs and the copyright owners DC Comics over the remuneration paid to the iconic character's creators. Siegel and Shuster were paid a simple $10 per page fee, totalling $130, for their Superman work on *Action Comics* #1. This unfair deal would later be seen as the 'original sin' of comic book history, the true tainted secret origin of all superheroes. They assigned the rights to Superman to DC Comics in return for a unique ten-year contract securing them additional work with the publisher. It was an agreement that would lay the foundations for a series of bitter legal disputes over ownership that continue to this day.

Neither the publishers nor the creators of Superman initially realized quite how successful the new character was, until reports started to filter back from news-stands that people were not requesting copies of *Action Comics*, but instead were asking directly for 'the magazine with Superman in it'. Almost immediately, the character had escaped the bounds of the comic book, leaping directly into the public imagination.

Initially, DC Comics' publisher Jack Liebowitz was cautious, keeping the print runs on *Action Comics* tight (around 200,000 for the earliest issues) even though it was regularly selling out. He also ran a variety of different characters on the cover. It soon became clear that Superman was driving sales, and from #11 onwards he was the only character featured on the front. *Action Comics* was selling almost half a million copies, and within another month that figure almost doubled. Superman was flying off newsstand shelves.

There had been little attempt to promote Superman: for the publishers the decision to print the strip was a happy accident. They hadn't briefed Siegel and Shuster what to write, happy to run whatever the pair came up with. Although Superman was from another world, much of the thirteen pages of the first adventure featured very current, real-world issues such as corruption in government, domestic violence, and injustice. Later stories would feature such contentious 'ripped from the headlines' issues as drink-driving, the arms race, slum housing, and workers' rights. This first incarnation of Superman was a hero for the Depression, fighting as much to improve the social conditions for the downtrodden in America as to right the wrongs of 'super-villains'.

The origin story fills less than a single comic book page. The first panel shows a baby launched into space by his father to escape the destruction of 'a distant planet' (Krypton is not named) about to be 'destroyed by old age'. In the second panel, a passing motorist discovers the alien baby crash-landed on Earth. The baby is put in an orphanage. The first act of super-strength is shown in the next panel, as the baby lifts a chair above its head with a single hand, amazing the orphanage staff with 'his feats of strength'. By the fourth panel, the now mature boy – called Clark – is testing his powers, including the ability to leap (the very specific) 'eighth of a mile', hurdle a twenty-storey building, run faster than a train, and lift huge weights. Superman's look and powers would gradually develop: he'd get the red boots in *Action Comics* #5, super-hearing in #8, and X-ray vision in #11. The final panel is his mission statement: '. . . he must turn his titanic strength into channels that would benefit mankind, and so was created 'Superman', champion of the oppressed . . .'

The rest of the first Superman strip depicted him going about the business of righting wrongs and helping people out, including saving a wrongly convicted innocent woman about to be executed by turning in the true perpetrator of the crime, saving another woman from her abusive husband, and rescuing his *Daily Star* co-worker Lois Lane from a gangster who abducted her (the incident depicted on the cover), and provoking a corrupt Washington Senator to confess. Shuster's cityscapes featured towering skyscrapers, the newest icons in the skylines of Chicago and New York, and the source of their nickname for their hero, the 'Man of Steel'. The strip also showed Clark Kent hiding his Superman costume under his regular clothes, an impractical arrangement given the cape, but part of the fantasy that would become iconic.

Ironically, the widest exposure of Superman was through the nationally syndicated newspaper strip from January 1939. Siegel and Shuster's original attempt to sell their Superman idea as a newspaper strip had been met with repeated rejection. By the end of 1939, the *Superman* newspaper strip would feature in more than sixty publications, with it eventually featuring in around 300. After the success of *Action Comics*, Siegel and Shuster had a chance to reinvent the origin story of their hero through their original dream of a daily newspaper strip. The first eight strips (across two weeks) expanded upon *Action Comics'* single page, giving names to the planet (Krypton, an advanced distant planet that 'bears a civilization of supermen'), Superman's father (Jor-L, later amended to Jor-El), his mother (Lora, later Lara), and finally his own name (Kal-L, later Kal-El). Scientist Jor-L leads his planet's attempts to create a 'space ark' to allow the population to flee their doomed world. A prototype ship is built, but further earthquakes and eruptions lead Jor-L to fear the end has come. He and Lora put Kal-L into the prototype (it can hold only one) and launch their baby son to planet Earth, the nearest world Jor-L has found that can support life. As Krypton explodes, Kal-L's vulnerable craft crosses the void, finally crashing upon Earth. The last strip of this sequence features the familiar *Action Comics* images of the discovery of Kal-L (there were no Kents yet), his youthful feats with a chair, his racing a speeding train, and his unveiling as Superman, 'champion of the oppressed'. It was an origin story that would become familiar worldwide through various retellings and reinterpretations in comic books, radio serials, television shows, and movies across many decades.

One interpretation of the name 'Kal-El' in Hebrew is 'voice of God', but like Jewish immigrants to America, the alien refugee from Krypton adopts a more American name in 'Clark Kent'. Whether it was intended or not, many have interpreted Superman as some kind of secular messiah, sent to Earth to save mankind. His true name may have Jewish origins, but growing up in Kansas (later central to the Superman origin story) made his upbringing Christian.

With the success of the character in *Action Comics* and the newspaper strip, executives at DC Comics were quick to develop a more heroic code of conduct for Superman. With a largely young and impressionable audience now following Superman's adventures, it was decided that he should never kill nor be responsible for the deaths of others, no matter the provocation. The character had become a valuable commodity, one that had to be protected at all costs – and that included from imitators, as well as his originators.

Within a year Superman was headlining his own comic book (*Superman* #1 was cover dated Summer 1939) – the first superhero character ever to do so – which featured yet another more expansive retelling of his origin story, including the addition of the Kent family, Kansas farmers who adopt and raise the young Kal-El. With their original superhero now firmly established, DC Comics began to look into developing others, aware that rival publishers were working on their own plans to snatch a slice of the comic book superhero market unexpectedly created by Superman. DC Comics second successful superhero would be the dark knight of Gotham City, known as the 'Bat-Man'.

4

BATMAN BEGINS: THE BIRTH OF THE DARK KNIGHT

With the rapid success of Superman, DC Comics was eager to repeat Jerry Siegel and Joe Shuster's feat and launch a second superhero they hoped would be just as popular with the increasing legions of young comic book readers. Non-superhero comic books had been selling in the region of 200,000 to 400,000 copies each month before Superman arrived, but *Action Comics* was regularly selling just under one million copies every month. When DC Comics launched *Superman* #1 it was soon selling on average 1.3 million copies monthly. The comic book business was a good business to be in, so another book featuring another Superman-like hero made good business sense. Limited progress was achieved until DC editor Vin Sullivan (the man who'd 'found' Superman) suggested to little-known cartoonist and occasional DC contributor Bob Kane that he should try creating a brand new superhero.

Kane had been born Robert Kahn in New York in 1915. He was high-school friends with *The Spirit*'s Will Eisner (Marvel's Stan Lee and Batman co-creator and writer Bill Finger also attended DeWitt-Clinton school). Kane's father worked for the *New York Daily News* (in a non-journalistic role) and regularly brought home the 'funny pages', inspiring his son's ambition to become a cartoonist. He changed his name to Kane at the age of eighteen and became a trainee animator at the Max Fleischer Studio in New York, famous for their Betty Boop cartoons (later the home of the animated Superman shorts). He freelanced occasionally at the Eisner & Iger comic book art shop and worked in a minor capacity for several comic books, including DC's *Detective Comics* (on *Oscar the Gumshoe*). He'd had to quit art school, due to the Depression and take up a job in a garment factory run by his uncle.

Although they'd attended the same school, Kane didn't properly meet Bill Finger (almost two years his senior) until they were both adults. Finger had been born in Denver, Colorado, but moved to New York City when he was very young. His father's tailor's shop had closed during the Depression, so Finger had taken on a series of menial odd jobs, including driving a cab, clerking in a hat store, and selling shoes. When he met Kane they discovered a mutual love of comic books and newspaper comic strips. Together they determined to break into the field, but Kane was more business-savvy than the insecure Finger. Their first work, which Finger wrote and Kane illustrated, included *Rusty and His Pals* and *Clip Carson* strips in DC's *Adventure Comics* and *Action Comics*. The credits for these mentioned only Kane.

Kane knew that Siegel and Shuster had secured not only regular work but also a higher income thanks to Superman. Encouraged by DC Comics, he deliberately set out to invent a similarly striking superhero. One Friday afternoon, Vin Sullivan had told Kane about the deal Siegel and Shuster were on and he'd mentioned DC's need for more 'mystery men' (as he described superheroes). Kane grabbed the opportunity, declaring he'd have a new character ready by Monday. Initially there was no backstory for his costumed hero, as an artist Kane simply concentrated on the character's look. 'Almost every famous character ever created had a kind of simplistic, definitive design that was easily recognizable,' said Kane. 'That's what I was striving for with Batman.'

Swirling around Kane's mind were ideas for the new character. He thought of Zorro, a masked hero, and he looked at Superman's distinctive dress. Just like Siegel and Shuster, Kane drew on images from movies. Douglas Fairbanks in the 1921 *The Mask of Zorro* was a prime influence in Kane's conception of a masked hero who was physically strong, fought for the weak against criminals, but was otherwise an unremarkable human, not a super-powered extraterrestrial. His first drawings were of a figure he dubbed the 'bird-man', a blond-haired hero wearing a domino mask like the Phantom, red tights like Superman, black trunks, and a yellow utility belt. He even had a pair of mechanical bird-like wings attached to his back, although he was depicted swinging, Zorro-like, from a taut rope. Kane's direct inspiration may have been a similar panel from a 1939 Alex Raymond *Flash Gordon* Sunday comic strip.

Kane took his sketch to Bill Finger, and his input would be crucial in the final formulation of the character as The Bat-Man (as he was initially dubbed). Kane often told his version, one that gave himself a solo role in coming up with the character (especially in his self-promoting autobiography, *Batman and Me*). He credited the initial inspiration for his use of the bat motif as coming from the work of Renaissance artist Leonardo da Vinci. He'd seen images of a bat-like flying machine known as an ornithopter drawn by the artist, and he combined this with figures he recalled strongly from childhood. A 1930 movie starring Chester Morris called *The Bat Whispers* (based on Mary

Rinehart's novel *The Circular Staircase*, previously filmed as *The Bat* in 1926) was also on Kane's mind. Of Morris, Kane noted 'He was the villain, but he wore a bat costume.' Finally, there was the image of Bela Lugosi's Dracula in the groundbreaking 1931 movie, with his arms holding his black cape aloft.

In his account Finger recalled that Kane '. . . had an idea for a character . . . and he'd like me to see the drawings. He had drawn a character that looked very much like Superman . . . no gloves, no gauntlets . . . He had a small domino mask [and] two stiff wings that were sticking out . . .' Recalling the dark and mysterious Shadow, Finger suggested giving the new hero a name that had something of a creature of the night about it. According to Jim Steranko's *History of Comics*, Finger pulled *Webster's Dictionary* from his shelves hoping to find an image of a nocturnal bat. 'I said [to Kane] "Notice the ears! Why don't we duplicate the ears?" I suggested Bob draw what looked like a cowl. I suggested he bring the nosepiece down and make him mysterious and not show any eyes at all. I didn't like the wings, so I suggested he make a cape and scallop the edges so it would flow out behind him when he ran and would look like bat wings. He didn't have any gloves on. We gave him gloves.'

From this disputed beginning Kane and Finger worked on developing Batman, giving him the cowl mask, bat-like ears, and a cape instead of wings, as Finger suggested. In his art Kane adopted a near-monochrome grey-black colour scheme and gave Batman's mask blank eyes to preserve his mystery. Finger came up with the name Bruce Wayne as Batman's civilian identity, and wrote the outline for what would become the first story. Kane had already sold DC on the character prior to Finger's involvement: he regarded Finger as his employee (the writer would go on to work directly for DC Comics, writing the earliest *Green Lantern* strips, among many others).

As with his previous practice on their work for DC together, Kane ensured he was the only one credited when the strip made its debut in May 1939 in *Detective Comics* #27. Despite the lack of credit, Kane eventually recognized the importance of Finger in the creation and development of Batman. 'Bill Finger was a contributing force on Batman right from the beginning. He wrote most of the great stories and was influential in setting the style and genre other writers would emulate. I made Batman a superhero-vigilante when I first created him. Bill turned him in to a scientific detective.'

DC Comics' editor Vin Sullivan was delighted by the new character but was apparently unaware of Finger's contributions. He commissioned Kane to produce a series of stories featuring Batman. In negotiating the contract, Kane not only learned from the mistake made by Siegel and Shuster, but he also had the aid of his father to ensure he would be paid for all ancillary exploitation.

There would be nothing to exploit – no animated cartoons, movies, newspaper strips, or merchandise – if he didn't have stories to tell. While Kane developed the image of Batman, it was down to Finger to come up with a backstory. To Finger, Batman had something of the detective about him (he was due to appear in *Detective Comics*, after all). He would have the intelligence of a modern Sherlock Holmes, combined with the heroism of Alexandre Dumas's *The Three Musketeers*. An avid reader of the pulps, Finger drew upon popular characters like the Shadow in developing Batman's identity. There were some previous bat-themed heroes that Finger may have been aware of, including the Black Bat who featured in 1933 issues of *Black Bat Detective Mysteries* (he didn't actually dress as a bat); The Bat, a wrongly-accused reporter who featured in *Popular Detective* (November 1934); and a story entitled 'Batman' from the February 1936 issue of *Spicy Mystery Stories* (one of Donenfeld's lurid pulps). The most interesting is the Bat, who adopted his alter ego identity after being inspired by a bat that flew in his window, a scene later faithfully recreated in the origin story for Batman.

The first ever Batman story appeared in *Detective Comics* #27 (May 1939). It was written by the uncredited Bill Finger, drawn by Bob Kane, and titled 'The Case of the Chemical Syndicate'. Finger admitted in *The Steranko History of Comics* that this first story was '... a take-off on a Shadow story'. This Shadow tale was uncovered in 2007 by researchers Anthony Tollin and Will Murray. It was 'Partners of Peril' from the 1 November 1936 issue of *The Shadow* pulp magazine. Written by Theodore Tinsley, an occasional stand-in for Shadow creator Walter Gibson, the story has a 'bat-like' figure stalking criminals, among several other key similarities. The haste with which Batman's first stories were created may explain why Finger and Kane drew on pre-existing sources, or their process might simply be comparable to that of Siegel and Shuster on Superman: they were influenced by everything that surrounded them, from pulp fiction characters to movie heroes. The rise of real-life gangsters, such as John Dillinger, 'Pretty Boy' Floyd, Bonnie and Clyde, Al Capone, and 'Dutch' Schultz was chronicled daily in newspapers and movies. Finger and Kane were immersed in this and it directly influenced their work.

The arrival of Batman would open the gates to a flood of superheroes at the start of the Forties. Between *Action Comics* #1, the first appearance of Superman, and Batman's arrival in *Detective Comics* #27, there had only been three other superheroes and each of them owed more to the pulp fiction of the past rather than the new breed. The Arrow (*Funny Pages* #21, September 1938) was the first American superhero to feature archery as a primary attribute. The Crimson Avenger (debuting in *Detective Comics* #20, October 1938) was a wealthy journalist who wore a red face mask when fighting crime. Sandman (*Adventure Comics* #40, July 1939) wore a green suit, a fedora and a gas mask as his crime-fighting attire (a character later completely reinvented by Neil Gaiman). After Batman, there would be many more costumed heroes fighting for young comic book readers' dimes.

Unlike the revised Superman, Batman was initially allowed to cause the death of villains in his battle against crime. He was a vigilante who considered pushing a villain into a vat of acid to be 'a fitting end for his kind'. Batman in his earliest stories was not above shooting villains dead (even if they were vampires, as in a September 1939 two-part storyline – elements of the supernatural were quickly dropped). Fairly soon, following the Superman model, fire-arms were phased out, as Finger and Kane turned to developing a series of remarkable gadgets for their superhero, and the strips turned somewhat lighter than the original 'angry vigilante' approach.

Of the famous supporting cast that has appeared in Batman stories throughout the years, only Commissioner Gordon appeared in the first outing. Unaware of Batman's double identity, Gordon believes Bruce Wayne to be 'a nice young chap' who must lead 'a boring life . . . seems disinterested in everything'. The story of 'The Case of the Chemical Syndicate' is a simple one of murder among business partners, interesting only in that it introduced a new hero. The same issue of *Detective Comics* featured a back-up strip by Siegel and Shuster titled 'The Mysterious Murders', and a Sax Rohmer story, 'The Insidious Dr Fu Manchu', among other run-of-the-mill strips.

Over the first few stories, Bill Finger developed the character of millionaire Bruce Wayne and his crime-fighting alter ego, as well as a supporting cast of denizens of Gotham City (although the location itself wouldn't be named until 1941), while Bob Kane refined his drawings of the newest superhero, giving him a stronger jaw (modelled after that of Chester Gould's newspaper strip detective Dick Tracy). Batman thwarted jewel thieves in his second appearance, while the third story 'The Batman Meets Doctor Death' (*Detective Comics* #29, July 1939) saw the appearance of Batman's first recurring villain. The story also established that, unlike Superman, bullets can harm Batman when he's shot by an armed thug. The escapade also saw the first use of Batman's now-famous utility belt, packed with crime-fighting gadgets. Writer Gardner Fox (a DC staffer who would become a significant Golden Age figure) took over for issues #31 and #32, introducing the 'Batgyro' and the 'Batarang' (the 'Bat-' prefix would rapidly become overused), as well as a quickly forgotten fiancée for Bruce Wayne. Fox kicked off Batman's love of extravagant gadgets, a trait that continues to this day in the comic books, as well as in animated television shows and movies.

It would be over six months before Batman was supplied with the kind of origin story (written by Finger) that Superman had in the first pages of his debut. In *Detective Comics* #33 (November 1939), a strip entitled 'The Batman and How He Came to Be' (itself merely a two-page introduction to that issue's main adventure, 'The Batman Wars Against the Dirigible of Doom') revealed that millionaire playboy Bruce Wayne was an orphan who had lost both parents in childhood when they were killed by an unidentified mugger (revealed in a 1948 version of Batman's origin to be small-time hood Joe Chill). The traumatized child nurses a thirst for vengeance as he grows up, eventually using his inherited wealth and years of mental and physical preparation to turn vigilante as a way of avenging his parents. While Batman's origin tale echoes some of that of Superman, his quest is personal, driven by dark tragedy rather than cosmic angst. Batman's entry into the world of crime and criminals as an avenger is shown to have been inspired by a bat that flies in through an open window, causing Bruce to adopt the guise of a 'bat-man' to hide his true identity. In dressing as 'a creature of the night, black, terrible' he sets out to frighten those who terrorize Gotham City through crime, regarding the city's criminals as 'a superstitious and cowardly lot'. The piece concluded: 'And thus is born this weird figure of the dark . . . this avenger of evil . . . The Batman!' By 1940 Batman featured in his own comic book, just as Superman did, while continuing to appear in *Detective Comics*. He and Superman would drive DC Comics to become the top-selling comic book publisher of the Forties.

During the first few strips published elements of the Batman myth and style accreted. The first Bat-vehicle, the Batplane, arrived in #31 (September 1939). Early on his underground activities made Batman as much a target of police investigation as the criminals he fought against. It was not a state of affairs that could exist for long (although Christopher Nolan's twenty-first-century film trilogy uses this opposition as a key element), with Batman eventually becoming an honorary member of the Gotham City police department.

Raised in wealth in what the later Sixties television show would memorably dub 'stately Wayne Manor', Bruce Wayne had the time and the money to prepare himself for a life fighting crime. Unlike Superman, who made a point in his Clark Kent guise of surrounding himself with ordinary humanity (like Lois Lane) to better understand them, Wayne was initially a loner, a vigilante who worked without help. However, as Bill Finger noted: 'Batman was a combination of Douglas Fairbanks and Sherlock Holmes. Holmes had his Watson. The thing that bothered me was that Batman didn't have anyone to talk to, and it got a little tiresome always having him thinking. I found that as I went along Batman needed a Watson to talk to. That's how Robin came to be.' The result was 'Robin, the Boy Wonder', introduced as similarly orphaned acrobat Dick Grayson in *Detective Comics* #38 (April 1940) – although

DC Comics' Jack Liebowitz was worried about putting a young character like Grayson in harm's way.

As with Lois Lane, the arrival of Robin served to humanize Batman. No longer the lone vigilante, he was now responsible for the safety of someone else. After they refused to pay up in an extortion scam, gangster boss Zucco killed Grayson's parents John and Mary (who lead the family acrobatic act the Flying Graysons), prompting Batman to investigate. As Bruce Wayne, he takes on responsibility for Dick Grayson, adopting him as his legal ward. Together they bring Zucco to justice, and as a result the young Grayson remains by Batman's side driven by a similar psychological need. Robin's costume – red tunic, yellow cape, green gloves, and boots – was deliberately modelled after that of Robin Hood (also the source of his superhero name). The bright colours of the sidekick costume stood in counterpoint to Batman's gloomy tones, serving to not only lighten the narrative but also brighten up the comic book page. Robin ends his first adventure as Batman's sidekick with the exclamation: 'Say, I can hardly wait until we go on our next case. I bet it'll be a corker!'

This first version of Robin would feature in comics by Batman's side from 1940 until the early Eighties when he would branch out on his own, adopting the superhero identity Nightwing. A second Robin – Jason Todd – would debut in 1983 in *Batman* #357 (March 1983). He would be murdered by recurring villain the Joker in the graphic novel *A Death in the Family* (1989, although Todd would later be resurrected as the Red Hood in *Batman: Under the Hood*, 2005–6). The third iteration of Robin was Tim Drake, who took on the mantle of Batman's sidekick in 1991. There was briefly a fourth, female Robin – Stephanie Brown – who later became Batgirl, and a fifth inheritor of the title was introduced in the 2009 series *Batman: Battle for the Cowl*. He was Bruce Wayne's son Damian Wayne (he'd be killed off in a 2013 comic, leaving the post vacant, although it will inevitably be filled once more).

After Robin's arrival in 1940, sales of *Detective Comics* almost doubled, with the young character having great appeal to the largely young comic book readership. While it would set a template for many of the superhero sidekicks who followed, the arrival of Robin also moved Batman away from the vengeance-driven dark loner character Kane had originally envisaged. Although he continued to be credited, Kane was by this point using 'assistants' to draft the *Batman* artwork for him. Prime among them was Sheldon Moldoff who soon moved on to work for DC Comics directly and who claimed to have given Kane the idea for 'a boy superhero'.

By the time 'Robin the Boy Wonder . . . The sensational character find of 1940' appeared, the *Batman* artwork was being completed by then seventeen-year-old Jerry Robinson. He was being paid directly by Kane to cover his expenses while he studied journalism at Columbia University. Working from a rented room in his family home in the Bronx, not far from Kane's own apartment, Robinson became the primary artist working on the *Batman* strip. Within a year Kane increasingly took a back seat, working primarily on the daily *Batman* newspaper strip and happy to enjoy the fruits of his creation. Kane would eventually move Robinson and another *Batman* artist, George Roussos, into an office he rented in Times Square where they'd work on the *Batman* strips producing around thirteen finished pages of artwork each week. Within another eighteen months, both artists as well as writer Bill Finger would be working directly for DC Comics at their Lexington Avenue offices.

A more unusual sidekick appeared in the saga in 1943 with the first appearance of Bruce Wayne's loyal butler Alfred Pennyworth, designed by Jerry Robinson. Originally created for the first Batman movie serial [see chapter

12], the character was introduced into the comic books (in *Batman* #16, April–May 1943) before the serial even reached cinemas, although the tubby comic book Alfred bore no relation to the screen's somewhat thinner actor William Austin (the character would also star in a long-running back-up strip, 'The Adventures of Alfred'). Alfred's comic book image would later be changed to better match that of the actor. He was one of the few characters in the comic books ever to know the secret identities of both Batman and Robin.

Another developing feature of the Batman mythos was the Dynamic Duo's primary mode of transport, the Batmobile. Although Batman had always driven around town in fast cars from his earliest appearances, they were little more than the usual Forties models available from dealers nationwide. His first car, a scarlet sedan, later became a blue convertible, complementing his superhero colour scheme. In 1941 this car was embellished with the addition of a distinctive hood ornament in the shape of a bat and the strip's writers began to refer to the vehicle as the Batmobile (from *Detective Comics* #48, February 1941). *Batman* #5 (Spring 1941) saw the arrival of the first purposely designed Batmobile, a dark-blue 'supercharged' car with a bat-wing tail fin and a huge bat's head battering ram. The Batmobile would be dramatically revamped in 1950 (by artist Dick Sprang), and its appearance has continued to change ever since.

Any superhero is often only as good as the villains he faces. Initially like Superman, Batman faced a series of classic Thirties gangsters and petty hoodlums of the type who'd been responsible for the death of his parents and those of Dick Grayson. However, the Batman villain menagerie would grow exponentially, providing a wacky rogues gallery of evil-doers for the Caped Crusaders to combat. Doctor Death (in *Detective Comics* #29, July 1939) was the first returning villain Batman faced, and he set the template for many of the more successful figures that followed. His racket was extortion, using the threat of the release of a deadly chemical weapon on Gotham City – he escapes thanks to a self-created explosion in his lab. He returned in the next issue, with a face disfigured due to the chemical explosion giving him a brown, skeletal appearance. The character wouldn't be seen again until brief revivals in 1982 and again from 2003 through to the 2006 year-long DC Comics publishing event dubbed '52'. Red-cloaked vampire the Monk appeared in *Detective Comics* #31 (September 1939), only to be killed by Batman in his coffin by the use of silver bullets. Like Doctor Death, the Monk was revived several times many decades later, including in 1982 (*Detective Comics* #515, June 1982) and the 2006 miniseries *Batman and the Mad Monk*. Supernatural villains, however, were to be few and far between in future.

This pair was only the beginning of the colourful array of malevolent misfits that Batman and Robin would face over the decades (with Kane and Finger taking their cue from the bizarre villains faced by Dick Tracy). One explanation is that the over-the-top ever more megalomaniacal villains of the comic books reflected a growing anxiety and fear over the rise of Fascism in Europe.

Professor Hugo Strange (*Detective Comics* #36, February 1940) was another professional scientist who turned his back on society. His 'concentrated lightning machine' generates a dense fog over Gotham, allowing his team of bank robbers to work undetected. Strange is already known to Batman, and in a Seventies story the malcontented professor would discover Batman's secret identity. Clayface (*Detective Comics* #40, June 1948) was an actor in B-movies who felt he hadn't received due recognition so adopted the guise of one of his earlier roles in a horror film to begin a life of crime. The name would be recycled for a variety of villainous characters in later Batman adventures.

Jack Schiff, the main editor on the *Batman* comics from the Forties to the Sixties, realized early on the need for distinctive villains. 'I wanted to get good opponents for Batman,' he said, 'somebody powerful to fight against so the kids could get interested.'

The publication of *Batman* #1 (Spring 1940) had allowed for an expansion in the number of villains with whom the vigilante hero could match wits. Prime among them was the Joker, 'the Clown Prince of Crime'. A criminal psychopath with a warped, mischievous sense of humour, the Joker would become Batman's prime antagonist through a variety of appearances across many different media, from comic books to movies and computer games. The exact origins of the character have been disputed, as Kane, Finger, and Jerry Robinson all claimed to have had the prime hand. Kane said that Robinson suggested the Joker playing card as the basis of a new villain, which he combined with his memories of a character played by Conrad Veidt in the 1928 silent movie *The Man Who Laughs*. Based on a Victor Hugo novel, this German Expressionist film saw Veidt play Gwynplaine with a disfigured face, an ear-to-ear grim grin. Kane would transpose this look directly to the Joker.

The purple-suited Joker regarded crime as fun, with his criminal acts accompanied by sick jokes or an undercurrent of dark humour. As a mirror image of Batman, the Joker employed a variety of gadgets, including such laugh-heavy devices as playing cards with blades embedded in them, pies filled with cyanide, exploding cigars laced with nitro-glycerine, flowers that squirt acid, and a deadly hand buzzer. These common joke shop items familiar to children were turned into malevolent trademarks, along with his insane laugh. The Joker relished his battles with Batman and Robin, almost hoping they would never end (he deliberately lets several chances to publicly unmask his adversaries go) and contrived to allow the Dynamic Duo's regular escapes.

The character was originally to be killed off at the climax of his second appearance later that same issue, but DC Comics' newest editor Whitney Ellsworth (replacing Vin Sullivan) suggested he be kept alive for a future return. An extra panel indicated his survival, allowing for a variety of seemingly 'fatal' near-death experiences the character somehow always managed to survive. In his first outing, the Joker carved his victims faces with a post-mortem smile resembling his own. It would become an enduring calling card, easily supplanting the intended playing card motif. That, combined with the bright red lips and emerald green hair, made for an unforgettable iconic villain. Almost a decade would go by before the character was given a full origin story, yet he proved to be one of Batman's most popular villains.

Also appearing in *Batman* #1 and destined to become a love-hate figure in Batman's life was jewel thief Catwoman (initially simply 'the Cat'). Selina Kyle is a self-sufficient burglar who likes the finer things in life. In early appearances she would wear a furry cat mask while engaged in a robbery, but not a complete costume. 'I always felt that women were feline,' noted Kane. As time went by, the character developed as a female counterpoint to Batman, with her costume sporting the same ears, cowl mask, and cape. As with Batman and the Joker, Kane had turned to the movies looking for an archetype for his new female villain, eventually settling on 'blonde bombshell' Jean Harlow, a popular female star and pin-up of the Thirties (she made six films with Clark Gable, one of the inspirations for Clark Kent's name). By her second appearance, she'd been dubbed the Cat-Woman (*Batman* #2, Summer 1940) and went up against the Joker in a quest to steal valuable jewels. Catwoman carried a whip and developed a complicated, sometimes romantic, relationship with Batman/Bruce Wayne, although she didn't gain her distinctive leotard-like costume until 1946. Catwoman thrived in the Forties, before the character fell foul of the Comics Code Authority in the mid-Fifties [see chapter 6], resulting in her disappearance from comics until revived in the mid-Sixties.

Popular villain the Penguin didn't make his debut until *Detective Comics* #58 in December 1941, just as America entered the Second World War. A devious crime boss, short, rotund Oswald Cobblepot takes after the Joker in his employment of deadly trick umbrellas, but adopts the guise of the Penguin to further his criminal ambitions, modelling much of his activities after those of birds. Bullies had taunted him as a child who likened his short, fat appearance to that of a penguin. Operating from the Iceberg Lounge nightclub, the vengeance-driven Penguin was a more comedic villain intended to compensate for the rather grim turn the Joker had taken. Unlike the Joker, the Penguin was depicted as perfectly sane and always in control of his faculties. He even, on occasion, became a source of underworld information for Batman. The mascot of Kool cigarettes – a penguin in a top hat holding an umbrella – had served as inspiration for Kane and Finger.

August 1942 saw the arrival of another iconic Batman villain: Two-Face. *Detective Comics* #66 introduced former District Attorney Harvey Kent (later renamed to the more familiar Dent, to distinguish him from Clark Kent) who'd had one side of his face horribly scarred when gangster Sal Maroni had thrown acid at him in court. The resulting mental anguish saw him commit a series of crimes based around the duality of his nature. He'd make major decisions by flipping a similarly damaged coin (retrieved from Maroni), giving the resulting fall of heads or tails power over his choices. Two-Face was another take on the tragedy of Batman, a crime fighter who had been changed due to his dual identity. While the psychology of Batman would be explored in later years, in the early days Two-Face was an effective way of suggesting this is what Batman could become. In the case of Two-Face, Bob Kane's inspiration was all-too-apparent – Robert Louis Stevenson's classic tale *The Strange Case of Dr Jekyll and Mr Hyde*. Again, it was the movies that gave Kane the idea, especially the 1932 version of the story starring Frederic March – the role won the actor an Oscar (the film had been remade in 1941 with Spencer Tracy, so might have been fresh in Kane's mind), although Jerry Robinson also had a hand in developing the character. Two-Face was used sparingly, only appearing three times in the Forties and only twice during the Fifties (several imposters did make appearances).

Exploiting his victim's fear, the Scarecrow (*World's Finest Comics* #3, Fall 1941) was the alter ego of psychologist Jonathan Crane, who turns to crime after he is fired from his university. Much developed in the later Silver Age, the Scarecrow only made two appearances during the Golden Age, but he proved to be another memorable villain who'd be used effectively by subsequent comics creators who'd grown up reading the earliest superhero comics. The Scarecrow drew from the American horror fable *The Legend of Sleepy Hollow* by Washington Irving (featuring Ichabod Crane). The Scarecrow's crimes are committed in the name of research, to further his study of fear (although later versions of the character emphasized his latent psychopathic tendencies). Captured by Batman, Crane spends two years in Gotham State Penitentiary only to escape (as depicted in *Detective Comics* #73, March 1943) and form his own gang of super-criminals. The Scarecrow would not be seen again until 1955 and not developed in any great depth until the late-Sixties.

The last of the major Batman villains was also a latecomer. The Riddler first appeared in *Detective Comics* #140 in October 1948. Edward Nigma (sometimes 'Nygma' – as used for the Jim Carrey version in *Batman Forever*, 1995 – or even 'Nashton' in the comic book, depending on the writer) was yet another riff on the extravagant comic crime boss. By then Kane had taken a back seat on *Batman*, so the credit for creating the Riddler went to writer Finger and artist Dick Sprang (a veteran of the pulps hired by Ellsworth in 1941). Obsessed with riddles, puns and word games, the Riddler was yet another villain who enjoyed playing games with Batman more than simply pursuing crime. Clad in a green suit and green bowler hat, the Riddler sported the old-fashioned domino style mask seen on the Phantom. Question mark symbols popped up on his clothing (such as on a tie), or on his props and accessories. The Riddler would entice Batman into his traps and schemes by supplying the police with clues, most often in the form of difficult-to-solve riddles. His need to reveal clues to his activities in the form of a riddle was later explained as a form of obsessive-compulsive behaviour, but initially it was nothing more than a flamboyant quirk for the last of the major Golden Age *Batman* comic book villains. The core members of Batman's rogues gallery were all in place as the Forties drew to a close. Many of these memorable Batman villains were inspired by figures from pre-code cinema (before the implementation of the 1934 Motion Picture Production Code) and several would fall foul of the comics' own moral code, imposed on the medium in the Fifties.

DC Comics editor Whitney Ellsworth took a more business-like approach to the publisher's developing superheroes than Vin Sullivan. He'd worked for the company in the days of Major Wheeler-Nicholson, but between 1940 and 1953 he was the editorial director for DC Comics, supervising and developing such key titles as *Action Comics*, *Adventure Comics*, *Batman*, *Detective Comics* and *Superman*. Especially during the early days of the *Batman* strip he got involved in softening the edges of Kane's vigilante killer. It was Ellsworth who'd eventually decreed that Batman wouldn't use weapons or kill criminals. He also saw the potential in returning villains, so he

softened the early ruthless characters of the Joker and the
Penguin, and saved the Joker from being killed off at the
end of *Batman* #1. Ellsworth hired new editors, including Mort Weisinger (who came from a background in the
pulps) and Jack Schiff (who'd edit the various *Batman*
titles for the better part of two decades). Schiff worked
closely with writers to tighten their stories, reducing them
to their basic cores so making them suitable for the panels
of comic book pages.

Eager to exploit the possibilities of Batman, it was Ellsworth who saw the potential in bringing the character to
newspaper strips, just like Superman. The daily newspaper strip – beginning in October 1943 and titled *Batman
and Robin* – was the first venue to name Batman's secret
lair the Batcave (developed by Bill Finger after he saw a
cross-section cutaway of an underground military base in
Popular Mechanics). Kane turned his focus to the newspaper strip (which would run until 1946, edited by Jack
Schiff), completely stepping back from his creation's comic
book adventures, leaving that to Robinson and Sprang who
mimicked Kane's style. The core talent on the comic book
throughout the Forties remained Finger and Sprang, who'd
introduce new ideas, concepts, settings, and characters to
the mythology.

While the era's two most prominent superheroes,
Batman and Superman, would appear together on the cover
of *World's Best Comics* #1 (Spring 1941, based on one-shots
produced for the World's Fair and retitled *World's Finest
Comics* from #2) and many a cover thereafter, they didn't
actually meet in the strips inside. It wouldn't be until
Superman #76 (June 1952) that the costumed crime fighters
would appear in the same story (other than a brief wartime
cameo in a 1941 issue of *All Star Comics*). Their first meeting, instead, happened on radio in the mid-Forties.

Batman never enjoyed a radio series of his own (despite
a couple of aborted efforts during and after the war), but

he and Robin appeared as supporting guest characters in *The Adventures of Superman* radio series [see chapter 12] on 5 September 1945. Superman comes to the rescue of Robin, who enlists the Man of Steel to rescue Batman from Zoltan's wax museum where he has been imprisoned in suspended animation. This was the first of thirteen appearances in *The Adventures of Superman* radio show for Batman and Robin. Often they were called in when Superman actor Bud Collyer needed a holiday, so Superman would be knocked out of action thanks to Kryptonite, clearing the way for Batman and Robin to fight crime in his stead. On radio Stacy Harris initially played Batman, followed by Matt Crowley who became more associated with the role. Ronald Liss voiced Robin.

Towards the end of the decade, Robin would enjoy solo adventures in DC comic books starting in *Star Spangled Comics* #65 (February 1947) – Batman would make occasional guest appearances, meaning he was now featuring in four different comics simultaneously (*Detective Comics*, *Batman*, *World's Finest Comics* and *Star Spangled Comics*). The Forties would end for Batman with some resolution to his driving motivation, his need for revenge on the killer of his parents. *Batman* #47 (June–July 1948) revealed that the man responsible for turning young Bruce Wayne into crime fighter Batman was trucking company owner Joe Chill. Once he tracks him down, Batman cannot bring himself to kill Chill, but neither is there enough evidence to see him convicted. Celebrating his apparent triumph over the Caped Crusader, Chill boasts to his fellow criminal cohorts who immediately turn on him, gunning him down – he was responsible for the creation of their greatest enemy, Batman. Chill dies in Batman's arms, signing off with the plaintive 'I guess you got me'.

Although this may have been the ideal moment to conclude Batman's adventures, the character was now too big, second only to Superman in the comic book superhero stakes. Batman and Bruce Wayne would carry on much as before, battling evil and righting wrongs, right through the war years of the Forties and into the more conservative post-war Fifties, when they'd encounter possibly their smartest opponent, Dr Frederic Wertham.

PART 2: CRISIS!

5

SUPERHEROES GO TO WAR!

The success of Superman and Batman led to a flood of comic book superheroes in the Forties, many from DC Comics and several from rival publishers who would make their own mark on the development of the comic book superhero. In the early Forties the Second World War saw these American superheroes put to patriotic ends, often personally taking on the bête noire of Adolf Hitler, most strikingly with the famous cover of *Captain America* #1 that saw Cap punching Hitler. Paper rationing and the loss of creators to military service affected the growth of the superhero, despite immense popularity. However, by the end of the decade superheroes would be in retreat . . .

Many of the new superheroes came from All-American Publications, closely associated with DC Comics through a financial investment and with the founding father of the comic book, Max Gaines, as editor. Among the popular characters from All-American were the Flash (who debuted in January 1940), Hawkman (January 1940), Green Lantern (July 1940), the Atom (October 1940), and Wonder Woman (January 1942). The other major publisher was Martin Goodman's Timely (later Marvel), launched in 1939 and home to Sub-Mariner (April 1939, the first super-hero to fly), the Human Torch (October 1939), and the iconic Captain America (March 1941). The biggest-selling title of the period was *Captain Marvel* (a Superman imita-tor who appeared in February 1940) from Fawcett Comics, who also included Minute-Man (December 1941) and Cap-tain Midnight (June 1942, from a radio serial) among their superheroes. Widely read was Will Eisner's newspaper strip *The Spirit* (June 1940). Lower down the pecking order came Quality Comics with their satirical superhero Plastic Man (August 1941), by Jack Cole.

The first directly influenced character to attempt to steal Superman's cape was Wonder Man (*Wonder Comics* #1, May 1939), created by Will Eisner, a friend of Batman's Bob Kane. Eisner was commissioned by Victor Fox of Fox Comics, a rival to Harry Donenfeld's DC. Seeing the sales figures of Superman, Fox fancied a slice of the superhero comic book action for himself, so set up Fox Comics. His brief to Eisner for 'Wonder Man' was simple: he wanted his own Superman. As a result of a lawsuit from Detec-tive Comics Inc. (part of DC), Wonder Man's appearance in 1939 was a one-off. The single Wonder Man story told of inventor Fred Carson who during a trip to Tibet is given a mystical ring by an ancient monk. The ring gives Carson super-strength and the power to fight evil. Directly copy-ing Superman, Wonder Man hides his red super-suit under his everyday clothing. Eisner admitted: 'We knew it was very like Superman, that it was imitative, but we had no idea of its legal implications.' At the trial in 1940, Fox lost the case. The would-be mogul failed to learn his lesson, and launched the Moth in 1940, imitative of DC's newest superhero, Batman. That brought further legal action that saw the Moth swatted out of existence after just four appearances.

The first two years of the Forties saw the establishment of a range of superheroes who would go on to not only survive but prosper. In January 1940, the Flash made his debut in *Flash Comics* #1. Created by writer Gardner Fox and artist Harry Lampert, the Flash was Jay Garrick, a college student who acquires the power of super-speed by inhaling 'hard water vapours' after falling asleep in a lab (revised in the Sixties to the slightly more scientific sounding 'heavy water'). Based upon the Roman God Mercury (whose Greek equivalent was Hermes), messenger to the underworld, the Flash can run at superhuman speeds and has incredibly fast reflexes. As well as becoming a football star, Garrick dons a red shirt with a lightning symbol emblazoned across it, and a stylized metal helmet complete with Mercury-style wings to fight crime as the Flash. Early on, it seems that Garrick's identity as the Flash is not really a secret, although later he'd fall into line with the superhero trope of separating his everyday life from his crime-fighting activities through an alter ego. His super-speed made him hard to photograph, and therefore difficult to identify.

The next month saw the arrival of Captain Marvel, a superhero with marked similarities to Superman but who temporarily escaped the legal troubles that wiped out Wonder Man. Created by writer Bill Parker and artist C.C. Beck, he first appeared in Fawcett Comics' *Whiz Comics* #2 in February 1940. Fawcett had been directly inspired to enter the comic book market thanks to the success of Superman. Captain Marvel outsold Superman, but it would be another decade before DC Comics' infringement lawsuit was resolved, killing off the character. Youthful radio reporter Billy Batson has the power to transform from weedy youth to super-powered Captain Marvel whenever he utters the word 'Shazam' – made up of the initials of historical or mythic characters whose attributes Marvel adopted: Solomon (wisdom), Hercules (strength), Atlas (stamina), Zeus (magic power), Achilles (courage), and Mercury (speed). Initially Captain Marvel was intended to feature a team of six superheroes modelled after these archetypes, before an executive decided to combine the powers in a single figure named Captain Thunder. That became Captain Marvellous, before being truncated to Captain Marvel. The character shared his core characteristics with Superman (a mild-mannered alter ego, super-strength and speed, science fiction adventures), but was distinctively different as his human alter ego was a teenager rather than an adult, appealing directly to the wish-fulfilment of the target readership. Like the Flash, Captain Marvel sported a red outfit with a lightning flash insignia, and a Superman-style cape. Captain Marvel's antagonists included mad scientist Doctor Sivana, wartime adversary Captain Nazi, and nuclear-powered robot Mister Atom. Through the Forties Marvel's regular enemies were Mister Mind and his Monster Society of Evil – Mister Mind was revealed to be a tiny intelligent worm from another world. The Monster Society gathered villains from past Captain Marvel stories into one evil supergroup.

The summer of 1940 saw the arrival of Green Lantern in *All-American Comics* #16 (July 1940). The Golden Age Green Lantern was Alan Scott, whose discovery of a magic lantern allows him to create a ring that endows him with great powers. Freelancer Martin Nodell created the character for DC Comics, inspired by the sight of a trainman waving a lantern in a tunnel at the 34th Street subway station in New York. Borrowing from Wagner's operatic *Ring Cycle*, as well as elements of Chinese folklore and Greek mythology, Nodell was paired with Batman writer Bill Finger to develop the character. Initially magical, the power ring was later reinvented in the Silver Age (1959–70) as a more scientific, technological (albeit alien) gadget.

The first significant superhero team-up (other than the

linking of Superman and Batman on the covers of *World's Finest Comics*) was the Justice Society of America (JSA) in *All-Star Comics* #3 (Winter 1940). The idea of gathering various heroes together was initiated by editor Sheldon Mayer and writer Gardner Fox. Although popular characters such as Superman, Batman, the Flash, and Green Lantern would be occasional members, the plan was to feature lesser heroes who might later be spun-off into their own titles. It proved to be a venue in which new superhero ideas could be tried out, promoted if they caught on or quietly dropped. The original incarnation of the JSA would run for just over a decade, until All-Star Comics became All-Star Western in May 1951. The initial members of the team included Doctor Fate (a sorcerer), Hour-Man (whose 'miracle vitamin' gave him super-powers for just one hour), the Spectre (a murdered cop who returned as a ghost, created by Jerry Siegel), the gas-masked business-suit-wearing Sandman (whose special weapon was sleeping gas), Atom (a crime-fighting strongman), and Hawkman (a reincarnated Egyptian priest, and the only JSA team member to appear in the full original run of All-Star Comics).

Other notable new Forties heroes included Daredevil (appearing in Lev Gleason Publications' *Silver Streak* #6 in September 1940, not to be confused with the later blind Marvel character), and Doc Strange (appearing in Better Publications/Nedor Comics' *Thrilling Comics* #1, no relation to the later Marvel character). Where Strange was a scientist whose 'sun atoms' serum gave him super-strength, invulnerability and the power of flight, Daredevil was the archetypal orphan figure who grows up to become a crime-avenging marksman (using a boomerang). This first flush of derivative characters, and the strong regular sales that allowed them to continue issue after issue, was a consequence of the superhero boom. Kids across an America emerging from the travails of the Depression were keen on escapism wherever they could find it, and one of the cheapest and most regular forms of escape (along with the movies) were the four-colour dime comic books.

The following year brought another wave of new superheroes, but it was clear that the range of potential superpowers had almost been exhausted. Created for a back-up strip in the DC Comics title *More Fun Comics* #73 (September 1941), Aquaman echoed legends of Atlantis in its story of an underwater society from which Arthur Curry/Orin came. As the 'sovereign of the sea' he could breathe through gills, swim at high speed and communicate with sea creatures – he would go on to become a key figure of the war years. Plastic Man, created by writer-artist Jack Cole, was a satiric superhero, appearing in *Police Comics* #1 in August 1941 from Quality Comics (later acquired by DC). Able to stretch his body into any form, his quirky adventures were intended as a spoof of the more straight-laced Superman. Green Arrow – real name Oliver Queen – was another Robin Hood-style archery hero, a counterpoint to Batman, introduced in *More Fun Comics* #73 in November 1941.

A very different type of hero arrived at the end of 1941 when Wonder Woman made her first appearance in *All-Star Comics* #8. An Amazon warrior princess (inspired by Greek mythology), Diana of Themyscira/Diana Prince was the creation of psychologist and writer William Moulton Marston and drawn by sixty-one-year-old H. G. Peter. A feminist theorist who lived with two women in a polyamorous relationship, Marston believed in the educational potential of the new comic book form and set out to redress the all-male domination of the world of superheroes. He created a model of the Forties liberated woman, giving his female character strength and power equal to any of the male superheroes. As he noted, 'Women's strong qualities have become despised because of their weakness. The obvious remedy is to create a feminine character with all the strength of Superman, plus all the allure of a good and beautiful woman.'

Originally called 'Suprema', Wonder Woman was created as a member of an ancient all-female utopia who becomes a crime-fighting US Government wartime agent, with the unique ability to force her captors to tell the truth thanks to her magic lasso (Marston had a hand in promoting the lie detector). Her heavy silver bracelets could also deflect bullets. Within six months, Wonder Woman was leading her own comic. Marston would write twenty-eight issues before his early death in 1947. Marston laced his tales of Wonder Woman with images of dominance and submission, bondage and female power – all topics that exercised him and were becoming prominent in the underground cultures of the Forties. Of the largely male readership of comics, Marston wrote 'Give them an alluring woman stronger than themselves to submit to, and they'll be proud to become her willing slaves!'

Wonder Woman was the last major superhero to emerge before America's entry into the war, and she suggested new directions superheroes might take. Before any of those could be adequately explored, the newly confident world of American comic book superheroes had to face two threatening upheavals: the Second World War, and the moral panics and censorship of the post-war Fifties.

Between 1940 – by which time most of the first-wave superheroes were established – and the end of the Second World War in 1945, sales of comics across the US tripled. It may have been the 'Golden Age' for creativity in the first flush of superhero comics, but it was also a golden age in terms of business for those companies who managed to capture the zeitgeist. During the war years that meant many American superheroes turned super-patriotic.

For the US, entry into the Second World War didn't come until December 1941 and the Japanese attack on Pearl Harbor. Across Europe the fighting had been under way for two years. American involvement had long been anticipated – not least in the world of comics, which was largely staffed by young men likely to face a call-up into the military. Since earlier in 1941 several publishers had their writers and artists working overtime to stockpile material to see them through the dark days to come. Artist Dick Sprang, hired to work on *Batman* in 1941, recalled DC Comics' editorial director Whitney Ellsworth indicating that his work might not see print for some time. 'He wanted to stockpile all he could,' recalled Sprang, 'in case he lost the artists.' While Sprang was spared from service (due to poor eyesight), others reported for duty including DC editor Mort Weisinger, and comics team Joe Simon and Jack Kirby. Artist Bert Christman, who drew the early Sandman strips, joined the Flying Tigers – US pilots flying with the Chinese Air Force – and was killed in action.

The shadow of war made itself felt in American comic books long before the US was formally involved. As early as January 1940 (almost two years before Pearl Harbor) German spies featured in *Pep Comics* #1 (MJL Publications, later Archie Comics). That same issue featured the first comic book hero whose costume was patriotically patterned after the American flag (Superman sported the red and blue, but the third colour in this chest shield and in his belt was more often yellow than white). The Shield – created by writer Harry Shorten and artist Irv Novick for Archie Comics – was Joe Higgins, chemist son of FBI agent Tom Higgins who'd been killed by a German saboteur. Tom had been working on a super-strength serum that the Nazis were after, so Joe sets out to complete his work and clear his father's name. His costume featured a huge chest insignia, shaped like a shield and patterned after the American flag. Working directly under FBI Chief J. Edgar Hoover (the only one who knew his secret identity), the Shield was soon joined by orphaned sidekick Dusty Simmons (another whose father was killed by foreign agents) to foil an invasion plot by Moskovia (a fictionalized combination of Nazi Germany and the Soviet Union). The early Forties were a time of extreme patriotism, and the Shield was the first superhero to capture that in his motivations and design. He wouldn't be the last nor the most successful.

Superhero comics were in transition in the social ideologies they expressed. The late-Thirties costumed heroes were a product of Franklin D. Roosevelt's New Deal social reforms. Superheroes targeted common criminals and corporate greed and stood up for the 'regular guy' against the system. As the Forties dawned and the prospect of war loomed, this switched to a more blatant patriotism that then evolved into what would now be seen as distinctly uncomfortably anti-foreigner (mainly German and Japanese) propaganda. Superheroes would go to war, battling both on the home front (Batman) or taking the fight to America's enemies (Superman and Captain America, among others). Superman was already a defender of 'truth and justice' at home. Now, 'truth and justice' were to be exported, forcefully, to Europe in the name of democracy, liberty, and freedom from oppression.

This repositioning required a significant change in the characters of several existing superheroes. In different ways, both Superman and Batman had been problematic for law enforcement, seen as sources of trouble equivalent to the criminals they'd vanquish. For the war effort, both icons had to become tools of the state, to be used as signifiers of 'truth and justice', in defence of the status quo. Any reforms they'd fought for at home had now to be fought for worldwide, and that included such key capitalist concerns as property rights and industrial monopoly.

Superman had fought for the welfare of the public against corporate greed, as well as against those in power who were corrupt or out for themselves, whether it be City Hall, labour unions, or organized crime. Targets included war profiteers, careless mine owners, and overbearing prison wardens. Now, in the Forties, the last son of Krypton would be battling Nazis, 'Japs' and fascists, and would become a defender of the American state. In defending American society from these external threats, wartime superheroes found themselves defending the establishment status quo.

The problem for Superman was that he could not be seen to stop the war single-handedly in comic books when it was continuing in real life. The wish-fulfilment of Superman's potential in a wartime context was too good to be entirely resisted. *Look* magazine commissioned Superman's co-creators Siegel and Shuster to devise a special comic strip for their 7 February 1940 edition explaining how Superman would bring an end to the war. This fanciful two-page tale saw the Man of Steel flying around the world, rounding up Hitler and Stalin (later an ally of the US) and dragging them unwillingly to Geneva to stand trial at the League of Nations. The 'power-mad scoundrels' are deemed guilty of 'modern history's greatest crime – unprovoked aggression against defenceless countries'. In his regular comic book adventures during wartime Superman could perform no such amazing deeds. He could sell war bonds, encourage the troops, and maybe engage in some low-level fighting, but he could not be seen to use his amazing powers to bring an end to a war that continued relentlessly in reality. Patriotic coverlines such as 'Knock out the Axis with bonds and stamps!' made regular appearances on Superman comic books.

One of the earliest of the new batch of superheroes created in Superman's image to take a stand against the aggression of Nazi Germany before the US was involved in the conflict was Namor the Sub-Mariner. Created by writer-artist Bill Everett for pulp publisher Martin Goodman through the packager Funnies Inc., Sub-Mariner was the mutant son of a princess from the mythical undersea kingdom of Atlantis and a human sea captain. Namor (whose name derived from the classical-sounding 'Roman', but spelled backwards!) enjoys super-strength, the ability to live under the sea and the ability to fly. He first appeared in *Marvel Comics* #1 (October 1939), but his first war-related cover was on the February 1940 edition of *Marvel Mystery Comics* depicting him tackling the crew of a submarine flying the Nazi flag. So successful was *Marvel Comics* #1 (which also featured the debut appearance of the original Human Torch – an android with the ability to control fire), selling close to 900,000 copies across two print runs, that Goodman rapidly set up his own comic book publisher called Timely Publications, head-hunting staff such as Joe Simon from his supplier Funnies Inc. (Timely would later become Marvel Comics, the biggest competitor to DC Comics). Sub-Mariner took on a more active role so that by early 1940 he was protecting the shipping lanes from attack and actively battling the Nazi threat. Stories had to have an American angle – as when Namor rescued American sailors (supplying much-needed food to Europe) from harassment by the German fleet. Eventually, the Sub-Mariner becomes a full part of the war effort, helping Allied forces fight the Nazi war machine, more than a full year before the US officially joined the war.

Also in 1940, writer Joe Simon conceived a patriotic character he'd dubbed 'Super American', but deciding there were already too many superheroes with 'super' as part of their titles, he settled for Captain America instead. As he said later: 'There weren't a lot of Captains in comics.' Simon was working for Timely as their first editor, having already worked for DC on Sandman. The first issue of *Captain America Comics* appeared in December 1940 (cover-dated March 1941), a year prior to Pearl Harbor. The now-infamous cover art drawn by Jack Kirby featured Captain America punching out Nazi dictator Adolf Hitler. Notably, Captain America's shield apes the symbol of the earlier Shield and fears of a potential lawsuit caused it to be changed to the more familiar round shield. That first issue sold almost one million copies. Simon and Kirby would work together on Captain America for the first ten issues, with Kirby joining Timely as the company's first art director.

Born in 1917 as Jacob Kurtzberg in New York's poor Lower East Side, Jack Kirby was one of the main influential practitioners during the Golden Age of American comic books. After co-creating Captain America (following a brief period at the Fleischer animation studios – just like Bob Kane – working on Popeye cartoons, and a spell with packagers Eisner & Iger) with Joe Simon, the pair moved to DC where they worked on Sandman and created Manhunter, a vengeance-fuelled crime fighter. Kirby served in the US Army from June 1943, landing at Omaha Beach in Normandy two months after D-Day. His art abilities saw him work in forward reconnaissance, sketching maps and pictures of strategic locations. After suffering frostbite, he returned to the US and spent six months in the motor pool before being discharged from the Army in July 1945. Simon spent the war in the US Coast Guard and working in military public relations. Thereafter he and Kirby worked in a variety of comic book genres in the post-war expansion, including Western, romance, and horror comics. Kirby would go on to draw Green Lantern for DC Comics in the Fifties, and then make his mark at Marvel in the Sixties where he worked closely with Stan Lee and co-created the Fantastic Four, Thor, the Hulk, Iron Man, the X-Men, Silver Surfer, Doctor Doom, Galactus, Magneto, and a whole host of other Silver Age superheroes and super-villains. Kirby would continue to make significant contributions to comics until his death in 1994, aged seventy-six.

Simon was clear that Captain America was a nakedly political creation: he wanted to reflect his own repulsion at the Nazi regime. He felt the anti-war movement was well organized, but those in favour of American involvement didn't have a platform. Captain America was his answer. The response was hugely favourable, but that didn't stop Simon receiving 'threatening letters and hate mail. Some people really opposed what Cap stood for'. Like many of the superhero creators, Captain America's everyday alter ego was the son of poor immigrants, Irish rather than Jewish. Steve Rogers was orphaned early in life and is studying art when the Second World War starts. Attempting to enlist, Rogers is rejected as he doesn't meet the physical requirements. He is signed up for the mysterious 'Project Rebirth', an experimental attempt to create a 'super-soldier' to fight the Axis powers. A serum created by a scientist is tried out on a willing Rogers, transforming the frail young man into a perfect human exhibiting extreme strength, stamina, intelligence, and resilience. The serum is lost when a Nazi spy kills the scientist, an act Rogers avenges as his first act as patriotic superhero Captain America.

Plans to unleash an army of super-soldiers are abandoned, but the one the US government has created is deployed as a strategic secret weapon to help defeat the Nazis. Posing as a clumsy infantry private, Rogers is deployed into the field when needed. He strikes up a friendship with another young recruit, 'Bucky' Barnes, who becomes his sidekick. President Franklin D. Roosevelt presented Captain America with a new round shield made of an alloy of steel and vibranium (a fictional metal that recurs in the Marvel universe). As well as fighting Nazis and Japanese, Captain America tackles disfigured Nazi agent the Red Skull and domestic villains such as the Black Talon.

Captain America was the first lasting superhero to come from Timely. With its patriotic approach, the strip won a legion of followers, shifting over one million copies each month, out-selling *Time* magazine. Among the contributors to Captain America's early development was the writer of a text story – 'Captain America Foils the Traitor's Revenge' – in issue #3: Stanley Lieber, later known as Stan Lee, the driving force behind Marvel Comics' rapid development in the Sixties. Following Simon and Kirby, other writers and artists took on the character after issue #10 (January 1942). Later, as the war drew to a close, Captain America and Bucky Barnes confronted Baron Zemo who attempts to sabotage a new experimental drone plane. In the course of defusing a bomb on board the plane, it explodes apparently killing both heroes, although Rogers is hurled into the freezing waters of the North Atlantic. With the war over, Captain America had served his purpose . . . for now.

As the war in Europe escalated through 1941, so too did its presence in American comic books. Many superheroes battled the Nazi menace on home turf, with the Human Torch defending ammunition factories from Nazi saboteurs, and Captain America rooting out fifth columnists and enemy spies. A little-remembered wartime superhero also used the flag as a significant part of his look. Captain Battle (created by Carl Formes and Jack Binder) featured in *Silver Streak Comics* #10 (until #23, the final issue). The title was part of Lev Gleason Publications, a small independent New York comic book publisher and one of the first to recognize adult interest in comic book heroes. Crime comics (like the much-imitated *Crime Does Not Pay*, 1942) and romance comics were the company's main titles, so Captain Battle was a bandwagon-jumping aberration. Suffering from an injury (the loss of his left eye) from the previous war, Jonathan Battle has a jetpack (called the 'luceflyer') among a series of amazing technological inventions (from his mountain laboratory) that he uses to thwart those who would bring the war to America. Red trousers, white boots, plus a blue top with a giant white star, formed his patriotic costume.

The surprisingly prophetic culmination of all this pre-entry activity was a December 1941 cover-dated (so released months earlier) edition of National Comics (confusingly published by Quality Comics, not DC) depicting 'Oriental' military forces launching an attack on US bases at Guam and Pearl Harbor, long before the real thing. This may have been informed speculation, as any Japanese attack would be expected to fall on the west coast, but it was still something of a harbinger of events yet to come.

Although the US was still over a year away from participating in the war, it made sense that Hitler would share the cover of *Captain America* #1. It wasn't his only comic book cover appearance. The cover of *Daredevil Battles Hitler* #1 had a fearful looking Adolf cowering before an onslaught of American superheroes. Hitler was a hate figure across the world, even before further nations added their weight to the fight against his Nazi regime. Perhaps more importantly, he was easy to caricature. His distinctive look was transformed into an instantly recognized character on the page. The angled cut of his hair, distinctive Charlie Chaplin-style moustache, and Nazi uniform were easily imitated and expanded upon for satiric effect. The outsized gestures and ranting speeches that captivated a certain section of the German audience made Der Führer something of a laughing stock elsewhere. His plans as German Chancellor made him an ideal real-world super-villain, even if paradoxically his Aryan supremacy message made some superheroes themselves look like the fulfilment of Nazi fantasy. Hitler became aware of his presence in American comic books and enlisted his propaganda chief Joseph Goebbels to attack the comics' largely Jewish creators, dismissing the material as 'Jewish propaganda' and Superman co-creator Jerry Siegel in particular as 'physically and intellectually circumcised'.

Generally, Forties American comic book villains were not widely inspired by real-life figures such as Hitler and

Stalin, but instead traded on caricatures fuelled by widespread jingoistic views of the nation's enemies, especially the Nazis and the Japanese. These views were partly fostered by official American policy towards such 'enemy' groups living within the US, with the Japanese in particular victims of internal internment from 1942 and promoted by government as enemies of the nation. Around 110,000 Japanese-Americans and Japanese living in America on the Pacific coast were forcefully shipped to 'War Relocation Camps' following the attack on Pearl Harbor.

Against this dark background, it was fairly easy for comic books to caricature their Japanese enemies as 'Japs' under the guise of 'patriotic racism'. That resulted in comic book covers such as *Action Comics* #58 depicting Superman operating a hand-cranked printing press producing 'patriotic' posters that read: 'Superman says: You can slap a Jap with War Bonds and Stamps!' *World's Finest Comics* #8 featured Superman, Batman, and Robin sharing a platform under a banner reading 'Sink the Japa-Nazis with Bonds and Stamps'. On the cover of *World's Finest Comics* #11, Superman, Batman, and Robin were shown working in a 'Victory Garden' growing fruit and veg. *Master Comics* boasted an American hero named 'Bulletman' who tangled with the evil 'world enemy no.1 Captain Nazi'. *Superman* #17 (July 1942) featured the Man of Steel hoisting aloft Adolf Hitler in his right hand and a caricatured Emperor Hirohito in his left, while issue #18 (September 1942) saw Superman straddle a bomb falling upon America's enemies promoting bonds and stamps which will 'do the job on the Japanazis'. In the Superman newspaper strip, the Man of Steel even rescued Santa Claus from the clutches of Hitler, Hirohito, and Mussolini.

MLJ Publications's *The Hangman* featured this coverline on #3: 'Nazi and Japs, you rats! Beware! The Hangman is everywhere!' A trio of patriotic figures – Yankee Doodle Jones, Dandy and Major Victory – appeared on the cover of *Yankee Comics* #2 (November 1941), while Captain Freedom adorned *Speed Comics* #19 (June 1942), about to clobber a buck-toothed, yellow-skinned caricature of a Japanese soldier. The Claw – an Oriental super-villain with huge fangs – appeared in Gleason Publications' *Daredevil*. Metaphorically giant versions of Captain America, the Human Torch, and Sub-Mariner are depicted on the cover of *All Select Comics* #1 (September 1943) storming a fortress labelled 'Hitler's Berchtesgaden'.

These jingoistic approaches and uses of superheroes may look alternately comic and simplistic today, but in a wartime context superheroes as propaganda became commonplace. Creators, writers, and artists – and their myriad creations – all played their part in the American war effort, and that meant turning the tools at their disposal – paper, pens, inks, and four-colour comics rather than bullets and bombs – to tackling the enemy. Some older readers may themselves have ended up in military service, with their reading matter shaping their attitudes.

The Asian enemy in particular was depicted in comics as a particularly alien 'other', impossible to understand or sympathize with. Ugly demonic-like creatures, often sporting fangs and actual yellow skin, Japanese officers were depicted as stupid, foolish, or cruel – sometimes all three at once. Incapable of inventing their own technology, the Japanese were out to steal American know-how, either in the shape of plans and blueprints or by kidnapping prominent scientists and engineers. This was a deliberate removal of humanity from an entire people, making it easier for them to be seen as deserving of American retribution following Pearl Harbor. The story titles featuring these caricatured Asians were almost all kids needed to read to get the message: 'Funeral for Yellow Dogs', 'The Terror of the Slimy Japs', and 'The Slant Eyes of Satan' all tell their own story. These depictions built on the long-standing 'yellow peril' concept, a metaphorical attack on Chinese immigrants who arrived on America's west coast in the late nineteenth century that had been deployed in stories in the Thirties pulps like those featuring Fu Manchu and movie serial villains such as Ming the Merciless.

The internment of Japanese-Americans or Japanese living on America's west coast was seen as a form of legitimization for the racist content in early-Forties comics. After all, the government had officially scapegoated the Japanese in America, so it couldn't be wrong for the comic books to do likewise – it was their patriotic duty. Fifth columnists – whether German or Japanese – were suspected of being everywhere, no one could be trusted. The anti-Japanese feeling that infested these comics seemed harsher than the regular attacks on the main enemy, Germany. Nazi caricatures didn't carry the racial overtones applied to the Japanese. Many Nazis were shown as foolish or misguided, but there was also a fear of their genuine threat encoded within their depiction: they were a menace to be taken seriously.

The titles of some of the new wartime comics betrayed their single-minded subject matter – Spy Smasher, The Fighting Yank, The Unknown Soldier. The patriotic names of some of the newest war-focused superheroes – Uncle Sam, Captain Victory, the Star-Spangled Kid, Captain Fearless – even had their female counterparts (following Wonder Woman) in Miss Liberty, Pat Patriot and Liberty Belle. The enemies of the US had similar evil flip-side names: Baron Gestapo, Captain Nippon, and Captain Swastika. The main instigator of this trend for ultra-patriotic superheroes and their racially denigrated antagonists, Joe Simon, later admitted, 'The whole reason we put Captain America out was that America was in a patriotic frenzy.' Editor Gardner Fox, co-creator of Sandman and a regular Batman writer, noted: 'If I could do it with a wave of my hand, I'd stop all this war and silly nonsense of killing people. I used superheroes' powers to accomplish what I couldn't do as a person. The heroes were my wish fulfilment figures for benefiting the world.'

None of this was accidental or merely the product of widespread jingoistic feeling, but a promoted policy of the American government. Official agencies, such as the Office of Facts and Figures and the Office of War Information, co-opted the media to support the war effort. Those producing entertainment were encouraged to think in terms of work that would contribute to the war effort. The official aims were to raise American morale, to identify the enemy Axis powers clearly, and to encourage public participation and communicate the government's war aims. This propaganda material was wrapped in otherwise entertaining content, so as not to put off those readers the government hoped would receive their messages. The enemies of the nation were foreign dictators like Hitler and Stalin, but also domestic profiteers and home-grown subversives. All this was filtered through the many (but not exclusively) Jewish comic book creators and emerged as the outlandish propaganda that swamped these titles.

While superhero comics offered succour to millions of young readers restricted to the home front during wartime, they also entertained millions of US troops stationed abroad, and reminded them what they were fighting for. According to Mike Benton in *Superhero Comics of the Golden Age: An Illustrated History* (1992), almost 44 per cent of US soldiers undergoing basic training were regular comic book readers. On military camps, comic books regularly outsold the *Saturday Evening Post*, *Life*, and *Reader's Digest* by almost ten to one. When troops were posted overseas, their families would meet their comic book needs with regular care packages. According to the *New York Times*, one in every four magazines sent to overseas troops was a comic book, while 35,000 special military copies of *Superman* went to those who'd enlisted every month.

The wartime economy was good for comic book

publishers, despite paper shortages (the need to recycle comics to produce paper is why wartime comics are notoriously rare on the collectors' market). According to *Publishers Weekly* and *Business Week*, around fifteen million comic books were being sold each month by early 1942. By the end of 1943, following the wave of wildly patriotic superheroes (some short-lived), comic book sales had reached twenty-five million, with as many as 125 different titles on news-stands each month. Retail sales for the comic book sector in 1943 added up to more than $30 million. There was money to be made in being patriotic through printed comic book entertainment.

Like Joe Shuster, Clark Kent had been rejected for military service due to a problem with his eyesight – as depicted in the *Superman* newspaper strip. He accidentally used his X-ray vision to read out the wrong eye chart from another room entirely rather than the one in front of him. Jerry Siegel was drafted in 1943, but didn't see any overseas action, remaining in Georgia working on the service newspaper *Stars and Stripes* for the duration of the war.

During the war years DC was publishing six regular comic books featuring their leading character. Superman became an icon of what Americans were fighting for: democracy, virtue, and wholesome values. Following the pre-war feature in *Look* magazine, Superman was largely confined to the sidelines, his super-powers simply too great to be used directly. In a *Superman* newspaper strip in 1942, he explains the reason for his non-involvement: 'The American armed forces are powerful enough to smash their treacherous foes without the aid of Superman.' The war didn't seem to reach Metropolis, except for the occasional cheerleading moment from Superman, those uber-patriotic covers, and some over-the-top flag-waving dialogue. The villains menacing the city were rarely Nazi saboteurs or Japanese agents, but fantasy creations like Mr Mxyzptlk, a malevolent imp from another dimension; mad scientists like the Ultra-Humanite (a variant on Siegel and Shuster's original 1933 'evil' Superman); the airship-inhabiting Lex Luthor hatching plans for world domination; the childish, middle-aged Toyman; and the practical joker and self-styled 'funniest man in the world', the Prankster.

During the war, Siegel and Shuster became separated from their creation – Siegel due to his war service and Shuster thanks to his worsening eyesight. Others worked on the strip, including writers Don Cameron and Alvin Schwartz, and artist Wayne Boring, under editor Jack Schiff. The team ran into trouble when Schwartz scripted a 1945 newspaper strip story about a cyclotron, a science gadget he remembered from a magazine article. This brought the interest of the War Department to Superman, as the cyclotron was a key element in the secret development of the atomic bomb. Many newspapers mysteriously dropped the strip, but the story was allowed to run through to its conclusion, the War Department having decided that by acting against it they might draw more attention to it.

The last year of the war saw a new character added to the Superman family, Superboy. He first appeared in *More Fun Comics* #101 (January–February 1945), depicting Superman's youthful years in his hometown of Smallville and on the Kent Farm. Superboy started out modestly as a few pages at the back of the comic, but soon expanded, leaving the humour-oriented *More Fun Comics* behind for a new berth in *Adventure Comics* in 1946 as the leading character, before winning his own title in 1949. Superboy combined the identification of young readers (usually with superhero sidekicks) with the wish-fulfilment of Superman's powers. Despite setting out to show the birth of a legend, the Superboy strip put the character in the distinctive costume, long before he supposedly developed his split identity. The contradiction was largely ignored, but it would create continuity problems for future DC Comics. Superboy gained a red-headed girlfriend named Lana Lang (continuing the alliterative Ls), and went to school in Smallville in the guise of Clark Kent (all this would later – minus the costume – form the basis of the hit television series *Smallville*, as well as the earlier, less-well regarded *Superboy* television show).

Siegel and Shuster did not approve of Superboy, with Siegel returning from war service to discover other hands writing stories for his characters, so depriving him of earnings. This unhappiness, combined with continuing resentment over their decision to sell the Superman rights to DC for a mere $130, led to an ill-fated 1947 lawsuit to regain control of their characters and $5 million in compensation. The court decided that the company retained legal ownership of Superman, but that Siegel and Shuster should be compensated for Superboy as their names had been used to promote the character in their absence. The judge's ruling noted that the character's creators 'had no property rights in Superman since they had assigned all rights to the publishers at the start of Superman's and their own career ten years earlier'. The pair were paid $100,000 for Superboy but had to renounce their claim on Superman. They stopped working for DC, who removed their credits from all the ongoing Superman comic books – this stalemate would last for the better part of thirty years until 1975 and further legal action.

Meanwhile, during the war Superman had conquered another medium (alongside radio and movie serials) by featuring as the central character in a novel, *The Adventures of Superman*, written by George Lowther, writer and narrator of the radio series. The novel featured Superman investigating a series of hauntings, which turn out to be a front for a gang of Nazi spies, but is also notable for offering further background to Superman's time on Krypton and his years growing up on the Kent farm, elements that would become central to the ever-growing Superman story.

In contrast to Superman, Batman wasn't as obviously

enlisted in the cause of wartime propaganda. His war-related cover appearances saw him more often shilling for war bonds (as on the cover of *Batman* #12, August/September 1942) than denigrating America's enemies. According to academic Will Brooker, during the war years Batman displayed a 'consistency and fidelity to a strangely removed ideal of urban crime fighting while the rest of his culture went to war'. One of a mere handful of war-themed stories was 'Swastika Over the White House' from *Batman* #14 (December–January 1943), in which Batman and Robin contrive to trap a Nazi gang on US soil under their own giant swastika flag. Unlike Wonder Woman, an unashamedly wartime creation whose early adventures were contemporary to the Second World War, Batman existed in a crime-ridden fantasy land of his own, separate from the travails of the real world. Bruce Wayne wasn't even drafted, clearly one of the privileges of wealth. The core characteristics of Batman remained largely unaltered by the war, and his lack of superpowers might be key. This folkloric Batman, the dark-caped avenger who fights crime, would be reinterpreted markedly in the years to come, but he remained virtually unaffected by the war that saw so many other superheroes rush to the patriotic barricades.

Steve Rogers fought the good fight as both super-powered Captain America and as ordinary Private Rogers, while DC's super-team Justice Society disbanded so that the individual members could enlist in the military and do their bit for the cause. *All Star Comics* #11 (June 1942) saw Hawkman, the Atom, Dr Fate, Hour-Man and Starman all enlist voluntarily in the US Army. Johnny Thunder joined the Navy, while Wonder Woman signed up for the Ambulance Corps, and Dr Mid-Nite enlisted as a surgeon. The group would come together as the Justice Battalion, including Siegel's Spectre. Superheroes' war efforts reduced the issues of participation to a black-and-white choice, with the costume-clad heroes backing the military without any reservations, influencing their young readership to take part in the battle to defeat the Nazis. Isolationists became spies or – worse – collaborators. The national ideology was enforced by the new entertainment form of comic books, previously regarded as a threat to education and morals. It would be again in the Fifties, after the pro-war patriotism had passed.

6

SUPERHEROES VERSUS THE COMICS CODE!

Superheroes faced two deadly enemies in the post-war years and into the Fifties: a declining readership and an enquiry by the US Government. With superhero comic book sales in free fall in the post-war era, publishers explored new concepts bringing them into conflict with US government committees and a notorious psychiatrist. This would lead to the imposition of the Comics Code which, in turn neutered the surviving superheroes resulting in a spate of silly, juvenile, and inoffensive storylines.

The Second World War had seen a boom in comic books, but the artistic legacy left behind was mixed. More people than ever before were buying a wider variety of titles: the comic book had become a staple of most American childhoods. The first quarter of 1946 had seen DC Comics alone selling over twenty-six million comics, an increase of 30 per cent on the previous year. Seventy million Americans

– almost half the population – read comics, according to the Market Research Company of America. Yet, within the pages there were insidious messages hidden under the guise of outspoken patriotism.

The simple American patriotism of characters like Captain America and Superman were ideal for providing those on the home front a way of understanding the war, but they faced difficult times ahead as the late-Forties and early-Fifties brought a huge backlash against comics, and the politics of the Cold War made such simplistic jingoism look old fashioned. Having fought Hitler and Hirohito, could America's superheroes simply return to battling bank robbers and criminal syndicates? In the years immediately after the end of the war, American youth's fascination with superheroes began to wane. By 1947 circulation for all superhero titles was on the slide from the wartime highs. Best-sellers like Captain Marvel were losing millions of sales every month. The jingoism of the patriotic superheroes faded away, as did many of the heroes themselves. Their work was done, and they were no longer needed.

In the Fifties comic books diversified into new genres, including humour titles, such as the best-selling Dell comics featuring cute animals from Walt Disney and Warner Bros. cartoons. These attracted bigger audiences than the adventures of humans and aliens wearing capes and tights. Romance, cowboy, and crime comics all caught up with the superheroes sales in the late-Forties. The biggest boom was in horror comics, launched in 1947 when William Gaines took over his father's EC Comics and began a series of garish titles, including *The Vault of Horror*, *The Haunt of Fear*, and *Tales from the Crypt*. By 1948 there were 425 comic book titles published regularly, a figure that grew to 592 the following year, and had reached a staggering 696 by 1952, but fewer of them featured superheroes.

All these comics were to bring unwelcome attention on the industry in the Fifties. It started slowly in 1948, when the senior psychiatrist of the New York Department of Hospitals, Dr Frederic Wertham, held a symposium on 'The Psychopathology of Comic Books'. Wertham's interest would grow, as would the threat to American comics – and now there were few superheroes on hand strong enough to deal with this menace, with only the central trio of Superman, Batman, and Wonder Woman continuing through the decade.

From the mid-Fifties, comics – including those featuring superheroes – came with a prominent seal of approval from the Comics Code Authority (CCA) on the covers. For almost sixty years, from 1954 until the early twenty-first century, this seal would mark out those publishers that had agreed to abide by the industry's self-imposed rules governing 'acceptable content'. The industry had come a long way from the early days when it was founded by would-be gangsters and ex-bootleggers, but the imposition of the CCA code was the result of a media storm, a rising fear of juvenile delinquency, and research by Dr Fredric Wertham (whose work, it would turn out, largely depended on faked results, as revealed in 2013). The rise of the horror comics brought the wrath of the public down on comic books and had resulted in the creation of the Comics Code Authority, but the Code would also change the destiny of the superheroes.

As early as 1948, citizen groups formed calling for the banning of crime and horror comics, and by the end of the year fifty US cities had restrictions on comic book sales, including on Army bases. From the late-Forties into the early-Fifties public concern about the disruptive content of comics read by teenagers continued to bubble under. ABC Radio broadcast a debate headlined 'What's Wrong with Comics?' in March 1948, while in February 1950 the Cincinnati Committee on the Evaluation of Comic Books published a study in *Parents Magazine* revealing that (in their view) 70 per cent of comic books contained some kind of 'objectionable' material. Articles expressing concern about the possible effects of comics on young minds appeared in popular magazines including *Collier's* (March 1948), *Reader's Digest* (August 1948), and the influential *Ladies' Home Journal* (November 1953).

With readers' interest in Caped Crusaders waning, the Fifties were ideally primed for the rise of the horror comic. A new generation of teenagers who'd missed the war due to their age now regarded superheroes as old hat and were looking for something to call their own, distinct from the comics favoured by their *Superman* and *Batman*-reading older brothers. EC Comics broke new ground in the graphic depiction of death, destruction, and mayhem in comics. These tales, graphic though they were, also contained a strong sense of macabre humour that lightened their impact. They quickly attracted a dedicated readership, providing an alternative to the few remaining costumed superheroes. By 1954, when the curtain began to fall on them, EC comics were selling 150 million copies every month, rivalling the biggest superheroes.

The titles from EC and the countless less-impressive imitators provoked a public backlash that built on the unease that many parents had been feeling from the late-Forties. Comic books came under renewed attack from the church, parents' groups, and teachers who claimed they contributed not only to juvenile delinquency, but also to the growing illiteracy of the younger generation. The final nail in the coffin was the 1954 publication of Dr Fredric Wertham's book *Seduction of the Innocent: The Influence of Comic Books on Today's Youth*. Wertham reinforced the public perception that comics were dangerous and a major contributor to Fifties' juvenile delinquency. His book was excerpted in *Ladies' Home Journal*, reaching a far wider popular audience.

Wertham's critical attack and growing public concern

resulted in the convening of a Senate subcommittee to Investigate Juvenile Delinquency in the United States in spring 1954 to specifically look at the effect of comics on American youth. Wertham was the chief witness. Many comic book writers, artists, and publishers were also called before the committee, with most admitting that there had been excesses and that comics had to be made suitable for younger readers. One hold out was EC's William Gaines, who saw nothing wrong in the cover art and contents of his horror comics. The subcommittee concluded that the comic-reading youth of America were being exposed to '. . . a constant diet of crime, horror and violence . . .', and maintained that this had to stop. While the Senate hearings – led by anti-crime crusader Estes Kefauver – were not followed in detail by America's parents, the newspapers wasted no time in heavily reporting the basic message: comic books were bad for your kids.

Wertham had not restricted his criticisms to just the crime and horror comics. Although the EC titles were his central target, he also used examples from superheroes to make his case. Wertham complained that Batman and Robin were depicted as homosexual partners, encouraging sexual 'deviancy' in youthful readers. He wrote that Bruce Wayne and 'Dick' Grayson '. . . live in sumptuous quarters, with beautiful flowers in large vases, and have a butler, Alfred. Bruce is sometimes shown in a dressing gown. As they sit by the fireplace, the young boy sometimes worries about his partner . . . it is like a wish dream of two homosexuals living together'. Wertham saw a relationship intended as that of a father/son or mentor/pupil (based on the testimony of those he surveyed) as presenting a model of homosexual life. While it is possible some of Wertham's correspondents saw in Batman and Robin gay role models, his accusations of a 'wish dream' are not without foundation. The pair do have a secret life (as superheroes), a constant anxiety of being unmasked, and they do wear elaborate costumes (the March 1957 tale 'The Rainbow Batman' in *Detective Comics* #241 has Batman trying out a variety of colourful crime-fighting outfits, including a pink ensemble and others coloured orange, lime, and yellow). They not only work together, but they have a joint domestic life. They are rarely out of each other's company. Batman and Robin do show great concern for each other (usually because the narrative demands of the serial form have Robin repeatedly kidnapped: in *Batman* #67, October–November 1951, the Joker kidnaps Robin from a fairground's Tunnel of Love!).

Batman wasn't the only superhero Wertham turned his firepower on. In the adventures of Wonder Woman he detected a bondage theme (something her eccentric creator William Moulton Marston had never denied), as well as evidence that her strength and independence from men suggested she was a lesbian. He saw Superman as both un-American and fascist, writing 'Superman (with the big S on his uniform – we should, I suppose, be thankful that it is not an S.S.) needs an endless stream of ever new sub-men, criminals and "foreign-looking" people not only to justify his existence but even to make it possible. It is this feature that engenders in children either one or the other of two attitudes: either they fantasize themselves as supermen, with the attendant prejudices against the sub-men, or it makes them submissive and receptive to the blandishments of strong men who will solve all their social problems for them – by force.' He compared the Fox/Charlton character Blue Beetle to a 'Kafkaesque nightmare', and asked 'Is that the best we can do for children, that we teach them the Green Lantern will help?' Wertham was the real-world super-villain the comic book superheroes could not defeat.

To avoid the threat of state regulation of comics, the remaining publishers still in business rapidly revived the late-Forties Association of Comics Magazine Publishers as the new Comics Magazine Association of America

(CMAA) in September 1954. Aiming to reassure the public and assuage the concerns of Congress, the new CMAA appointed New York magistrate and expert in juvenile delinquency Charles F. Murphy as its head (after Wertham declined). He was charged with devising a 'code of ethics and standards' for the industry that would allow self-regulation, rather than state control. Murphy established the Comics Code Authority (CCA) that devised a new code.

Banned from comics under the Code was the depiction of violence and gore, especially in (but not limited to) crime and horror comics. Sexual content was also outlawed, even mild forms of sexual innuendo, as were depictions of drug usage. Disrespect for authority – whether in the form of a policeman, judge, government official or respected institutions – was prohibited, while a requirement that 'good should triumph over evil' was enforced. Illustrations in comics must not be 'lurid, unsavoury [or] gruesome'. The words 'terror' and 'horror' could not be used in titles, ending Gaines's plans to launch further EC horror comics. Feeling he'd been specifically targeted, Gaines cancelled all his horror titles and focused exclusively on *Mad*, his new satire magazine. These defensive actions largely avoided individual States establishing local ordinances banning crime and horror comics from stores. Comics that did not feature the CCA seal, designed to look like an official stamp, would not be carried by major distributors or sold through major retailers, forcing most large publishers to sign up to the CCA and so abide by the Code.

In 2010 Wertham's original research data that provided the backbone of his claims in *Seduction of the Innocent* and the attack on comic book content became available to researchers. Investigating his research, Carol Tilley, Assistant Professor at the Graduate School of Library and Information Sciences at the University of Illinois, discovered that 'Wertham manipulated, overstated, compromised and fabricated evidence – especially that evidence he attributed to personal clinical research with young people – for rhetorical gain'. Tilley's work (published in 2013) revealed that Wertham used a non-representative sample of young people who came from troubled backgrounds, that he took colleagues' information and claimed it as his own, and that he dropped testimony where it conflicted with his thesis and also manipulated the statements of many of his adolescent subjects so they better conformed with his criticisms of comics. His aim overall was to present his evidence as objective scientific truth, and in that he succeeded, bringing about the creation of the CCA and the adoption of the censorious Comics Code that controlled the content of most widely available comic books for almost sixty years.

The decline of superheroes in the post-war period and the shakedown in the comic book world following the creation of the Comics Code Authority, combined to create a space where a new type of comic book could prosper. The big winners in the mid-Fifties were the child-focused comics produced by Dell, featuring Mickey Mouse, Donald Duck, and clean-cut heroes such as Tarzan and Roy Rogers. Circulations for these family-friendly titles soared while the superhero, crime, and horror comics nosedived.

Several superheroes found themselves benched as a result of falling circulations and changing tastes. Timely Comics' *Marvel Mystery Comics* (featuring the Human Torch), *Sub-Mariner Comics*, *Captain America Comics* (retitled *Captain America's Weird Tales* in an attempt to cash in on the EC horror titles, and billing Captain America as a 'Commie Smasher!'), were cancelled, with the company adopting the Atlas Comics name and logo from late-1951 as part of an attempted rebranding. That same year DC Comics' *All Star Comics* (featuring the JSA superhero team) was retitled to capitalize on the latest trend to *All-Star Western*, keeping continuous numbering from #58.

The Silver Age revival, the second great period of

superhero comic book creation and success, was kicked off by DC Comics' *Showcase* #4 (September 1956). The idea behind *Showcase* was to try out a new character in each issue. 'In the Fifties,' recalled DC editor Julius Schwartz, 'we were really suffering.' The first old superhero to be revived was the Flash, whose eponymous comic book *Flash Comics* Schwartz had cancelled in 1949.

Assuming that mid-Fifties comic book readers – and potential readers – would not even remember the old Flash, Schwartz took the opportunity to reinvent the character in the light of the new 'jet age'. The new Flash was police scientist Barry Allen, who gains his super-speed when caught in a spill of toxic chemicals during a lightning storm. In a neat form of self-referentiality, Allen takes on the alter ego of the Flash after reading the Golden Age comic book (put out by Schwartz). The look of the superhero was redesigned by artist Carmine Infantino who'd contributed to the original Flash Comics, as well as working on Green Lantern and Justice Society of America. Infantino would go on to become DC Comics' editorial director in the late-Sixties and eventually publisher from 1971, and was still drawing the Flash in the early-to-mid-Eighties. He retired in the Nineties and died in 2013, aged eighty-seven.

Sales of *Showcase* #4 unexpectedly went through the roof, so follow-up issues featuring the Flash (issues #8, #13, and #14) led to a relaunch of the stand-alone title *The Flash* (from spring 1959, and picking up the numbering of the old *Flash Comics* from #105 after a decade). For the first time, the Flash had a cowl mask, as well as a one-piece red suit augmented by yellow slashes at the waist and cuffs, with yellow boots. He kept the lightning 'flash' insignia on his chest, but also sported a pair of dainty ears, indicating Mercury's wings. This Flash had his very own Lois Lane, in the shape of reporter Iris West, and a batch of the usual super-villains to combat, including the blue hoodie-wearing Captain Cold (a variation of Batman's Mr Freeze, who also made his debut in 1959), head of the villainous cabal known as the Rogues; Mirror Master, a criminal who manipulates mirrors and reflections to baffle his pursuers; and Weather Wizard, a green-clad figure who controls the weather with a wand. This reinvention of the Flash pointed the way for revivals of other comic book superheroes through the Fifties and into the Sixties.

The Fifties were a troubled time for Superman, falling from favour in the first half of the decade before returning in triumph as a new generation of readers enthusiastically rediscovered the iconic superheroes of the Forties. His origins had been retold in greater detail by writer Bill Finger in *Superman* #53 (July/August 1948), just in time for the character's tenth anniversary (it would be done again in 1961 by Otto Binder in *Superman* #146, July 1961, in 'The Story of Superman's Life' which added honorary membership of the United Nations to Superman's achievements). The radio serial *The Adventures of Superman*, which had been running since 1940, had ended in 1951, with Michael Fitzmaurice playing Superman, having just taken over from Bud Collyer who'd played the role for a decade. It had originated several novel elements of the mythos that were adopted by the comics (including *Daily Planet* editor Perry White, copy boy Jimmy Olsen, and Superman's nemesis Kryptonite). Superman had also appeared in the movies [see chapter 12] in two live actions serials: *Superman* (1948), and *Atom Man vs Superman* (1950), both with Kirk Alyn. From 1952 chunky George Reeves would play Superman in 104 episodes of the television series *Adventures of Superman*, until his mysterious death in 1959. It was from the television show's opening narration that Superman became defender of 'the American way'.

While Superman was flying high on radio and on the small screen, he was reinvented in comics. The television series had lead to a proliferation of Superman spin-offs, including *Superman's Pal Jimmy Olsen* (from 1954), and the younger skewed *Adventure Comics* (which had been running since 1938, but enjoyed a sales boost thanks to television), and Superboy (in his own title since 1949). There were other additions to the Superman family in the Fifties. Following the Jimmy Olsen book there was *Krypto the Superdog* (from 1955), and *Superman's Girl Friend Lois Lane* (from 1958), as well as additions to the main books, such as Supergirl (from 1959). Superman's dog was introduced as a test subject for Jor-El's rocket to Earth, with the rocket knocked off course and arriving on Earth long after Superman. Unfortunately, the super-animals didn't end there, with later comics featuring the whimsical likes of Streaky, the Super-Cat, and Comet, the Super-Horse. This was a symptom of a wider move to juvenile fantasy following the imposition of the Comic Book Code.

There had been several previous attempts at a female equivalent of Superman. The Woman in Red, created by writer Richard E. Hughes and artist George Mandel, had appeared in *Thrilling Comics* #2 (March 1940, published by Nedor Comics), a policewoman who donned a red cloak and hood when off duty to fight crime. Not super-powered, but perhaps a female equivalent to Batman, she is the first female hero preceding Wonder Woman. She continued having adventures in *Thrilling Comics* for the next five years. Another female superhero was Satanna, the Tiger Girl, scientist and surgeon Sara Descari, and an enemy of Hawkman (featured in *Flash Comics* #13, January 1941). Another similar Forties heroine was the dark-haired and buxom Phantom Lady, created in the Eisner & Iger shop for Quality Comics, first appearing in *Police Comics* #1 (August 1941, an anthology title that included the debuts of Plastic Man and the Human Bomb). She was the socialite daughter of a US Senator who donned a yellow bathing suit and a cape to fight crime.

Wonder Woman appeared in 1942, and was quickly

followed by Mary Marvel in *Captain Marvel Adventures* #18 (December 1942). Created by pulp writer Otto Binder and Marc Swayze (who modelled her after Judy Garland), she was the twin sister to Billy Batson, and a member of the growing Marvel family in Fawcett Comics, including Captain Marvel, Jr. Other significant heroines included the Blonde Phantom, a masked crime fighter from Marvel predecessor Timely. Louise Grant was the secretary for a private detective who took on her own cases, clad in a red evening gown and wearing a domino mask. She appeared in the final issue of *All Select Comics*, #11 (Fall 1946 – it became *Blonde Phantom Comics* from the following issue and ran until 1949), and was one of a number of female characters introduced to comics just as superheroes began to temporarily disappear from news-stands (including patriotic wartime character Miss America; Captain America's sidekick Golden Girl; female Sub-Mariner, Namora; the Human Torch's secretary Sun Girl; and Venus, an avatar of the goddess Aphrodite). Many of the female characters of the time – like Black Canary, introduced in *Flash Comics* #86 (August 1947) – were simply non-super-powered vigilantes who donned outrageous costumes to battle crime, often alongside or instead of a male hero. By the Fifties, around 25 per cent of the comic book marketplace was taken up by female-focused romance comics featuring the domestic exploits of models and nurses. Many of the other popular female characters featured in jungle comics – such as Sheena, who dated back to 1937 – and were clearly aimed at male readers.

Superman's super-powered female co-stars included Lois Lane temporarily becoming Superwoman in a dream (*Action Comics* #50, May 1943); a Latin-American athlete joining Superboy as 'Super-Girl' (*Superboy* #5, November–December 1949); and Jimmy Olsen using a magic totem to wish into existence a 'Super-Girl' to help out Superman. The real deal arrived in *Action Comics* #252 (May 1959), when Superman's cousin Kara Zor-El, the last survivor of Argo City – blasted through space with the destruction of Krypton – arrived on Earth. With powers identical to Superman, and the Earthbound alter ego of Linda Lee, she became an occasional sidekick to the Man of Steel.

The decade brought Superman a significant new super-villain called Brainiac who collected cities from throughout the universe shrunken down in bottles, like model ships. He first appeared in *Action Comics* #242 (July 1958), when Superman discovers one of the cities Brainiac has in his bottles is Kandor, capital of Krypton. Superman rescues the city and keeps it in his Fortress of Solitude, discovering he can shrink himself and explore the trapped city. Along with a shrunken Jimmy Olsen, they become the Batman and Robin of Kandor City (named Nightwing and Flamebird).

The Superman titles were still under the editorial control of Mort Weisinger during the Fifties. Kryptonite came to comic books under Weisinger's watch, after it had been resisted for years. Introduced into the radio serial in 1943, it was taken from an unpublished Jerry Siegel story from around 1940 about 'K-Metal' from Krypton, in which Superman not only falls prey to this Achilles heel but also reveals his secret identity to Lois Lane. Editors at the time hated both ideas and spiked the story, but the concept of a metal from Krypton that could nix Superman lived on, and after the radio serial it was used again in the first movie serials. Weisinger felt one way of keeping Superman fresh was through gimmicks, as seen in his various 'Superman family' spin-offs, and Kryptonite – the radioactive remains of Superman's home planet of Krypton – was too big a gimmick to resist. It was introduced (coloured red) in *Superman* #61 (November–December 1949), and when recoloured green for its second appearance, the deadly metal became a regular feature.

Kryptonite wasn't always deadly: in various doses it

could lead to paralysis, loss of consciousness, or just general weakness in Superman. As soon as he discovered its existence, super-villain Lex Luthor attempted to synthesize it to use it against the Man of Steel. Red Kryptonite made a return in *Adventure Comics* #252 (September 1958) in which Superboy found it was ten times stronger than green Kryptonite. In future appearances red Kryptonite would be unpredictable, causing new effects as and when required editorially, leading to any number of off-the-wall plots until attempts were made in the early-Seventies to dilute its effects on Superman.

With the success of Superboy with younger readers and the rise of the newly labelled 'teenager', there was an attempt to reflect the readers in the comic book pages, as with the superhero team the Legion of Super-Heroes. It began with an Otto Binder story in *Adventure Comics* #247 (April 1958) that introduced three teen heroes from the future (the thirtieth century) who come to the aid of Superboy: Cosmic Boy, Saturn Girl, and Lightning Boy. They test Superboy for membership of the League (a superhero club of the future inspired by Superboy himself), pretending he'd failed their tests when in reality he'd passed. The story was intended as a one-off, but the next appearance of the time-travelling superhero squad came twenty issues later in *Adventure Comics* #267 (December 1959) – Lightning Boy had now become the suitably alliterative Lightning Lad.

The Legion of Super-Heroes proved popular, so returned regularly in issues of *Adventure Comics*, *Action Comics* and other titles supervised by Weisinger. The team was filled out by a host of new additions, including the self-explanatory future teen heroes Chameleon Boy, Invisible Kid, Colossal Boy, Triplicate Girl, Shrinking Violet, Sun Boy, Phantom Girl and Ultra Boy. Many of their attributes played upon teen concerns, such as being invisible to others or trying to be in three places at once to cope

with the demands of homework, chores, and the new lei-
sure activities of the Fifties (movies, television, the mall,
comic books). The Sixties would see the similar Teen Titans
(a 'junior Justice League' team of sidekicks like Robin and
Kid Flash) find success.

Following the unexpected comeback success of the
Flash, DC Comics' Julius Schwartz was looking for other
previously 'retired' superheroes to revive. Next on his list
for a makeover was Green Lantern, whose last appearance
had been as part of the Justice Society of America super-
team in *All Star Comics* #57 (March 1951). The dedicated *Green Lantern* comic book had been cancelled years
before, with the last issue being #38 (May–June 1949). In
Showcase #22 (September–October 1959) Schwartz relit
the Green Lantern.

Schwartz's new angle was to increase the science fiction
elements, rather than the fantasy aspects of the original
character Alan Scott. Where Scott had a magic lantern and
stories that played on the tale of Aladdin and his magic
lamp, the new Green Lantern, test pilot Hal Jordan, was
given a 'power ring' by dying alien Abin Sur. This made
Jordan a member of the Guardians of the Universe as well
as a member of the Green Lantern Corps, a group of inter-
stellar police. Schwartz brought a cosmic scale to superhero tales, combining the science fiction of other worlds
and alien beings with the more Earth-bound heroics of the
regular superheroes.

Artist Gil Kane was charged with giving shape to the
new Green Lantern, abandoning the usual superhero costume for a sleeker transformation. The character featured
in the next two issues of *Showcase* following his debut,
before launching in his own title, *Green Lantern* #1 (July–
August 1960). The team of pulp writer John Broome and
Kane kept the title fresh and the character developing for
several years, with the next major revisions not coming
along until 1970.

The Fifties saw Superman co-creator Jerry Siegel working at DC Comics once more following an intervention by
his wife, Joanne. Despite the legal problems over Superman and Superboy, Siegel was rehired to work on Superman
scripts (including the Legion of Super-Heroes), but without credit. His bosses were now Weisinger and Schwartz,
his one-time contemporaries. His speciality became the
so-called 'imaginary stories', tales that deviated from
established Superman continuity. He wrote stories that
saw Superboy captured by the government where he establishes an evil dictatorship, and a Supergirl tale that saw Mr
Mxyzptlk temporarily resurrect her Kryptonian parents.
In *Adventure Comics* #271 (April 1960), Siegel gave Luthor
the first name of Lex and revealed that he and Superman
had grown up together in Smallville, while in *Superman*
#141 (November 1960), Siegel had Kal-El witness the
last days of Krypton as a displaced time-ghost incapable
of interfering. In particular, Siegel made significant – if
largely unsung – contributions to the teen-heroes of the
Legion of Super-Heroes, creating characters such as Brainiac 5, Lightning Lad and Spider Girl. It was a way to earn
money and keep working, but Siegel's old resentments still
burned deep and he and Joe Shuster would be back in court
attempting to wrest control of Superman from DC Comics
in the Seventies.

Along with Superman, Batman was one of just a handful
of the original superheroes to be continually published
through the war years and into the era of the Comic Code
Authority. As with Superman, there was a focus in the
years after the war on lighter material, with far less social
commentary. Where Superman had added various, notably
younger 'family' members in Superboy and Supergirl, so
Batman also entered the realm of juvenile fantasy. Far from
his bleak origins and his battles against the dark, menacing urban world of the Forties, Batman in the Fifties was

depicted as a respectable citizen, even a paternal figure to sidekick Robin, enjoying clean-cut adventures in a colourful and optimistic environment (in response to Wertham). It was very different to the Batman that had come before, and distinct from the dark reinvention he would undergo in the mid-Eighties.

Although they'd appeared together on covers of wartime issues of *World's Finest Comics*, Superman and Batman actually first teamed up in a strip in the June 1952 issue #76 of *Superman* in a story appropriately titled 'The Mightiest Team in the World'. Each having booked on to a crowded ocean cruise, Clark Kent and Bruce Wayne end up sharing a cabin and discovering each other's superhero identities. Also on the cruise is Lois Lane, so the two crime-fighters have to protect their secret identities from her. The cover depicted both heroes attempting to rescue Lois, each declaring this was uniquely a job for them . . . The success of this gambit saw the format of *World's Finest Comics* revised so that both superheroes would share adventures. This proved to be one of the few sure-fire superhero success stories during the Fifties, and the format endured until the comic finally folded in 1986.

Following the criticisms from Wertham and others, the Senate hearings, and the establishment of the Comics Code, Batman took a lighter turn for the rest of the decade. The idea to create a family of characters for Batman, like those developed for Superman, came from the book's then-editor Jack Schiff. Gone were the gritty crime stories, and gone was the close relationship between Batman and Robin, Bruce Wayne and his 'ward' Dick Grayson. To counter Wertham's claims, more women were introduced to the lives of Batman and Bruce Wayne, as with Batwoman (from 1956). Wealthy heiress Katherine Kane is introduced in *Detective Comics* #233 (July 1956) as the motorcycle-riding, black and yellow-clad Batwoman. Inspired by the example of the 'notorious' Batman, Kane has decided to put her wealth and resources in the service of fighting crime in Gotham City. Kathy – as she was known – was clearly intended as a love interest for Batman/Bruce Wayne. She was followed by her niece, Betty Kane (named after Bob Kane's wife) who doubled up as Bat-Girl and a romantic interest for Robin. Instead of a utility belt, Batwoman had a 'utility purse' packed with gadgets and weapons disguised as typical female items such as lipstick, bracelets, cosmetic compacts, and hairnets. In their desperation to show Batman wasn't gay, the creators of the comic ended up featuring a stereotypical female character filtered through male eyes, thus doing no one (let alone the few female readers of comics in the Fifties) any favours. Even Alfred was replaced by the 'safer' female figure of Aunt Harriet...

As the decade progressed, the *Batman* strips became more science fiction oriented, in keeping with the atomic age as depicted in science fiction movies such as *The Day the Earth Stood Still* (1951), *It Came from Outer Space* (1953), *This Island Earth* (1955), and *Forbidden Planet* (1956). The range of characters expanded and became sillier, including Ace the Bat-Hound (the Bat-equivalent of Krypto the Super-Dog), Bat-Mite, and Bat-Ape. Ace first appeared in *Batman* #92 (July 1955) and was a German Shepherd dog, like canine movie heroes Rin Tin Tin and Ace the Wonder Dog. Adopted by Batman, the dog had a hood matching Batman's own and a bat-emblem dog tag. The spurious reason for dressing up his dog in such bizarre fashion was that as Bruce Wayne he'd placed several ads in his hunt for the dog, which featured a prominent star marking on its head. Worried that the easily recognized dog might be connected to him and so reveal his identity as Batman, Wayne decided to disguise the dog in an appropriate super-dog costume! The Bat-Hound would become a regular in Batman comics through to the mid-Sixties.

Bat-Mite was a little different, and even more off-the-wall.

First appearing in *Detective Comics* #267 (May 1959), Bat-Mite was an imp-like character (echoing Superman's frequent antagonist Mr Mxyzptlk – the two even teamed up four times in the pages of *World's Finest Comics*) introduced in the story 'Batman Meets Bat-Mite'. A tiny being who lived in the 'fifth dimension' and possessed advanced technology, Bat-Mite's skills appeared magic. As Bat-Mite idealizes Batman, he dresses in a similar style whenever he gets involved in adventures with his (super)hero, even instigating strange happenings to capture Batman's attention. Neither villain nor friend to Batman, Bat-Mite is really more of a nuisance. As with the Bat-Hound, the character would reappear until the DC titles were revamped once more in the mid-Sixties.

The Fifties saw a new roster of super (and not-so super) villains take on the caped crusader. Assassin for hire Deadshot made his debut in *Batman* #59 (June–July 1950). As a child, Floyd Lawton had accidentally killed his brother, saving the father he hated – ever since, he'd developed his marksman skills to ensure he never missed a target again. After attempts to take over the Gotham criminal underworld failed, Deadshot ended up in jail. Later he'd join the Suicide Squad, determined to exit life in the most spectacular way possible – instead circumstances made him an anti-hero fuelled by the need for revenge when his own son is killed. He'd go on to become a member of Lex Luthor's super-villain gang, the Secret Six, and form a close bond with Catwoman.

Killer Moth (in *Batman* #63, February–March 1951) was a less successful new bad guy. As a costumed anti-Batman figure, he aimed to help criminals the way Batman helped ordinary citizens. Minor criminal Drury Walker was obsessed with fame, so adopted a Bruce Wayne-style identity as a wealthy playboy, but also a costumed 'hero' identity as Killer Moth. He was a miserable Batman wannabe, regularly defeated. He'd go on in later comics to sell his soul to a demon and be transformed into a genuine moth-creature, losing his humanity in the process. The Firefly continued the insect theme (*Detective Comics* #184, June 1952), in reality Garfield Lynns, a pyromaniac petty criminal and ex-movie effects expert who burnt down large parts of Gotham. Horribly scarred after being caught in one of his own fires, Lynns wears an all-over flame-retardant suit. At one point he was even the protégé of Killer Moth.

Before the decade was out, Batman was assailed by the Terrible Trio, a triple threat of the Fox, the Shark, and the Vulture (*Detective Comics* #253, March 1958) who wore animal hoods and business suits, and Calendar Man (*Detective Comics* #259, September 1958) who was determined to keep a date with Batman. All his crimes reflected significant dates or holidays, and he'd adapt his costume to fit. Doctor Double X made his debut in *Detective Comics* #261 (November 1958). He was Dr Simon Ecks, an unstable scientist who created a 'energy duplicate' of himself, a cruel and evil figure who quickly took him over. Another obvious riff on Robert Louis Stevenson, Doctor Double X would become a recurring foe for Batman and later need two superheroes to defeat him when Batman called upon Superman for help.

The most successful and longest lasting of all the Batman villains of the Fifties was Mr Zero – or Mr Freeze as he later became. *Batman* #121 (February 1959) introduced Dr Victor Fries (pronounced 'Freeze') as another of Gotham City's seemingly endless parade of misguided scientists. Having frozen his wife Nora in the hope of finding a cure for her degenerative disease, Fries is transformed when the corporation funding his experiments cuts off his cash flow, leading to an accident with his cryogenic equipment that changes him into a creature that can only exist at sub-zero temperatures. Developing a protective cryogenic suit, he embarks upon a quest to revenge himself and save his wife. Batman is in his sights as he holds him partially responsible for thwarting his attempts to rob banks to fund his research. Initially adopting the guise of Mr Zero, Fries reinvents himself as Mr Freeze and begins an on-going battle of wits with Batman and Robin. Freeze was a clever combination of then-newsworthy technology with the best attributes of the comic book super-villain. After a few misfires and abortive attempts, the writers and artists behind Batman in the troubled Fifties had discovered a super-villain who'd last, even if they'd had to freeze him to do it.

The Fifties was a period when Batman's gadgets and crime-fighting technology was refined, taking shapes very familiar to Bat-Fans today. A new model Batmobile, a new jet-age Batplane, a flying Batcave mobile HQ and the underwater Bat-Marine were all introduced, while the origins of the Batsuit were revealed. All Batman's gadgets, technology, and whacky vehicles were more than enough to make up for his lack of superpowers and the Fifties were a time of huge technological innovation, especially in the areas of transport, from cars to planes. In *Detective Comics* #156 (February 1950) an all-new Batmobile ('one I've been planning for a long time,' says Batman) was intro-duced after the previous version was destroyed in pursuit of a criminal gang. The new vehicle was 'ten years ahead of anything else on wheels', and resembled an elongated Studebaker featuring a built-in laboratory, a 'knife-edge' nose for breaching barriers, a roof-mounted searchlight, a Bat Signal projector, and rocket thrusters. The Batmobile would continue to evolve through the decades, with new gadgets constantly added.

Inspired by the first helicopter flight in 1939, Batman already had an experimental Batgyro, but it was the coming of the age of jet travel that allowed him to upgrade his flying machine to the '100-miles-an-hour' jet-propelled Batplane in *Batman* #61 (October–November 1950). The vehicle was also fitted out as an 'aeraquamobile', allowing it to travel on land and function as a speedboat, as well as fly in the air. In *Detective Comics* #257 (July 1958) Batman and Robin would be kitted out with personal flying machines known as Whirly-Bats. The Batcave also took to the air in *Detective Comics* #186 (August 1952). Essentially a giant helicopter, the Flying Batcave provided Batman and Robin with mobile headquarters that contained all the crime-fighting and data analysis equipment they were used to having access to, including panoramic surveillance capabilities and a smoke generator to provide cloud cover for hiding in. Towards the end of the decade, Batman was using the Bat-Copter (from *Detective Comics* #254, April 1958) – a tricked-up super helicopter. Of course, Batman's villains had to have their own equivalent vehicles, including the Freezemobile and the Joker's Goon Car.

Although it had begun as little more than a tunnel between Wayne Manor and an old, deserted barn, the Batcave (Batman's rather nearer-to-hand equivalent of Superman's Fortress of Solitude) had evolved from its humble beginnings to become a technology-laden subterranean lair. The Batcave's origins were revealed in *Detective Comics* #205 (March 1954), drawing upon its depiction in the Forties cinema serials. A secret door in Wayne Manor, hidden behind a grandfather clock (sometimes a bookcase), allows access by setting the time on the clock to 10:47 (poignantly the time young Bruce Wayne's parents were murdered – a constant reminder of his motivation for fighting crime).

Batman ended the decade by joining the superhero team the Justice League of America in *The Brave and the Bold* #28 (February 1960), reappearing several times during the year. Following *Showcase*, Julius Schwartz was using *The Brave and The Bold* as another try-out title, where he could run new ideas and see if any of them caught on. The Justice League of America was one such, a reinvention of the old Justice Society, a title that Schwartz found 'uppity'. The title of 'League' made this superhero team sound like a gathering of elite sportsmen and women, rather than a club for malcontents. Initially comprising the revamped League were Green Lantern, the Flash, and new hero Martian Manhunter (he'd first appeared in a back-up story in *Detective Comics* #225, November 1955). A green-skinned alien from Mars, the Manhunter was accidentally teleported to Earth where he is stranded. He naturally enough decides to become a costumed crime-fighter, while waiting for his Martian chums to rescue him, or for Earth technology to develop to the stage where he can be sent home. He was more a detective than superhero, despite his alien origins. Also joining the League were Wonder Woman and Aquaman. Superman and Batman would play supporting roles in the League's adventures. This enduring team set the template for superhero groups and would feature in their own titles from the end of 1960, going on to become a major feature of the comic book landscape of the Sixties.

Following the death of her creator, William Moulton Marston, in 1947, the task of supplying stories for Justice League member Wonder Woman had fallen to Robert Kanigher, the co-creator of the second (and best-known) version of the Flash. Without Marston's firm guiding hand, some of the edges were smoothed out in Wonder Woman's character and she became a more conventional superhero fitting better with DC housemates Superman and Batman. The effect of Wertham's attacks, combined with the Senate hearings and the new writer, softened Wonder Woman, so she became less of a feminist and fell into the traditional role of pining after a man, pilot Steve Trevor (as well as later infatuations with Merman and Birdman).

Following the death of originating artist H. G. Peter, new artists Ross Andru and Mike Esposito revamped the character in 1958, with *Wonder Woman* #105 offering up a new origin story for the Silver Age. This revealed her super-powers to be gifts from the gods (shades of the Greek heroes), with her blessed with the attributes of Aphrodite (beauty), Athena (wisdom), Hercules (strength) and

Mercury (speed) while still in her crib. Her Second World War origins were erased, and by 1960 a second title had been introduced featuring Wonder Girl (the youthful Wonder Woman, just as Superboy was the youthful Superman). The times were certainly changing as a new decade loomed and a major new player prepared to shake up the cosy world of superhero comics.

PART 3: EXCELSIOR!

7

MARVEL RISING

No new superheroes had matched the seismic impact of the originals, Superman and Batman. Wonder Woman was the first successful female superhero, despite her sometime status as the secretary for the Justice Society (a position that had obliged her to sit out much of the war). Captain Marvel had challenged Superman on his own turf, but had disappeared along with publishers Fawcett in 1953. It was only with the arrival of the tumultuous decade of the Sixties that a genuine challenger to DC Comics would arise in the form of the revived Marvel Comics and its roster of more 'realistic' superheroes. The driving forces behind this new era in superhero history were Stan Lee and Jack Kirby.

Marvel had its beginning in the original superhero boom at the end of the Thirties. Publisher Martin Goodman established Timely Comics in 1939 after a period as a salesman during the Depression and a career in pulp magazines producing Western, sports, and detective magazines.

Jumping on the superhero bandwagon Goodman launched *Marvel Comics* #1 (October 1939) using material supplied by packager Funnies, Inc. Among the characters in that first Marvel comic book were the Human Torch and the Sub-Mariner. Goodman built his own staff, head-hunting creators from Funnies, Inc., including Joe Simon. Joined by artist Jack Kirby, Simon created Timely's third superhero, Captain America, in 1941. When Simon and Kirby left after ten issues, Goodman hired Stan Lee to be the company's new editor.

Stanley Martin Lieber was born in 1922 in New York City to Eastern European Jewish immigrants. His childhood hero was Errol Flynn, and heroic action movies would have a major impact on his future work. Sharing a bedroom with his younger brother, Larry, the teenage Lieber was happy to spend his days at DeWitt Clinton High School in the Bronx. Reading and writing occupied him, and he began to dream of writing 'the great American novel'. Part-time roles as a stringer for a news service and as a writer of press releases brought him to Goodman's Timely as an editorial assistant in 1939, aged just seventeen: he had an advantage as his cousin, Jean, was married to Goodman. His first work, a filler text story in *Captain America* #3 (May 1941), saw him adopt the pen name Stan Lee, which he has used ever since, and later adopted as his legal name.

The post-war years and the Fifties afforded Lee the opportunity to learn the skills and build the experience he would apply to the new superheroes from Marvel in the Sixties. As the first flush of superhero success faded, Goodman instructed Lee to chase whatever new genre looked likely to sell. That saw Timely move into romance comics in the late-Forties, horror comics in the pre-Code early-Fifties, Western adventures in the middle of the decade, and finally comics featuring giant monsters, driven by the success of the Godzilla movies, at the end of the Fifties. Lee spent three years during the war in the US Army Signal

Corps, where he created manuals and training films. Married and with a daughter, Lee was living in Long Island. History repeated as DC's superhero revivals saw Goodman instruct Lee to chase success once more with a new line of superheroes for the renamed Marvel Comics.

According to legend, Goodman was inspired to return to superheroes during a game of golf with DC's Jack Liebowitz in 1961. Perhaps foolishly, given they were professional rivals, Liebowitz confided in Goodman that DC's ad-hoc superhero team of Superman, Batman, Wonder Woman, and Green Lantern in the Justice League of America had been a huge hit. The information was soon imparted to Stan Lee as an instruction that Marvel should have its own superhero team. However, the almost-forty-year-old Lee was ready to pack in comics. His wife, Joan, suggested as he was thinking of quitting anyway he could respond to Goodman by doing whatever he liked. Lee saw an opportunity to create a superhero team he really believed in, and his experiment led to the debut of the Fantastic Four.

Jack Kirby co-created the Fantastic Four with Lee. After the war he'd worked for a variety of publishers, creating romance comics with Joe Simon (as well as their own short-lived joint company, Mainline Publications), before joining Timely/Atlas in the mid-Fifties. He worked on Western hero Black Rider, and the Yellow Claw, a Fu Manchu 'yellow peril' villain. Following a couple of years back at DC where he retooled Green Arrow, Kirby found a niche at Atlas working on their 'weird monster' anthology comics, such as *Strange Tales*, *Tales to Astonish*, and *World of Fantasy*. Like Lee, Kirby was beginning to tire of comics, but he felt trapped. When the opportunity came to launch new superheroes, Lee turned to Kirby, although the artist still harboured resentments over disagreements between them dating back to the Forties.

The Fantastic Four was the first new superhero team of the Silver Age not to come from DC, who up to now had been content to recycle key superheroes from the Golden Age. Lee's approach was straightforward: although his heroes would be super-powered, they'd also be real, relatable people, unlike powerful figures such as Superman. After two decades, Lee felt the superhero field had become complacent, the leading characters serving as idealistic role models with an unattainable perfection. There were no ongoing repercussions for Superman/Clark Kent and Batman/Bruce Wayne. Nothing ever really changed for them, and they seemed to have nothing but the most superficial of 'real' lives outside of their superhero adventures. Lee wanted to explore the consequences of being a superhero on a group of otherwise 'ordinary' people.

However, the humans who made up the Fantastic Four were far from ordinary. Reed Richards (Mister Fantastic) was a genius scientist. His eventual wife, Sue Storm, and her impetuous teenage brother Johnny, joined Richards and co-pilot Ben Grimm in a test flight of their space rocket. Their prototype ship is caught in a 'cosmic storm' and the four crew members are exposed to extremes of radiation. Upon returning, they discover each has developed weird, but very particular, superpowers. Richards can stretch his body to any lengths and into any shape, Sue can become invisible, and Johnny can surround himself in flame (like the Human Torch) and fly. Perhaps worst off is Ben Grimm, buried under orange stone-like skin (more monster than a hero), but exhibiting powerful strength and endurance. The team prove just as likely to use these powers in mundane, everyday life as they are battling monsters and super-villains.

According to Lee, 'The characters would be the kind I could personally relate to: they'd be flesh and blood, they'd have their faults and foibles, they'd be fallible and feisty, and – most important of all – inside their colourful, costumed booties they'd still have feet of clay.' Lee and Kirby would brainstorm ideas together, before Lee handed the story outline to Kirby who rapidly drew the art, delivering his finished work back to Lee, who filled in the dialogue balloons and captions. This collaborative approach became known as the 'Marvel method' and would become their standard way of working within a year.

The exact details of who came up with what concept during the creation of the Fantastic Four have been lost, with both Lee and Kirby offering variants. Much of the success of Marvel in the Sixties was laid at the feet of Lee, with only comics fans appreciating the importance of artists such as Kirby, and Steve Ditko (on Spider-Man). Some of Kirby's previous work (notably *Challengers of the Unknown*, created for DC in the mid-Fifties) resembled the Fantastic Four, but it took the combined efforts of both Kirby and Lee to produce the superhero team that launched Marvel in a fresh direction. As comics historian Mark Evanier (an assistant to Kirby in the Seventies) noted, the general feeling at the time was that the Fantastic Four 'was created by Stan and Jack. No further division of credit seemed appropriate'.

It took a few issues for the Fantastic Four to properly find their feet. The team didn't have costumes initially, it was only in *The Fantastic Four* #3 (March 1962) that the distinctive blue jumpsuits with the black trim and the large '4' encased in a white circle on their chests made their appearance. That issue also brought a couple of other innovations: Lee emblazoned the front cover with the slogan 'The Greatest Comic Magazine in the World' (it became 'The World's Greatest Comic Magazine' from #4, and the slogan remained in use until the Nineties), and he introduced a letters column (DC's Superman had featured a basic letters page since 1958). In early science fiction fandom and later comic book fandom, letter columns put young fans in touch with each other and allowed readers to strongly identify with 'their' magazine or comic. It was a great way of generating reader loyalty, offering the

readership a sense of ownership of their favourite superheroes. By 1963 Lee claimed he was receiving around 100
letters from fans each day.

As the issues progressed the Fantastic Four gained
many of the traditional superhero accoutrements, from the
FantastiCar (their Batmobile) to a well-equipped secret lab/
hangout. In keeping with a team of four, the flying FantastiCar could split into four separate vehicles, one for each
member. Some of them, especially moody teen Johnny
Storm (who briefly quit almost immediately in issue #3)
and the downright angry Ben Grimm, didn't take naturally
to unwanted superpowers. Grimm, in particular, had real
problems with his transformation into the Thing, and his
self-pity was a trait that soon came to the fore. These were
superheroes with real-world emotions, and they reacted to
their predicament as readers might. They argued among
themselves about how to use their powers. Lee brought
melodrama and even soap opera into comic books.

The success of the romance comics rubbed off on these
new superheroes. Not only were Sue Storm and Reed
Richards engaged, but the Thing gained a blind girlfriend,
Alicia. In reflecting the real world of the Sixties, the Fantastic Four were the first superhero team to embrace their
resulting celebrity. Far from hiding from the world like
Superman and Batman, these four heroes were happy to
attend ticker-tape parades in their honour. They also had
real-world problems, such as in #9 (December 1962) when
they were nearly evicted from their headquarters as they
couldn't pay the rent. The comic book superhero would
never be the same again.

Every good superhero team needs a villain to test their
mettle. Issue #4 (May 1962) saw the reintroduction of a
figure from Timely's past: Bill Everett's Namor, the Sub-
Mariner. He had previously enjoyed a very short-lived
revival in the Fifties (alongside Captain America, who
couldn't escape his wartime roots, and the original Human

Torch). There had been hopes for a television series, following the George Reeves' *The Adventures of Superman*, but when that didn't surface, the Sub-Mariner's second attempt at superhero longevity died with *Sub-Mariner Comics* #42 (October 1955). In the spring of 1962, Lee had Fantastic Four member Johnny Storm discover Namor living as an amnesiac tramp in Manhattan's Bowery. He returns to Atlantis (named as his home for the first time) after Johnny helps him recover his identity. Discovering his underwater world destroyed and his people missing, Sub-Mariner becomes an anti-hero (returning the character to his 1939 roots), declaring war on humanity and aligning himself with the Fantastic Four's regular antagonist, Dr Doom. In a melodramatic move (further evidence of the influence of romance comics), he develops feelings for Sue Storm.

In issue #5 (July 1962) Lee introduced the armoured villain who would do much to define Marvel's signature antagonists. Jack Kirby drew Doom as an armour-encased super-villain, his suit containing not only a damaged body but a damaged mind. Victor von Doom is initially described as an old college classmate of Richards, expelled after an experiment to revive the dead went awry. Attacking the Four's Manhattan high-rise headquarters in the Baxter Building, Doom takes Sue Storm hostage, luring the others into a time-travel experiment to find Blackbeard's lost treasure. There's little detail of Doom's background – readers would have to wait a full two years before his origin story was revealed in *Fantastic Four Annual* #2 (September 1964). Lee and Kirby's story 'Origin of Doctor Doom' depicted the young Doom exploring magic and science to avenge the death of his father. He encounters Richards at State University and the two become rivals. Despite Richards highlighting the flaws in Doom's experiment to raise the dead, he goes ahead almost destroying himself. A period in Tibet strengthens his mysterious powers, and

Doom creates an armoured costume, hideously scarring his face when he dons the metal helmet before it had fully cooled.

The unexpected sales success of *The Fantastic Four* #1 (November 1961, the title was initially bi-monthly) saw Lee reconsider his career plans away from comics. He decided to stay with Marvel, believing the new opportunities were worth exploring. It was the biggest-selling title that Lee had worked on for years, and the level of fan mail suggested readers were hungry for new superheroes. With the Fantastic Four, Lee and Kirby laid the groundwork for a huge expansion of the Marvel Universe of superheroes.

To begin with, the stories were self-contained and featured repeated appearances by the team's antagonists, Namor the Sub-Mariner and Dr Doom. Gradually the stories expanded, becoming multi-part, more complex tales featuring a host of emotional entanglements for these unwilling heroes. This epic world-building approach would lend itself to eventual movie dominance in the twenty-first century. The longevity of the run afforded Lee and Kirby (who quit Marvel in 1970, after 102 issues of *The Fantastic Four*) the opportunity to develop an unusually complex, coherent, and interconnected universe.

The pages of *The Fantastic Four* engaged in discussions and depictions of topics like the 'Red Menace', America's fear of Communist infiltration. The second issue (January 1962) introduced the Skrulls, shapeshifting aliens infiltrating humanity unobserved. In a weird case of intertextuality (a developing Marvel trait), Richards defeats the alien invaders by exposing them to images of Earth's greatest defenders – characters from the pages of Marvel's comics. The Skrulls would appear in a variety of Marvel publications, often matched against another alien race, the Kree. The issue that introduced Dr Doom (#5), also saw Johnny Storm reading the first issue of *The Incredible Hulk*, and commenting on the Hulk's similarity to Ben Grimm.

Later, in *The Fantastic Four* #10, Doom would even invade the Marvel offices.

The first 100 issues of *The Fantastic Four* took the heroes through the Sixties, and introduced a roster of imaginative villains and weird characters. These included evil stage hypnotist Miracle Man (#3); the controlling Puppet Master (#11); Soviet space scientist Red Ghost and his trained primates the Super-Apes who planned to populate the moon (#13); Uatu, first of the alien Watchers who warn mankind of the coming of cosmic entity Galactus (who would arrive in #48, alongside his 'herald' the Silver Surfer, who'd later headline his own title, but would never command huge popularity); and the weird advanced race of Inhumans (#45). Marvel broke new ground with the introduction of the Fantastic Four's Native American ally Wyatt Wingfoot (#51) and the first mainstream African American superhero, Black Panther (#52–53; Marvel would also later introduce the Falcon and Luke Cage).

Other notable antagonists included the sonic-powered Klaw (#53), the original Human Torch revived for a battle with Johnny Storm (Annual #4), the leonine alien outlaw Blastaar (#62), and the Christ-like Adam Warlock (originally billed simply as 'Him', #66). Marvel's newest superheroes (the Hulk, Spider-Man, the Avengers, and the X-Men) would slowly eclipse the Fantastic Four, but it was this quartet of all-too-human heroes who first paved the way for a contemporary take on the genre.

The question facing Goodman, Lee, and Kirby as 1962 dawned was: how could they follow the Fantastic Four? It would turn out to be a banner year. The new interest in superheroes appeared more than a passing fad, but the only way Lee could find out if that were true would be to put more superhero comics into the market place. Lee had access to limited distribution slots due to an unfortunate deal with the DC-owned distributor Independent News.

After self-distributing through Atlas, Marvel had relied on American News in the late-Fifties to get its comics on news-stands. The collapse of American News saw Marvel fall back on Independent News, but DC Comics (who controlled the company) didn't want too much competition, so restricted Marvel to just eight monthly titles. This required Lee to carefully manage his range of comics. Publishing bi-monthly allowed for sixteen individual titles, while he replaced older comics with new ones, or incorporated superhero 'try-outs' into Marvel's anthology titles. Rather than producing quantity regardless of quality, Lee found the limited number of outlets meant he was better able to control the content himself, improving the storytelling quality at the expense of quantity.

The next Marvel superhero success was the Incredible Hulk, building on the success of the Thing, the single most popular character in the Fantastic Four. Lee – drawing on thoughts about Quasimodo and Frankenstein's creature – set about creating another Thing-like figure for whom readers could have sympathy. 'I decided I might as well borrow from Dr Jekyll and Mr Hyde as well – our protagonist would constantly change from his normal identity to his superhuman alter ego and back again,' said Lee.

Marvel was back in the superhero business just as the Cold War was kicking into high gear, with the Cuban Missile crisis just months away. The atomic threat was on everyone's minds, so many of Marvel's new breed of heroes would be ordinary people, often scientists, transformed by out-of-control atomic science into super-powered creatures (the pre-war equivalent had been the ubiquitous 'super serum'). Also feeding into Lee's creation of the Hulk was the Jewish legend of the Golem, a magical hulking humanoid creature created from inanimate matter, best known from the story featuring the late-sixteenth-century rabbi of Prague. However, this first iteration of the Hulk was rather different from the one that would endure.

In *The Incredible Hulk* #1 (May 1962), the tightly emo-
tionally controlled Dr Bruce Banner works for the US military and is about to test detonate a gamma bomb (when
desert atomic tests were at their height). However, the
intervention of a Communist spy causes the bomb to detonate early while Banner is rescuing a reckless kid named
Rick Jones from the test site. Caught in the violent gamma
ray blast, Banner is soaked in deadly radiation (in a more
affecting sequence than that which showered the Fantastic
Four in cosmic rays). Banner survives and is quarantined.
At night he undergoes a shocking transformation: growing to a huge size, his skin turning an unhealthy grey. An
anger-fuelled orgy of destruction followed, wrecking army
jeeps and weapons. Escaping the military, but pursued by
General 'Thunderbolt' Ross (father of Banner's girlfriend
Betty), Banner is helped by Rick Jones, the kid he saved,
who locks him up at night for his own safety and that
of others when he 'hulks' out. There's something of the
pathos of the unwanted transformations of Lon Chaney's
Larry Talbot in the 1941 film *The Wolfman* in Banner's
predicament.

Unhappy with the look of the grey Hulk in the first
issue, Lee had the character's colour changed to green (to
avoid any particular ethnic group). This origin story would
be recoloured green whenever it was reprinted, until *The
Incredible Hulk* #302 (December 1984) reintroduced the
grey Hulk, allowing for the origin colouration to be reinstated. Whatever his colour, this first version of the Hulk
only survived six issues, with the series cancelled with the
March 1963 cover-dated issue. In keeping with the emerging habit of having Marvel characters meet each other
across various comics, the Hulk stayed around despite
losing his own title, turning up in *The Fantastic Four* #12
(March 1963), and then becoming a founding member of
the Marvel superhero team the Avengers (in September
and October 1963). More guest appearances followed as

the Hulk bounced around from comic to comic, including *The Fantastic Four* and *The Amazing Spider-Man* through 1964. Towards the end of that year the Hulk returned as a regular character in *Tales to Astonish* #60 (October 1964) – his transformations now caused by rage – with artists from Kirby and Ditko to John Buscema, Bill Everett, and Gil Kane working on the title. Throughout, Banner retained an ambivalent attitude towards his uncontrollable transformations, fearing what he might be responsible for as the Hulk. Regular villain the Leader was introduced (*Tales to Astonish* #62, December 1964), a menial worker whose brain power is boosted during a chemical accident unleashing his desire for world domination, as well as the Abomination (*Tales to Astonish* #90, April 1967), another gamma-irradiated creature lacking in Banner's benevolent outlook. The Abomination was Emil Blonsky, a Soviet spy who deliberately exposed himself to gamma radiation in order to become even more powerful than the Hulk.

The Hulk was an odd sort of superhero. Banner certainly set out to help people and thwarted various enemies, but – as with the Fantastic Four – he was more often depressed by his condition, and on several occasions was shown contemplating suicide. Marie Severin, a rare female contributor to Marvel's male-dominated comics, was the last writer-artist to work on the run of the Hulk's adventures in *Tales to Astonish*. The book was retitled *The Incredible Hulk* from #102 (retaining the previous numbering) in April 1968, and heralding what Lee dubbed 'The second age of Marvel Comics'. The not-so-jolly green giant entered the Seventies still struggling with anger management.

In 1962, Stan Lee's creativity was free flowing. After the Fantastic Four and the Hulk, his new superheroes emerged fully formed and took the comic book marketplace by storm. Ant-Man (never a major figure) emerged in *Tales to Astonish* #27 (January 1962), but the adventures of scientist Hank Pym would have a regular place in Marvel's line-up.

Working with Steve Ditko, Lee came up with a character that drew on another member of the Fantastic Four: Johnny Storm, the moody teenager who'd been gifted unwanted superpowers. Lee repeated the trick with young high schooler Peter Parker, who when bitten by a radioactive spider develops spider-like skills, including the ability to effortlessly climb walls, as well as great strength and agility. Already ostracized by his classmates, Parker is a loner who enters a wrestling contest during which he wears a mask to hide his identity. He later appears on a television show wearing a home-made red-and-blue 'Spider-Man' costume, complete with arachnid insignia and web patterns. Rushed by a criminal, Parker fails to intervene, learning only later that the same man is responsible for killing his Uncle Ben. Distraught, Parker dresses as Spider-Man once more, tracks down the thug and turns him into the police. Lee's story concludes with the warning that 'With great power, there must also be great responsibility' (a quote from French Enlightenment philosopher Voltaire).

This ground-breaking strip ran in the pages of *Amazing Fantasy* #15 (August 1962). Tales that climaxed in surprise twists had been the comic's formula, but publisher Martin Goodwin had marked the title for cancellation. Given the limited outlets Lee had to try out new superheroes, he took the opportunity of a dying title to deliver a teenage orphan (once thought sidekick material) as a new kind of angst-driven, youthful superhero. Despite Goodman's reservations that using an insect motif was 'distasteful', Spider-Man was an immediate hit. *Amazing Fantasy* disappeared from newsstands anyway. It would be several months before Spider-Man returned, headlining his own title.

Artist Steve Ditko added some key characteristics to Lee's concept of Spider-Man, coming up with the wrist-mounted web-shooters and the idea of hiding Parker's face under a mask in order to generate an air of mystery. Ditko had been born in Pennsylvania in 1927, spent a short time in the Army after 1945, and then studied under *Batman* artist Jerry Robinson (Ditko was turned on to comics by Batman, and Eisner's *The Spirit*). He turned professional in 1953, working for Simon and Kirby's studio, Charlton Comics, and Atlas, among others. He'd worked on the Marvel monster comics with Lee, but the editor had first taken the idea for Spider-Man to Jack Kirby. When Kirby failed to produce the visuals Lee had in mind (calling Kirby's version 'too heroic'), he turned to Ditko. 'One of the first things I did,' recalled Ditko, 'was to work up a costume. A vital, visual part of the character. I had to know how he looked . . . before I did any breakdowns. For example: A clinging power so he wouldn't have hard shoes or boots, a hidden wrist-shooter versus a web gun and holster . . . I wasn't sure Stan would like the idea of covering the character's face, but I did it because it hid an obviously boyish face.'

Ditko and Lee would work together on thirty-eight issues of *The Amazing Spider-Man* (between March 1963 and July 1966), but once Ditko left, Lee continued to write the title through to its 100th issue. With Peter Parker, Lee created a superhero that was an ordinary American teen, cursed by superpowers and a sense of responsibility about how he should use them. As often as he'd battle outlandish villains, Parker was shown worrying about where his rent would come from or about the health of his widowed Aunt May. Parker was romantically torn between red-haired party girl Mary Jane Watson and the more sophisticated blonde Gwen Stacy, a dilemma lifted from romance comics. As a freelance photographer for the *Daily Bugle*, Parker used his unique 'connection' with Spider-Man to capture exclusive photographs of the web-spinner (although his editor J. Jonah Jamieson used the pictures for anti-Spider-Man stories, considering him a public menace). Lee combined Clark Kent's newspaper base with Jimmy

Olsen's teenage enthusiasm and Batman's wrong-side-of-the-law ethos. While Ditko could easily tackle the mundane scenes, his art sprang to life depicting the web-slinger swinging from building to building across the New York skyline, possibly the only time Parker escaped his troubling thoughts about being a superhero and really soared.

In elevating a teenager to the lead superhero rather than the sidekick, and giving him doubts and concerns about his powers, Lee and Ditko tapped into a powerful connection with the youthful readers of Marvel comics. Spider-Man was a different take on the superhero than Superman or Batman (or even the nearest equivalent, Captain Marvel's teen wish-fulfilment). He was of the moment, unarguably contemporary, and *The Amazing Spider-Man* showed that over 20 years since they began, superheroes still had new places to go.

Major villains Spider-Man dealt with in the Sixties echoed many of the scientific concerns of the time. Doctor Octopus (#3, July 1963 – but he turned up again in #11–12 and #31–3) was scientist Otto Octavius, who develops a set of mechanical arms to aid his research into atomic particles. An accident in the lab sees 'Doc Ock' (as Spidey calls him) dosed in radiation and fused to the metal arms, which he can now control with his mind. Rejected by science, he's driven into a criminal career to continue his research. Anxiety about the atomic age, with nuclear power replacing the nuclear bomb as the primary fear, was behind many of Marvel's characters and it shows up repeatedly in the origin stories of many heroes and villains. A nasty dose of radiation (whether through a spider bite or from 'cosmic rays') was enough in Stan Lee's mind to explain any number of mutations and superpowers. Doctor Octopus would later form the Sinister Six (*The Amazing Spider-Man Annual* #1, 1964), an anti-Justice League of crime comprising Vulture (*The Amazing Spider-Man* #2, May 1963), Electro (who gained control of electricity after being struck by lightning in *The Amazing Spider-Man* #9, February 1964), Kraven the Hunter, Mysterio, and Sandman, all of whom had appeared previously in *The Amazing Spider-Man*.

Spider-Man's signature antagonist was the Green Goblin, first seen in *The Amazing Spider-Man* #14 in July 1964. Initially depicted as a green-skinned imp-like creature, the origins of the Goblin remained mysterious until *The Amazing Spider-Man* #39, the issue on which John Romita replaced Ditko as artist. Lee and Ditko had a difficult working relationship, with the reclusive artist rarely venturing into the Marvel offices. Their ideas over the direction the stories and art should take were often very different. Despite this, they managed to tolerate each other, but a serious disagreement as to who the mysterious Green Goblin should be unmasked as had left his origins unexplored. As soon as Ditko left, Lee revealed the Goblin as Norman Osborn, an industrialist introduced two issues previously. Ditko argued it would be more realistic for the Goblin to have been a previously unknown character. With his Goblin Glider and pumpkin bombs, the Goblin may have appeared frivolous, but over the years he has proven to be 'the most dangerous foe Spidey's ever fought' (as claimed in a coverline for his first appearance, and actively displayed in his role in the later death of someone close to Peter Parker).

Romita was of Italian descent, and had graduated from Manhattan's School of Industrial Art in 1947. Two years later he broke into comics on *Famous Funnies*, freelanced for Timely and others, and worked on the mid-Fifties short-lived revival of *Captain America*. Romance, war, and horror comics kept him busy (including freelancing on Marvel's *The Avengers*), before Lee had him take over *Daredevil* and then *The Amazing Spider-Man*. It would be Romita's Spider-Man that would become the most well-known portrayal, eventually serving as Marvel's mascot. Romita's work became a house style, with him as Marvel's de facto art director. He taught artists how to draw for Marvel comics following Kirby's style. From *The Amazing Spider-Man* #39 (August 1966), Romita worked on the title (with three other artists) through until #95 in April 1971.

One of the most acclaimed Spider-Man stories came in the mid-Sixties when the title was still under Lee and Ditko. *The Amazing Spider-Man* #31–33 presented 'If This Be My Destiny . . . !' in which Peter Parker begins university (meeting Harry Osborn – son of Norman – and girlfriend Gwen Stacy) and Spidey encounters technology thief the Master Planner (revealed as Doctor Octopus). He has stolen a rare isotope that could save Aunt May's life, but Spider-Man is trapped under heavy machinery. Sheer force-of-will and thoughts of his family allow him to summon the brute strength required to escape, depicted in some of the most powerful images yet seen in comics. Critic and historian Les Daniels said of the sequence: 'Steve Ditko squeezes every ounce of anguish out of Spider-Man's predicament, complete with visions of the uncle he failed and the aunt he has sworn to save.' In a 2001 poll, readers voted the story #15 in the *100 Greatest Marvels of All Time*. It stands as one of the most dramatic and well-realized sequences in superhero history.

The late-Sixties saw *The Amazing Spider-Man* focus as much on Peter Parker's life as a young man caught up in the events of his day – such as the Civil Rights movement, the exposure of corrupt politicians, and the protests against the Vietnam War – as much as on his superhero battles against outlandish creations like criminal mastermind the Kingpin (introduced in #50 in June 1967, before featuring as the main recurring villain in *Daredevil*), and the Rhino (#41–3, October–December 1966), a criminal thug from an Eastern Bloc country who volunteered for an experiment that bonded a super-strong new polymer to his skin, giving him super-speed and making him impervious to attack. He featured in battles against both Spider-Man and the Hulk through to the end of the decade. Having escaped from the comic page to television in the animated *Spider-Man* series of 1967 [see chapter 13], the web-slinger became one of the icons of the era, the Sixties' signature character equivalent to Superman in the Thirties and Batman in the Forties.

The final major superhero from Marvel in 1962 was Thor, a dramatic departure from doubtful and angst-ridden young heroes. The origins of many superheroes can be traced back to the myths and legends of gods who enjoyed powers beyond ordinary men [see chapter 1], and with 'The Mighty Thor' Lee drew directly from the well of legend, adapting Norse mythology. Thor's dialogue was cod-Shakespearean, but he featured in such a wide-ranging mythological playground that he couldn't fail to resonate with the times, an 'ancient aliens' stew laced with fashionable Eastern mysticism.

Looking for a character stronger than the Hulk, Lee decided he needed a genuine god rather than merely an altered human. Assuming Marvel was attracting an educated readership (as demonstrated by the popularity of their superhero comics with the college crowd), Lee decided '. . . readers were already pretty familiar with the Greek and Roman gods. It might be fun to delve into the old Norse legends . . .' In his mind, the Norse gods resembled Vikings, all 'flowing beards, horned helmets, and battle clubs'. Lee tried out the new character in the pages of *Journey into Mystery*, an anthology that needed 'a shot in the arm'. He tasked his brother Larry (employed in a junior role at Marvel) to write up a script for Jack Kirby to illustrate.

The results appeared in *Journey into Mystery* #83 (August 1962). In the first tale, Dr Donald Blake is on vacation in Norway (in a story with the pulpy title 'The Stone Men from Saturn') when he discovers Thor's magical hammer, Mjolnir. Striking it upon a rock, Blake is transformed into Thor, complete with cape, boots, and winged helmet. Blake/Thor adopts a superhero double life, living as a medical student (with his nurse girlfriend Jane Foster), while as Thor, the Thunder God, he protects humanity. A later backstory explained that Thor's father Odin decided Thor needed to learn humility, so he removed his powers and placed him in the body of disabled medical student Donald Blake.

The strip, under the title *The Mighty Thor*, continued in *Journey into Mystery*, plotted by Lee, scripted by Larry or Robert Bernstein, and drawn by a variety of artists, including Joe Sinnott, Don Heck, and Al Hartley. From *Journey into Mystery* #101 the title settled into a consistent approach under the control of Lee and Kirby, running through until the middle of 1970 (#179, retitled simply 'Thor'). In keeping with the source material, the adventures of Thor would develop into an all-encompassing and imaginative saga.

Thor's presence on Earth comes to the attention of his evil half-brother, Loki, in *Journey into Mystery* #85 ('Trapped by Loki, the God of Mischief', October 1962). Loki was quickly followed by three other villains – the Absorbing Man, the Destroyer, and the Wrecker – all helped into existence by Loki (he alters a beat-up boxer into the Absorbing Man when he laces his drink, while the Destroyer is animated armour forged by Odin and used by Loki, and the Wrecker is a demolition expert turned super-villain who accidentally encounters an enchantment intended for Loki). Loki would become obsessed with Earth and with defeating Thor, so became a recurring antagonist. Beyond the Asgardians, Thor would also deal with more down-to-Earth (if no less outlandish) enemies like Zarrko the Tomorrow Man, an evil scientist from the future (#86, November 1962); Chinese Communist and nuclear physicist Radioactive Man (#93, June 1963); the Human Cobra, a Dutch lab assistant researching snake venom (#98, November 1963); and mad scientist Calvin Zabo, who – obsessed with Robert Louis Stevenson – transforms himself into Mister Hyde (#99, December 1963). During the 1964 and 1965 run, Thor returned to Asgard, in defiance of Odin, where he battles several creatures such as fire demon Surtur, and Skagg the Storm Giant, before he is dragged before a court to prove his worthiness in 'The Trial of the Gods' (*Journey into Mystery* #116, May 1965). The plots would become more cosmic, in keeping with the rising 'Age of Aquarius' (an astrological term referring to the 'New Age' self-help spiritual movement), while still grounding Thor in his love for Jane Foster. However, she is forbidden to him, and is given the chance to prove herself to Odin through a series of trials. These she fails, even when Thor tries to help, leaving the Asgardian warrior heartbroken. No matter how crazy the stories got, Lee and Kirby made them relatable to contemporary readers, while still attempting to blow their minds.

In less than a year, between 1961 and 1962, Marvel had transformed the comic book superhero. Stan Lee had been the driving force, using his limited publishing opportunities to create an inter-connected universe of ordinary people turned superheroes, a grand cosmic soap opera. With dynamic artists such as Jack Kirby and Steve Ditko bringing his creations to colourful life, the Marvel comics of the Sixties captured the zeitgeist, sparking a fresh sense of invention and innovation at rival DC Comics, where Superman and Batman were looking rather tired compared with the youthful new blood brought to the medium by Spider-Man and Thor.

8

THE MARVEL AGE

Marvel was on a roll with their new-age superheroes. The following year, 1963, would see the creation of Iron Man, the X Men, and the Avengers (one of whose founding members was the Hulk) – all characters and superhero teams who would do much to power the future of comics. First on to the page was Iron Man, appearing in *Tales of Suspense* #39 (March 1963), one of the old monster anthologies (*The Amazing Spider-Man* #1 had replaced a cancelled soap opera/romance title *Linda Carter, Student Nurse*). Unlike Peter Parker, inventor and millionaire Tony Stark did not suffer from a lack of confidence or a dearth of social skills. He was a magnet for trouble. Created by Stan Lee, he had his brother Larry Lieber write the first Iron Man script, with Don Heck drawing the interior pages and Jack Kirby contributing the cover (as well as designing the iconic costume).

With Stark, Lee created a seemingly invulnerable

character who has it all – money, women, fame – yet is crip-
pled by an infirmity that also functioned as a heavy-handed
metaphor. He had a real-life model in mind: 'Howard
Hughes was one of the most colourful men of our time.
He was an inventor, an adventurer, a multi-billionaire, a
ladies' man, and finally a nutcase. Without being crazy,
[Iron Man] was Howard Hughes.' When he is kidnapped
by Chinese Communists, Stark's heart is gravely injured.
He's forced to work upon a super-weapon for Wong-Chu,
the 'Red Guerrilla Tyrant', but constructs an armoured
suit that will both protect him and maintain his heart until
he can find medical help. The first Iron Man suit was a
heavy, grey, inelegant creation, clearly built from materi-
als to hand. By the second story (#40, April 1963) the suit
had been replaced by a golden version. The best-known
red-and-yellow armour didn't appear until the end of the
year in #48 (December 1963), drawn by Steve Ditko (with
a Kirby cover).

The stories were about the man, not the armour. With
the Vietnam War heating up, Stark was pressed into service
as an anti-Viet Cong agent as well as an all-round anti-
Communist (he was an idealization of the successful
American Capitalist businessman). This new wartime patriotism saw *Tales of Suspense* running Captain America
stories as back-up strips from #59 (November 1964), before
the book was renamed *Captain America* following #99
(March 1968), when Iron Man gained his own title.

Stark was a superhero whose powers were conferred
through technology. Only his sense of right or wrong dic-
tated his actions. His heart trouble remained, so each suit
had built-in mechanisms for the continuation of his heart
rhythms (until replaced by a synthetic heart in *Iron Man*
#17–19, September–November 1969). The focus would
later move to military defence and Government contracts,
putting Stark in a compromised position where he prized
his independence while serving his country. As well as

signifying the obvious 'broken heart' (Stark is a woman-izer who is in love with his secretary, Pepper Potts), his vulnerability is a classic Achilles heel imperfection, his Kryptonite.

The Cold War turned hot after the Cuban Missile Crisis, and the exploits of Tony Stark provided an internationalist outlook, more than the 'home front' Fantastic Four, Hulk, and Spider-Man. Following the Fantastic Four model, Stark made himself a celebrity and had to deal with the fallout from fame. Stark was a founding member of the Avengers, appearing in issue #1 (September 1963), as well as in one-shot Iron Man and Sub-Mariner (April 1968), before making his solo debut in *The Invincible Iron Man* #1 (May 1968). Artist George Tsuka began a decade run drawing this techno-hero from #5 (September 1968).

The Fantastic Four had been created directly in response to DC's Justice League of America. If the format was suc-cessful once, reasoned Lee, there was no reason it couldn't work again. The remainder of 1963 would see two superhero super-groups from Marvel, the X-Men and the Avengers. These teams, along with the Fantastic Four, would become the cornerstones of the Marvel Universe, with their mem-berships fluctuating across the years.

DC Comics had tried to match Marvel's invention, introducing a new superhero team in June 1963. The Doom Patrol comprised a selection of super-powered misfits, more freaks than heroes. Among these angsty heroes was Robotman (a crash survivor whose brain was housed in a robot body, the equivalent of the Thing), Elasti-girl (a female equivalent to Mister Fantastic), radioactive monster Negative Man, and their mysterious wheelchair-confined 'Chief'. Together they were billed as 'the World's Strangest Heroes'. The series would end with the entire team killed off in 1968.

Responding to his publisher's Doom Patrol-influenced request for a team of 'super mutants', Lee decided to go with the X-Men instead of Goodman's suggested 'The Mutants' (with the 'X' alternatively explained as from their telepathic mentor, the wheelchair-bound Professor Xavier, or because these unlikely mutant superheroes each carried a mysterious 'X-gene' that gave them their powers). The Marvel team debuted just three months after DC's *Doom Patrol*. *The X-Men* #1 (September 1963) featured mutant heroes Cyclops (Scott Summers, whose visor prevents his deadly optical-rays from escaping uncontrolled), Marvel Girl (Jean Grey, who can move objects by her mind), Angel (Warren Worthington III, who sports a pair of wings), Beast (Hank McCoy, a super-strong ape-like character, who later becomes the blue-furred version seen in the X-Men movies) and Iceman (Bobby Drake, a frosty version of the Human Torch). The line-up would change, but their enemy would often be Magneto (introduced in #1, later revealed to be a concentration camp survivor) and his Brotherhood of Mutants (from #4), a militant faction of mutated antiheroes. Magneto believed that the super-powered should rule the human race, while Professor Xavier opposed such self-centred use of the powers his students exhibited. The Brotherhood included Scarlet Witch, her twin brother Quicksilver (both of Roma descent), Toad, and Mastermind.

While Marvel's earlier heroes were ordinary people transformed due to cosmic accidents into reluctant super-heroes, the X-Men were all born different with little choice but to grow up coping with and hiding their various abilities. Themes included prejudice, acceptance, tolerance, and racism, following the real world Civil Rights movement. Their powers – which usually emerged at puberty – made the X-Men attractive to adolescents who felt a sense of isolation. Not immediately popular, it took time for the X-Men to catch on. By 1969 young writer Roy Thomas (who'd become Marvel's editor-in-chief early in the Seventies, succeeding Lee) was revamping the X-Men to include new figures Havok and Polaris, but the title eventually stopped running new material with #66 (March 1970), with reprints filling out the last issues until the comic was cancelled with #93 (April 1975). Some of the more popular members (such as Wolverine and Storm) would not appear until the mid-Seventies relaunch of the new X-Men in *Giant Size X-Men* #1 (1975).

Where the heroes of the X-Men had all been born with their mutant gene superpowers, the various members of the other Marvel super-team, the Avengers, had come across theirs in diverse ways so they had little in common. The X-Men had been created as a team, but with the Avengers, several existing characters were united. The idea had again come from Goodman, who wanted a book that would bring all Marvel's new superheroes under one title. With *The Incredible Hulk*'s first title cancelled after just six issues, he became the core around which the Avengers assembled.

'Earth's Mightiest Heroes' – as *The Avengers* #1 (September 1963) billed them – were Iron Man/Tony Stark, the oddball pairing of Ant-Man (scientist Hank Pym who can shrink to insect size) and his wife, the Wasp (B-level heroes from *Tales to Astonish*), the Hulk and Thor (not actually from Earth). Captain America – revived after being discovered frozen in ice since the Second World War in #4 – joined the team. As with the X-Men the core members would vary, but their central aim – to fight 'the foes who no single superhero can withstand' – remained constant. The original comic book run, initially written by Lee and illustrated by Kirby, would continue until #402 (September 1996), alongside a variety of one-shots, spin-offs, and mini-series.

By *The Avengers* #3 (January 1964), the Hulk had turned bad guy and teamed up with the ever-restless Sub-Mariner to take on his erstwhile team mates. In #4 (March 1964), a thawed-out Captain America joined (deliberately ignoring his brief Fifties revival as a 'Commie Smasher'). By 1965 Captain America would take charge, although he was the only 'big name' superhero left, as the rest included Hawkeye (a skilled human marksman), and reformed villains Quicksilver and the Scarlet Witch. Lee had found it difficult to keep his stories straight when his lead characters were having adventures in their own books, but also teaming up with each other in *The Avengers*. Villains the Avengers faced in the Sixties included the Masters of Evil (a super-villain gang), Wonder Man (quickly dropped when Wonder Woman's DC complained), Swordsman, Power Man and the Fantastic Four's regular antagonist, Dr Doom. A crossover featuring the X-Men and the Avengers was inevitable, and it featured in *The X-Men* #45 (June 1968) and *The Avengers* #53 (June 1968). By the end of the Sixties, heroes and villains featured in the Avengers included Hercules, Black Panther, the Grim Reaper, and the Vision (an android created by Ultron, an artificial intelligence built by Henry Pym).

The human Nick Fury – originally a Second World War hero in Lee and Kirby's *Sgt. Fury and his Howling Commandos* – was updated to 1965 to run SHIELD, a counterespionage group connected to the Avengers through Tony Stark. Created by Lee and Kirby for *Strange Tales* #135 (August 1965), Fury was a gadget-obsessed hero battling the evil HYDRA. Artist Jim Steranko took over from #151 (December 1966) and then added writing duties from #155 (April 1967). Comics historian Les Daniels wrote of Steranko's work: 'With each passing issue Steranko's efforts became more and more innovative. Entire pages would be devoted to photo-collages of drawings [that] ignored panel boundaries . . . pages became incredible production numbers.' Steranko popularized the use of 'op art' and psychedelia in Marvel's comic books.

This Sixties period of comic book experimentation also gave rise to the magical Doctor Strange, created by

Spider-Man's Steve Ditko. Strange had once been a neuro-surgeon, but in keeping with the developing psychedelic philosophy, he'd become a practising sorcerer who served the Sorcerer Supreme – a personified 'Earth force' protecting the planet from magical incursions and mystical threats. The character first appeared in *Suspense Tales* #110 (July 1963), sharing the book with the Human Torch (until #134) and military hero-cum-spy Nick Fury (until #168). Strange's origin story would not appear until #115 (December 1963) and Ditko stayed with the title until #146 (July 1966). During his tenure, Doctor Strange explored Marvel's weirder side, tapping into head-trip, drug-taking youth culture. The colourful visuals and weird occult arcana made Doctor Strange a trippy favourite on college campuses. Ditko's triumph was a multi-part storyline featuring Eternity, a silhouetted personification of the universe (some of the ideas in Doctor Strange influenced Neil Gaiman's *Sandman* in the Eighties). Running for a year across *Strange Tales* #130–146 (July 1965–July 1966), the story developed the cosmic reach of Marvel, with Eternity eventually 'ret-conned' (fitted into a developing continuity retroactively) as a 'Cosmic Power' of the wider Marvel Universe.

Comics historian Bradford W. Wright cited the art of Salvador Dalí, popular in the US in the Sixties, and the fiction of the Beat poets as influencing Ditko and co-writer Lee in creating Doctor Strange. Wright noted that 'Doctor Strange remarkably predicted the youth counterculture's fascination with Eastern mysticism and psychedelia. Never among Marvel's more popular or accessible characters, Doctor Strange still found a niche among an audience seeking a challenging alternative to more conventional super-hero fare.'

Strange would pop up across the Marvel titles, with guest appearances in *The Fantastic Four* #27 (June 1964) and *The Amazing Spider-Man Annual* #2 (1965). Following Ditko's

exit, Roy Thomas and Dennis O'Neil (a young writer/
artist head-hunted by Thomas from DC) each had a stint
on the title, with Bill Everett eventually taking over until
#152. Eventually *Strange Tales* #168 morphed into the reti-
tled *Doctor Strange* (numbering continued from #169).
Lee, Thomas and others took the character through the
remainder of the decade, developing such new cosmic villains as the Living Tribunal (*Strange Tales* #157, June 1967),
who challenge Doctor Strange to prove that Earth is worth
saving. When Gene Colan took over as artist in 1968,
Doctor Strange became a more conventional Marvel superhero, including having a secret identity. Sales collapsed and
the title was suddenly cancelled with #183 (that final issue
carried an unfulfilled 'Next Issue' blurb), with the remaining stories wrapped up in *Sub-Mariner* (#22, February
1970) and *The Incredible Hulk* (#126, April 1970). A hero
of his time, Doctor Strange faded away just as the Sixties
ended – he'd return to the Marvel universe a changed man.

Daredevil was the name of a previously unsuccessful Lev
Gleason superhero from the Forties, revived in the Sixties
and attached to a completely different character. The new
Daredevil was Matt Murdock, a lawyer blinded by 'radioactive cylinders', but whose other senses were extraordinarily heightened. Created by Stan Lee and Bill Everett (the
title went through a succession of artists after Everett only
managed to complete two-thirds of the first issue – Ditko
finished it off, with Kirby on covers and character origina-
tion), his origin story was the centrepiece of *Daredevil* #1
(April 1964). Based on the notion that 'Justice is blind', Lee
depicted a driven vigilante whose super-powers are mild,
but whose sense of vengeance after the death of his father at
the hands of a corrupt boxing promoter is fierce.

Artist Wally Wood provided some stability on the title
between #5 and #10, introducing Daredevil's enduring red
costume in #7. After a brief run under Kirby and John
Romita, *Daredevil* fell to Gene Colan, beginning with #20

(September 1966) encompassing all but three issues through to #100 (June 1973). It was Colan who was the quintessential Sixties artist on *Daredevil*, working from Lee's plot outlines. The Daredevil strip Lee was most proud of saw Murdock defend a blind Vietnam veteran in *Daredevil* #47 (December 1968), although he turned writing chores over to Thomas from #51. Never as popular as others in the Marvel fold, and featuring a series of B-villains, Daredevil enjoyed a crossover with Spider-Man (#16, May 1966) and a troubled romantic history with Karen Page, who learns of his secret identity (#57), but – in true Marvel soap opera style – has difficulty dealing with it.

As well as creating enduring characters, Stan Lee also mythologized life behind the scenes at Marvel through his Marvel Bullpen Bulletin. The concept of the Bullpen, a special page in which initially Lee and later other editors would chronicle life at Marvel Comics, originated in *The Fantastic Four* letters page, but took off across all of Marvel's titles from 1965. With many writers and artists working freelance from home, this idyllic workplace full of camaraderie and banter was as fictional as any of the superheroes chronicled in the comics. It was good PR and great for engendering reader identification with Marvel, the creators, and the characters, an important weapon in the battle between Marvel and DC for the attention of readers and the increasingly important collectors. Beyond the regular Bullpen communications, Lee launched a dedicated Marvel fan club aimed at comic-reading kids and the growing college audience. The Merry Marvel Marching Society (1965) membership cost $1 and included stickers, a membership card, a badge, and a five-minute flexi-disc featuring fans' favourite writers (mainly Lee) and artists offering up a heavily rehearsed, stiltedly delivered glimpse inside the fictitious Marvel Bullpen. Readers who wrote in to point out continuity errors in the comics and who offered their own ways of fixing them would receive the infamous Marvel

'No Prize', an envelope with text that read: 'This envelope contains a genuine Marvel Comics NO-PRIZE which you have just won!' The envelope was empty . . .

For many observers, Stan Lee was Marvel Comics. For all that a growing comic book fandom was aware of the work of individual artists, casual readers and the wider media were not. Across the pages of all Marvel titles, it was Lee's name ('Stan Lee presents . . .' headed each story) and distinctive editorial voice that stood out. He used his 'Stan's Soapbox' column to write about life at Marvel (in their new offices at the heart of New York's fashionable ad-land in Madison Avenue) and to hype future plans. It was here he'd deploy his trademark phrases, such as 'Face front!' (from his military service), calling Marvel fans 'True Believers', wrapping up opinions with ''Nuff said!', and signing off with 'Excelsior!' (pinched from New York State's motto, which means 'ever upwards'). Lee spent increasing amounts of time touring college campuses giving talks to captivated students and appearing on television chat shows where he promoted the legend of Stan Lee as much as Marvel Comics. He was truly the one-and-only ringmaster of the Marvel comic book circus.

What Lee, his writers, and often unsung artists created in the first half of the Sixties was a self-contained, self-aware comic book universe to rival that built by DC Comics across the previous two decades. Lee's core superheroes – Spider-Man, the X-Men, the Avengers – would endure to become central characters in the superhero movie boom of the twenty-first century, alongside DC's older Superman and Batman. Marvel's mutants and misfits were superheroes for a new atomic age of anxiety. They were ordinary people, some of them teenagers like the readers, with ordinary concerns and worries transformed by extraordinary events. Gone (for the most part) were the secret identities adopted by the previous generation of DC superheroes. Instead, the Fantastic Four and Tony Stark embraced media fame (as did Lee), and 'monsters' like the Thing and the Hulk discovered they could also be heroes.

If DC were the establishment, then Marvel were the rebels, the drop-outs who presented a fresh take on superheroes (even though many of the creators had been working in comics for twenty years). Stan Lee – finally given a chance to shine – in combination with idiosyncratic artistic talents like Jack Kirby and Steve Ditko, unleashed a fresh take on the idea of what superheroes could be, and who could be superheroes. 'We were trying to elevate the medium,' said Lee in 1968. However, by the start of the Seventies, Lee had lost both Ditko and Kirby (who left in spring 1970 to go to DC, increasingly dissatisfied by Marvel's exploitation of his work without due compensation or credit). It was the end of the first Marvel age.

It had all been about attitude at Marvel, resulting in the company shifting almost one million comic books every week by 1968. That success finally allowed publisher Martin Goodman to not only dump his restrictive distribution arrangement with the DC-owned Independent News that limited Marvel to eight titles per month, but also to sell the entire company to the Perfect Film and Chemical Corporation. The deal saw Goodman retained as publisher, to run Marvel as a separate subsidiary, and Lee tied to a long-term contract as editor-in-chief. It was only the first of several changes of ownership for Marvel that would see them endure tough times and finally re-emerge triumphant and re-energized as part of the Walt Disney Company in the twenty-first century.

The Sixties saw the rise of often self-published, but defiantly independent comic books dubbed 'underground comix', inspired by and reacting against the products of Marvel and DC. The creators of these publications (distributed in 'head' shops and record stores) tackled subjects mainstream publishers could not, mainly those forbidden by the

Comics Code, such as drug use, sexuality, and violence. They grew out of the wider American underground culture (yet had their roots in older suppressed graphic forms like Tijuana bibles) and flourished between 1968 and 1975. Key figures included writers and artists like Robert Crumb, Gilbert Shelton (*The Furry Freak Brothers*), Gary Panter, Art Spiegelman (*Maus*), Melinda Gebbie and Harvey Pekar (*American Splendor*).

Largely personal works, often autobiographical, the underground comix were not a natural breeding ground for superheroes, but they would have an influence on mainstream publishers, leading to a maturation of their approach and a lessening in the grip of the Comics Code. *Zap Comix* #1 (October 1968) originated in San Francisco and featured the work of Crumb, among others. Within the pages could be found Wonder Wart-Hog, the Hog of Steel, a violently reactionary superhero parody. His alter ego Philbert Desanex is a pig-faced creature who disguises himself as a rubber-faced human. Created by cartoonist Gilbert Shelton and Tony Bell, the character first appeared in Pete Millar's independently published *Drag Cartoons*, and then went on to appear in two issues of *Wonder Wart-Hog Quarterly*, before enjoying an afterlife in underground newspapers and in Shelton's *Rip Off Comix* anthology.

Zap Comix was to underground comics what Superman had been to the mainstream: it resulted in a host of imitators and independent spin-offs. Harvey Kurtzman and Wally Wood had been spoofing Superman for some time in William Gaines' *Mad* magazine as Superduperman, but there were other underground superheroes. Larry Fuller's *Ebon* (1970) featured an African-American superhero (beating Marvel's Luke Cage by two years; other black superheroes Black Panther and Falcon were supporting characters, not leads). Larry Welz parodied Marvel's output in *Captain Guts*, while 'Spain' (Manuel) Rodriguez created Trashman, a working-class, radical, left-wing, shapeshifting superhero battling a fascist police state future America. According to Clay Geerdes, English professor and drama critic, '[*Zap*] was the book that turned on all those light bulbs and taught people they did not have to submit to the East Coast comic book monopoly, and wait for acceptance or rejection. *Zap* taught them they could do their own.'

The anti-authoritarian streak in underground comix was reflected in Marvel's superheroes. Although Stan Lee was of an older generation, he was wise enough to tune in to what was happening in the wider culture and bring on younger writers and artists, such as Roy Thomas, Archie Goodwin, and Jim Steranko, to reflect that world in their comic books. DC also hired younger contributors such as Len Wein, Marv Wolfman, and Mike Frederich who all brought a flavour of the underground to mainstream superheroes. Marvel and DC both featured socially conscious stories in their late-Sixties, early-Seventies comics to appeal to young hip readers. A character such as Wolverine, the most popular of the X-Men to come out of the mid-Seventies relaunch, had more than a flavour of the anti-authoritarian underground comix. The socially relevant comics featuring Green Lantern, Green Arrow and Spider-Man in the early-Seventies also reflected the underground publishing of the Sixties.

Mainstream comic creators would also owe the pioneers of underground publishing a debt in the area of creator rights. This became a hot topic within comic book publishing in the Seventies, with practitioners such as Neal Adams becoming advocates for the likes of Siegel, Shuster, Jack Kirby, and others. The growing movement to secure the return of artists' original artwork and to implement royalty payment schemes for creators, and the rise of creator-owned characters into the Eighties, all had roots in Sixties underground comix.

* * *

While they faced new competition from the nascent super-heroes at Marvel, the creators at DC had a few innovations of their own. Their iconic Thirties and Forties superhe-roes, while still selling, needed updating. The values of the Depression no longer sat well in the swinging Sixties.

The biggest innovation came in *The Flash* #123 (Septem-ber 1961) in a story entitled 'Flash of Two Worlds'. Editor Julius Schwartz, writer Gardner Fox, and artists Carmine Infantino and Joe Giella developed the concept of Earth-Two. This placed the original versions of the Thirties and Forties DC superheroes on an alternative Earth, while the modern reinventions existed in the present, dubbed Earth-One (Earth-Prime was inhabited by DC Comics' real-life readers). This idea of the DC Multiverse would be built upon for years to come, allowing for huge diversification of their characters and concepts.

As depicted on the cover, the two versions of the Flash meet in *The Flash* #123. Vibrating his molecules to achieve invisibility (as part of a magic show), the Flash (Barry Allen) falls into an alternate dimension (Earth-Two, although it is not actually named until 'Crisis on Earth-One' in *Justice League of America* #21, August 1963) where he encounters Jay Garrick, the Golden Age Flash. It is suggested that comic book writer Gardner Fox must be mentally in tune with Earth-Two as the source of his stories is in his dreams.

The DC shared universe had been slow to change, with their original heroes inhabiting completely separate, dis-tinct worlds. Slowly, team-ups began: it was hard to resist uniting Superman and Batman. Similarly, a handful of sto-ries in the past found it useful to feature alternative ver-sions of Earth, but they were promptly forgotten once they'd served their purpose. In the Sixties, as Marvel was successfully doing, DC attempted to unite not only its cur-rent roster of superhero comics and characters, but also all those of the past two decades into one coherent universe, even if the concept of a multiverse had to be invoked to shoehorn in Golden Age characters. The original Justice Society encountered the new Justice League in *Justice League of America* #21 (August 1963) and #22 (September 1963), under artist Mike Sekowsky. In #29 readers were introduced to another alternate universe. On Earth-Three everything was topsy-turvy, with Lex Luthor a hero and most of the other superheroes were super-villains, part of the Crime Syndicate of America. It was a neat solution to proliferating characters, and an innovative way of keeping up with Marvel, but sometimes the implications of these rapidly diversifying DC universes could prove to be head-scratchingly confusing, not only for the readers but also for the writers and editors . . .

At the start of the Sixties DC was located on Lexington Avenue in New York, headed up by Irwin Donenfeld (son of the late founder Harry, who died in 1965 aged 71) and Jack Liebowitz. Superman was under the watchful eye of Mort Weisinger, while Jack Schiff continued to oversee the Batman titles. Robert Kanigher was running the romance comics, but he also edited *Wonder Woman*. Editor Julius Schwartz oversaw everything the company was producing. Like Stan Lee at Marvel, most of the senior staff had begun in comics during the Golden Age and had weathered two decades of ups and downs, but there wasn't one controlling editorial voice in the way that Lee commanded Marvel.

Feeling abused and neglected by DC, who had built an empire on the back of Superman, Jerry Siegel still wrote for the company, although his feelings about how he'd fared in relation to his most successful creation might have been reflected in his 1961 story 'The Death of Superman' (in *Superman* #149, November 1961). This was one of several 'alternate reality' stories that allowed creators to explore the superhero mythos without inflicting lasting changes on the characters. Siegel had Lex Luthor triumph over Superman through the use of Kryptonite, but he was eventually trapped in the Phantom Zone (sourced from the 1949

Superman movie serial). Siegel would see out the decade proof-reading comic pages for Marvel, given a 'pity job' by Stan Lee.

Artist Curt Swan (who'd drawn Siegel's 'The Death of Superman') revamped Superman's appearance, creating the definitive look (replacing Wayne Boring). He was particularly prolific when teamed with writer Dennis O'Neil on Superman through the Seventies. Swan reduced some of the more cartoony elements of the Man of Steel, such as his outsized jaw, tending towards a more realistic look for the original Golden Age superhero. Julius Schwartz rang the changes on Superman, removing the Fifties crutch of Kryptonite, and ditching 'all the robots that used to get him out of situations'. He also set about updating Clark Kent, with modern tailoring (his regular suit still seemed to date from the Forties), and moved him on in career terms away from the *Daily Planet* and into television (where Schwartz reckoned most young readers were getting their news – a similar updating would see the twenty-first-century Clark Kent become an Internet blogger, rather than a newspaper reporter).

One of the oddest, but best remembered, 'imaginary' Superman stories of the Sixties appeared in *Superman* #162 (July 1963). 'The Amazing Story of Superman-Red and Superman-Blue' splits the Man of Steel into two distinct Supermen after an ill-fated experiment with Kryptonite. One wears an all-red outfit, while the other is all blue. The combined brainpower of the two Supermen leads to the reconstruction of Krypton from fragments scattered across the galaxy and the removal of all evil on Earth thanks to an 'anti-evil' ray. Superman Red marries Lois Lane and starts a new life on New Krypton, while Superman Blue marries Lana Lang and retires, leaving his robot duplicates to take care of any natural disasters. The final panel asked readers: 'Suppose this Imaginary Story really happened! Which couple do you think would be happiest?' It was a tale that seemed to draw a line under the domestic sitcom period of Fifties' slapstick family adventures.

After a brief period at Marvel (where he reintroduced Professor Xavier in *The X-Men* #65, with artist Neal Adams) Dennis O'Neil re-joined DC in 1968 and would make a significant impact on the company's titles in years to come. Initially he tried creating new characters, such as the Creeper with Steve Ditko, but eventually he took a shot at revamping some of the company's older super-heroes. In the face of increasing Sixties 'women's lib' and feminism, O'Neil with artist Mike Sekowsky removed Wonder Woman's powers, turning her from an Amazonian super-heroine into a self-styled Sixties secret agent involved in international intrigue (riffing on contemporary hits like the James Bond movies and Diana Rigg's Emma Peel in British television series *The Avengers* – unrelated to Marvel). *Wonder Woman* #179 (November–December 1968) saw Diana Prince renounce her powers rather than leave Earth with her Amazonian sisterhood. The following issue killed off her longtime love interest Steve Trevor. O'Neil hoped to capture the modern Sixties liberated young woman in the new Diana – after all, women could be 'Wonder Woman' without super-powers – but the gambit backfired when feminist Gloria Steinem criticized the move as effectively reducing the strength of an important female icon. The change lasted for twenty-five issues before O'Neil restored the status quo.

The Sixties were a better decade for Batman. Following the bizarre cod-science fiction shapeshifting adventures of the Fifties under Jack Schiff, the arrival of Julius Schwartz as editor in 1964 saw him returned to his roots as a dark figure of the night, avenging crime. Even though in the late-Fifties and early-Sixties the Batman titles had gone down a similar 'family' spin-off route to Superman (with Bat-Hound, Bat-Mite, Batman even became Bat-Baby!), it was easier to restore equilibrium. *Detective Comics* #327

(May 1964) saw the arrival of a 'new look' (as the cover billed the redesign) for Batman, crafted by artists Carmine Infantino and Joe Giella. 'The Mystery of the Menacing Mask' rescued the comic from cancellation, as falling sales reflected readers' lack of patience with the out-of-place weird science that dominated. There was a conscious effort to return Batman to reality (in comic book terms). Clad in trench coats, the Dynamic Duo looked set to finally fulfil Batman's original billing as 'the world's greatest detective'. The Batcave was made over in a more realistic manner, while the now internationally recognized Batman logo, with the bat symbol encased in a yellow oval on Batman's chest, was introduced across the three ongoing Batman titles (*Detective Comics*, *World's Finest*, and *Batman*).

Schwartz's first issue of *Batman* was #164 (June 1964) and featured a revamp of the Batmobile, turning it into more of a sports car than a Forties sedan. He banished the habit of regularly transforming Batman, eliminated all alien beings and trips to outer space, and banned all mention of any of the members of the Batman 'family'. The next step was the rehabilitation of old villains, with the Riddler reintroduced in #171 (May 1965), eighteen years after his last appearance. New villains were developed, including the enduring Poison Ivy (#181, June 1966). However, the unexpected success of the camp spoof *Batman* television series of 1966 [see chapter 12] rapidly undid many of these developments as the Batman comics were rapidly changed to fit better with the wildly popular camp version of the Dynamic Duo now on television.

Despite these changes, DC Comics remained the stiff-necked establishment to Marvel's burgeoning, free-wheeling counterculture. DC heroes were still clean cut (like their Fifties counterparts), and rather than side with Vietnam protestors or students (in the way Marvel appeared to), DC stuck to its inherently conservative outlook on American life. The fall out from the Fifties censorship and

Comics Code had a greater and longer-lasting resonance at DC, where the writers, editors, and artists were more willing to self-censor.

Inevitably, the newly resurgent Marvel was seen as the outsider rebel (despite the company having been in the comics business almost as long as DC), willing to experiment and try anything to curry favour with readers. DC would not be swayed by such tactics – with Superman and Batman it was largely steady as she goes . . . The characters remained establishment figures, with Superman continuing to defend 'the American way', while Batman and Robin were both deputized by the Gotham City Police Force. Non-conformity was often equated with criminality, another hangover from the conventional Fifties.

DC belatedly tried to jump on the teen superhero trend ignited by Marvel's Fantastic Four and especially Spider-Man. Their response was *The Teen Titans* (#1, January–February 1966, after a try-out in *The Brave and the Bold* #54 in 1964), consisting of a foursome of youthful sidekicks – Kid Flash, Aqualad, Batman's sidekick Robin, and Wonder Girl. Aqualad was later replaced by Speedy, the Green Arrow's sidekick. Unlike Marvel's seemingly effortless ability to connect with Sixties youth culture, DC's attempts appeared strained. Stage magician and sorcerer Zatanna (who first appeared in *Hawkman* #4, October–November 1964) and Nightshade (in *Captain Atom* #82, September 1966), as well as Batgirl, were worthy attempts to reach out to female readers but often came across as halfhearted tokenism.

Overall, DC Comics did little to directly engage with the success of the new Marvel titles. The creative forces there, rather stuck in their ways, even consoled themselves with the idea that it was the 'bad art' and 'juvenile puns' that were making Marvel's superheroes momentarily successful and that their success could not last. They didn't recognize that the inherent humanity in Marvel's superheroes was precisely what was missing from their own characters. The Seventies would see DC having to face up to Marvel's new stable of superheroes and refresh their own offerings accordingly.

DC was bought by Kinney National Services in 1967, a company formed from the merger of car parking and cleaning companies. Kinney also bought the struggling Warner Bros. movie studio, sowing the seeds of the entertainment giant Warner Communications that eventually became Time Warner, the company behind the superhero movie successes of the twenty-first century. Kinney wanted DC for distributor Independent News, while Perfect Film and Chemical Corporation were after Goodman's men's magazines rather than Marvel comics. Both companies would find that the incidental comic book lines they inherited would turn out to be much more valuable in the long run.

By the end of the decade several of the original innovators that DC had relied on had hung up their pens. Superman's Jerry Siegel and Joe Shuster were largely a spent force, and Batman creator Bob Kane withdrew from comic books in 1967 to focus on television cartoons. DC editor Mort Weisinger retired in 1970 (he'd die eight year later), and was replaced by the promoted Julius Schwartz. The comics old guard were leaving the page, clearing the way for a new generation to forge a new direction for the superheroes in the Seventies.

PART 4: TURMOIL!

9

SUPERHEROES OR ANTI-HEROES?

Two key events marked the end of the Silver Age in 1970: Jack Kirby quit Marvel, sundering the partnership with Stan Lee that had resulted in a whole slew of successful new superheroes, and long-term DC editor Mort Weisinger retired after masterminding many of the original superheroes since starting at the company in 1941.

A new generation of storytellers was ready to take these now-venerable superheroes in new directions, or return them to their roots. This younger generation had grown up as comic book fans, so brought a return to the social awareness of the Thirties and Forties. This 'Bronze Age' stretches from 1970 to the mid-Eighties, when superheroes took a turn for the dark and serious. The origins of that revisionism sprang from the socially relevant Seventies.

The move towards modern social relevance had begun in the late-Sixties, as Stan Lee realized that Marvel's new characters were a big hit on college campuses. Lee determined to reflect recent student activism in his most popular comic. *The Amazing Spider-Man* #68 (January 1969) depicted the webbed wonder swinging his way through a crowd of multi-cultural placard-brandishing students. 'Crisis on Campus' told how the Kingpin's plot to steal an ancient tablet from Empire State University is thwarted by a sit-in by students. Spider-Man treads a middle ground, neither endorsing nor decrying the students, but the plot came from real demonstrations at Columbia University.

Also following wider real-world political developments was the Falcon, the first genuine mainstream African-American superhero (Black Panther, introduced three years previously, had been African by birth). Created by Lee and drawn by Gene Colan, the Falcon first appeared in *Captain America* #117 (September 1969). Colan recalled that '... [with the] Vietnam War and the Civil Rights protests, Stan [Lee] always wanted to be at the forefront of things ... [He] started bringing these headlines into the comics'. Colan ensured characters he depicted, especially in *Captain America*, were of mixed ethnicity, and he claimed to have sold Lee on the idea of an African-American lead. A reformed gangster, the Falcon became Captain America's right hand (although sidekick status brought criticism, he did step into Cap's shoes for a while).

Within a couple of years, Luke Cage was headlining his own title: *Luke Cage, Hero for Hire* #1 (June 1972). Created by writer Archie Goodwin and artists George Tuska and John Romita, Cage was a black youth jailed for a crime he didn't commit. Offered early parole, Cage takes part in an experiment to create immunity that instead leaves him with skin hard as steel and impervious to bullets. Escaping prison, Cage becomes a freelance superhero. The suspicion remained that Luke Cage's creation was less a desire to depict racial equality than to cash in on the then-prevalent 'blaxploitation' craze in movies. As kung fu movies became popular, Cage gained a kung fu side-kick named Iron Fist. Cage's identity was further 'main-streamed' when he adopted the title Power Man (the comic's title changed in 1978 to *Power Man and Iron Fist*, giving his martial arts sidekick equal billing).

The question of ethnic superheroes was first properly addressed in the Seventies. The Hulk would make common cause with a black teenager, who complained that the larger world hated them both. Following Black Panther (headlin-ing his own comic, *Jungle Action*, from 1973 – with Marvel avoiding the 'Black Panther' title due to its militant politi-cal connotations) and Luke Cage, there were a handful of others. Blade was a black superhero vampire hunter intro-duced in *Tomb of Dracula* #10 (July 1973) as a support-ing character, followed by solo appearances in *Adventure into Fear* #24 (October 1974); *Vampire Tales* #8 (December 1974); and *Marvel Preview* #3 (September 1975). However, it would be the Nineties before he was properly explored, leading to the Wesley Snipes movie trilogy [see chapter 13]. The relaunched X-Men saw Storm join, whose origins as the former queen consort of Wakanda would quickly be forgotten (her backstory was established in *The X-Men* #102, December 1976). A version of DC's Green Lantern featured John Stewart as a black Lantern, first appearing in *Green Lantern* #87 (December 1971/January 1972), a back-up to Hal Jordan's Lantern. Stewart's racial origins upset Jordan, provoking the Guardians who appointed the Lan-terns to accuse him of bigotry. Perhaps one of the silliest stories was the *Superman's Girl Friend, Lois Lane* (#106, November 1970) instalment 'I Am Curious (Black)', where Lois became a black woman for a day in order to understand Metropolis's minority culture! It was well-intentioned, but in hindsight simply looks naïve, as does its titling after an infamous movie. Although relying too heavily on the kung fu vogue, other non-white DC superheroes included Bronze Tiger and Black Lightning, followed by Vixen and

Cyborg. It took time for them to develop, but the further from their blaxploitation and kung fu origins they were, the stronger they became. The writing may have been direct, but it made for an interesting debate in a medium widely perceived as 'childish'.

Alongside race, domestic US politics was high profile as the hangover from the Vietnam War fed the Watergate scandal that brought down President Nixon. Between 1973 and 1975 a long-running story in *Captain America* drew on Watergate. Written by Steve Englehart, 'Secret Empire' suggested there was a conspiracy within the US Government to undermine democracy. Englehart recalled: 'I was writing a man [Captain America] who believed in America's highest ideals at a time when America's President was a crook. In the Marvel Universe, which so closely resembled our own, Cap followed a criminal conspiracy into the White House that saw the President commit suicide.' The story concluded, after Nixon resigned, depicting the President as the head of the shadowy 'secret empire'. Shaken by this, Rogers temporarily abandoned his Captain America identity, becoming 'Nomad', a man without a country.

While Marvel was reflecting the wider political atmosphere of mid-Seventies America, DC was travelling a more personal road. Green Arrow was added to the April 1970 issue of *Green Lantern*. Artist Neal Adams updated the look of the character, sparking writer Dennis O'Neil – who drew upon the 'new journalism' of Tom Wolfe and Hunter S. Thompson – into overhauling Arrow's outlook. Both men were from a new generation of comic book creators under thirty. Oliver Queen loses his fortune, becoming a spokesperson for society's underprivileged. Green Arrow was brought into *Green Lantern* #76, stepping up from a supporting character in the Justice League to become a voice of dissent beside Hal Jordan's establishment figure – in his first appearance he upbraids Green Lantern for saving a suited businessman, revealed as a slum landlord. O'Neil and Adams explored social and political issues through the clash of ideas between these two, often depicting Queen advocating direct action while Jordan lectured about achieving change by working within the system. Travelling the country in an old pick-up, the pair witnessed the 'real' America, and were involved in stories reflecting modern corruption, as well as stories based in racism, religious cults, the 'generation gap', the plight of Native Americans, poverty, overpopulation, and environmentalism. Stories were taken from the headlines, such as that appearing in *Green Lantern* #78–9 (July, September 1970) entitled 'A King of Loving' that saw Black Canary fall in with a Manson-like cult. This series tapped into the same college audience turned on to Marvel's Spider-Man, but it also had crossover appeal, with mainstream media such as the *Wall Street Journal* and the *New York Times* citing these tales as evidence that comics had reached a new form of maturity.

Where these stories succeeded was in personalizing big issues so they affected individuals, even if they were superheroes. The most effective and best-remembered was the drug addiction story in *Green Lantern* #85–6 (August–November 1971), 'Snowbirds Don't Fly'. The striking cover featured the strapline 'The Shocking Truth About Drugs!'. It depicts Jordan and Queen looking on in horror as Queen's former sidekick Speedy shoots up heroin. The main cover line reads 'DC attacks youth's greatest problem . . . Drugs!'. With Queen focusing on his social crusades, he'd neglected his personal responsibility, unaware of Speedy's growing addiction. The story brought a letter of congratulations from the then-mayor of New York, but, as so often, Stan Lee's Marvel had prepared the ground for DC.

The US Department of Health, Education, and Welfare had officially approached Lee asking if Marvel would be willing to use Spider-Man to educate young readers about the dangers of drugs. While keen to do so, Lee found himself running afoul of the mid-Fifties Comics Code Authority guidelines that banned the depiction of drug use. His tale 'Green Goblin Reborn!', in *Amazing Spider-Man* #96–8 (May–July 1971), saw Harry Osborn battle drug addiction, but also caused the CCA to refuse its seal of approval which did little to deter Lee, despite pressure from within Marvel. This led to a revision of the Code, allowing the depiction of drug use as long as it was clearly exposed as 'a vicious habit'. As a result, the following issues of *Green Lantern* dealing with Speedy's narcotic problem carried the CCA seal missing from the earlier *Amazing Spider-Man* drug issues.

Post-1968 even that tool of the military-industrial complex, Tony Stark, found himself distanced from the establishment and fighting on behalf of the common man. Like several superheroes, Iron Man preached a non-violent solution to problems. One of Iron Man's enemies was Firebrand (*Iron Man* #27, July 1970), once all-American kid Gary Gilbert, but now a violent anti-industrialist vigilante who lost faith in peaceful protest. Having accidentally killed his own father, Firebrand becomes an alcoholic. The dichotomy of violent insurrection versus peaceful protest caused an inrush of mail to Marvel, with just as many siding with Firebrand in his radical approach as did with Iron Man. By 1971, Stark was battling US Senators who saw the 'youth of today' as an un-American breed out to bring down the Government. Siding with the American people, Iron Man was labelled an anarchist by the authorities. At the same time, Stark and his weapons factories were targets of student demonstrations. One of the few Marvel comics to directly tackle the Vietnam War, *Iron Man* had Stark distance himself from the conflict and withdraw from creating weapons, focusing instead on consumer goods and environmental products. The story 'Long Time Gone' (in *Iron Man* #78, September 1975) had Stark review his own conversion from anti-Communist fighter to anti-Vietnam campaigner. While questioning his moral authority – and that of his government – Stark reaffirms his status as a superhero out to help those at the mercy of such governmental-industrial-military forces that he once represented.

A more personal plight for Tony Stark was featured in the classic nine-issue 'Demon in a Bottle' storyline (*Iron Man* #120–8, March–November 1979), written by David Michelinie and Bob Layton, and illustrated by John Romita, Layton and Carmine Infantino. The series chronicled Stark's descent into alcoholism as a result of the business and personal pressures he faced. Troubled by his seemingly malfunctioning armour and having lost his position as leader of the Avengers, Stark turns to drink. Discovering his armour failures have been caused by rival businessman Justin Hammer to discredit him, Stark is hunted by a team of Hammer's super-villains. Falling further into alcoholism, Stark argues with his butler Jarvis, and his girlfriend Beth, who nonetheless helps him through alcohol withdrawal.

The bottle and its contents were, according to Michelinie, 'our villain of the month'. Winning the 1980 Eagle Award for 'Favourite Single Comic Book Story', the 'Demon in a Bottle' tale proved influential in fusing super-heroics with real-world personal problems. It humanized Tony Stark in a way that had never been attempted as successfully before. His recovery from addiction brought a real-world everyday issue many readers may have experienced within their own families to the pages of a four-colour superhero comic. These superhero stories of the Seventies were relevant, but not radical, reflecting contemporary events and attitudes. However, they failed to stop the slide in sales, and the exhaustion of the superhero form became more evident.

The changes in the CCA Code saw several other types of comic book make a return. With supernatural creatures

such as vampires, werewolves and ghouls now permitted
again, a whole raft of titles such as *Ghost Rider*, *Swamp
Thing* and *The Tomb of Dracula* appeared, alongside many
fantasy heroes such as Conan the Barbarian, Tarzan, John
Carter, and Solomon Kane (all based on the work of pulp
novelists). The most interesting was *Swamp Thing*, created by Len Wein and drawn by Berni Wrightson, who
first appeared in anthology title *House of Secrets* (#92,
July 1971). Cashing in on the contemporary horror boom,
Swamp Thing enjoyed his own series (labelled for 'mature
readers'), running for twenty-four issues between 1972
and 1976. Writer Alan Moore would radically reinvent
this unlikely superhero in the Eighties. Despite this devia-
tion into atmospheric horror, the core of many superheroes remained personal stories, directly relevant to the
readership.

Comics had previously been rather cavalier in the way
they'd killed off many incidental characters, but the death
of Spider-Man's girlfriend Gwen Stacy in 1973 was a serious moment of tragedy and heartbreak. This was a personal blow that reflected larger issues, and brought many
younger readers to confront death meaningfully for the
first time. She had first appeared in *Amazing Spider-Man*
#31 (September 1965) as a fellow student when Peter Parker
attended Empire State University. Their romance unfolded
gradually, including a temporary dalliance between Parker
and Mary Jane Watson, Gwen's friend. Foreshadowing her
own death, Gwen's police captain father is killed in *Amazing Spider-Man* #90 ('And Death Shall Come', November
1970) when he is hit by falling masonry while trying to save
a young boy – the debris caused by a battle between Spider-
Man and Doctor Octopus. Gwen blames Spider-Man for
her father's death, while hoping Peter will propose to her
– but he can't due to his guilt. In *Amazing Spider-Man* #121
(June 1973), the Green Goblin – who knows Spider-Man's

secret identity – kidnaps Gwen and holds her captive on top of the George Washington Bridge. As most readers would expect, Spider-Man appears to save the day, defeating the Goblin and apparently rescuing Gwen by stopping her fall when he catches her with his webbing, exclaiming 'Did it!'. It is only when he pulls Gwen back up that he realizes she is dead. In shock, Spider-Man attacks the Goblin, almost killing him but pulling back at the last moment. Neither Peter Parker nor the Goblin really know how Gwen died, with only the reader privy to the subtle 'snap!' sound effect suggesting her neck was broken when Spider-Man's webbing abruptly broke her fall. This was a shocking dose of reality for the fantasy world of superhero comics.

The death of Gwen Stacy changed something. Superheroes had previously rarely been seen to fail, or if they did, that failure was immediately followed by a moment of triumph. Neither were characters close to the heroes, whether sidekicks or love interests, killed off in such perfunctory fashion. The idea for the death of Gwen Stacy had come from artist John Romita to shake up the otherwise cosy world of superhero comics. Gerry Conway wrote the story and the unforgettable art was by Gil Kane, with the spoiler title 'The Night Gwen Stacy Died!' only revealed on the final page. For many, the formal end of the Silver Age came with this issue of *Amazing Spider-Man*, when comic book superheroes lost their innocence. Marvel didn't shy away from exploring the repercussions of Stacy's death: Peter and Mary Jane both gained a new maturity and developed a deeper relationship, while the Green Goblin went on to surpass Doctor Octopus as Spider-Man's number one villain. The death of supporting characters (and superheroes) would become more common in years to come, especially during 'event' series from both Marvel and DC in the Eighties and Nineties, but it was in the mid-Seventies that this original death made its biggest impact on a whole generation of readers and creators.

*   *   *

By the end of the Sixties it seemed Marvel's mutant superhero team, the X-Men, had reached the end of the road,
with later issues filled with reprints. Not wanting to let the
title lie fallow, a new creative team was put in charge and
the characters relaunched in *Giant-Size X-Men* #1 (May
1975). Written by Len Wein, with support from editorial
assistant Chris Claremont (who would become the defining creative force of the X-Men over the next fifteen years),
and illustrated by Dave Cockrum, the sixty-eight-page
special kick-started the new X-Men after a five-year hiatus
from new material. The story had Professor X recruiting
a new team, intending to rescue the original X-Men who
have vanished while on a mission to the island of Krakoa.
The new international team (based on a suggestion from
Marvel's corporate owners – now named Cadence Indus-
tries – that they needed characters with 'foreign' appeal)
consisted of original member Cyclops, plus Sunfire (from
Japan, who quickly quit), and Banshee (Irish, both from
earlier appearances), plus Wolverine (from Canada) – a new
character introduced in *The Incredible Hulk* #180 (October 1974) who would become the most popular member.
They appeared alongside newly invented Storm (African-
American of Kenyan descent), Nightcrawler (from Germany), Colossus (Russian), and Thunderbird (an arrogant
American Indian killed off almost immediately, demon-
strating the new characters' vulnerability). The island is
revealed to be a living giant mutant, which the new X-Men
destroy (by firing it into space) while rescuing the original
team. The issue closes by pondering the future of the now
newly enlarged team of thirteen X-Men.

Claremont took over writing duties full time. The X-Men
were ideally placed to take advantage of the vogue for
social relevance in superhero comics: each was a symbol of
prejudice, disguised in comic book terms as mutant super-
powers. The popularity of the revived X-Men outstripped

the originals, suggesting the metaphor-laden storylines were striking home with teenage audiences: whether black, homosexual, or otherwise 'different', most teenagers felt apart from the dominant culture. Their story continued in regular title *The X-Men* (revived from #94), with these 'all new, all different X-Men' (as the cover boasted) effectively melding Marvel's emotional soap opera with high-flying fantasy stories, threaded through with the kind of real-world social concerns that gave superheroes a new relevance.

Following the unexpected death of Thunderbird (in #95, seen as too similar to Wolverine in temperament), Claremont continued to evolve the X-Men in unexpected ways, while developing their emotional sides. He brought back the mutant-hunting robotic Sentinels (the Mark III versions, from #98, best used in the apocalyptic 'Days of Future Past' in *The Uncanny X-Men* #141–2 in 1981 – 'Uncanny' was added to the title from #142) and used telepath Jean Grey as the basis for the 'Phoenix/Dark Phoenix' saga (1977–80), both stories repurposed in the twenty-first-century X-Men movies. Saving her fellow X-Men while piloting a shuttle, Grey was exposed to cosmic rays, which seemingly killed her, although she returned in the form of Phoenix (having bonded with a cosmic entity), with a new set of dramatic powers (*The X-Men* #101–8, 1977). Corrupted by her new powers, she is transformed (partly due to the villainous Hellfire Club) into Dark Phoenix, and eventually becomes a threat to the universe (*The X-Men* #129–138, 1980). Only her suicidal sacrifice in #137 prevents universal destruction.

Canadian John Byrne had replaced Cockrum on art, and the Claremont-Byrne team produced a run of impressive stories that propelled the X-Men to Marvel's top sellers by the end of the decade (that popularity never left the series). The deliberate internationalism of the X-Men saw the development of a Canadian team following the success of Wolverine. Alpha Flight (comprising Sasquatch, North-star, Snowbird, Shaman, Guardian, and Aurora) debuted in *The X-Men* #120 (April 1979), created by Byrne as part of the previously unexplored backstory for Wolverine before spinning off in their own titles in the Eighties. Among other significant characters introduced to *The X-Men* in the Seventies were Mystique (*Ms. Marvel* #16, April 1978), a super-villain shapeshifter who would become central to Magneto's Brotherhood of Mutants, and Proteus (*The X-Men* #125, September 1979), a Scottish mutant who breaks free from his mother Moira MacTaggert's isolated genetic research laboratory.

Martin Goodman had retired from Marvel in 1972. Stan Lee took less interest in the day-to-day running of Marvel Comics as he was promoted to Publisher, so spent more time working on the business side than on the creative. He would spend two decades involved with largely futile attempts to launch movie versions of Marvel's characters. Others took over the titles he'd been writing, with Roy Thomas on *The Amazing Spider-Man*, Archie Goodwin on *The Fantastic Four*, Gary Friedrich on *Captain America* and (youngest of them) Gerry Conway on *Thor* – he'd have a chance to work on many titles, including *Daredevil*, *Iron Man*, *The Incredible Hulk* and *The Fantastic Four*. Lee dubbed this period as 'Marvel: Phase Two'. It saw a series of writers step up as Editor-in-Chief (filling Lee's shoes), but few lasted long. In turn, Thomas (until 1974), Len Wein (nine months), and Marv Goodman (one year), Conway (one month), Goodwin (eighteen months), and Jim Shooter took on the role during the decade – Shooter would hold the position for nine years. Each (other than Shooter) came to the conclusion they were happier writing comics than managing them, and each left in turn to take up a freelance editor/writer role with a batch of Marvel titles. Replacing Lee proved impossible: when he oversaw just eight comics per month the job was feasible, but with the proliferation of titles and the exponential growth of the Marvel Universe, it was often beyond a group of writers who saw themselves as mavericks, not management. While the story content of many Marvel comics had turned cosmic between *2001: A Space Odyssey* (1968) and *Star Wars* (1977), it was the best-selling comic of the latter movie that got Marvel out of dire financial straits as the decade ended and sales collapsed.

Over at DC, Jack Kirby spent much of the early Seventies developing his 'New Gods/Fourth World' series. Kirby took on scripting and art duties on *Superman's Pal, Jimmy Olsen*, a little-regarded member of the Superman 'family' books left over from the Fifties and DC's lowest seller. Upset by his lack of ownership of characters he'd co-created with Lee at Marvel, Kirby brought several concepts to DC and used the *Jimmy Olsen* book to introduce them. Drawing on Thor, Kirby conceived of warring gods on an interplanetary scale, envisaging the work being collected in individual volumes. In the pages of *Jimmy Olsen*, Kirby introduced the genetic engineering experiment Project Cadmus (#133, October 1970), a version of Darkseid (#134, November 1970 – later one of the most powerful characters in the DC Universe), and the artificial planet Transilvane (#142–3, October–November 1971). Kirby further explored his concepts in three inter-related comics – *The Forever People* (1971, eleven issues), *Mister Miracle* (1971, eighteen issues), and *The New Gods* (1971, eleven issues) – pioneering a new grand-scale comic book storytelling. Kirby's galactic conflict between the forces of light and dark was never completed to his satisfaction, with titles cancelled or redirected to other creators by 1973 (mainly due to the antipathy of Carmine Infantino). Kirby's 'New Gods/Fourth World' would prove long-lasting, evolving through the input of many others from the Eighties (after a brief 1977 revival), becoming integral to the DC Universe in later years.

Kirby worked on other DC titles, including a one-shot of *The Sandman* with old partner Joe Simon (their last collaboration), but he found the production line qualities of DC as frustrating as those at Marvel. At a MarvelCon fan event in 1975, Stan Lee announced Kirby was returning to Marvel, where he scripted and drew *Captain America* and created *The Eternals* (#1, July 1976), introducing the superhuman defenders of Earth created by the alien Celestials. Kirby continued to develop the 'New Gods/Fourth World' concepts (ironically the new version faced a similar fate when it was cancelled incomplete in 1978). Lee and Kirby's final collaboration came with the 1978 revival of the *Silver Surfer* as the only non-reprint edition of Marvel's graphic novel-like 'Fireside Books' (an early 'graphic novel'). Kirby also worked on *Black Panther* and several non-superhero titles before leaving the company to explore television animation at the end of the decade.

By the Seventies, DC Comics was firmly under the editorial guidance of artist-editor Carmine Infantino. He encouraged younger talents, giving O'Neil and Adams their chance on *Green Lantern/Green Arrow*, and their 'realistic' revamp of Batman. They reacted against the camp of the television show, returning the character to his vigilante roots, although it was not enough to slow the fall in sales. Batman was once more the lone avenger, with Robin sent off to college. Starting in *The Brave and the Bold* #79 (August/September 1968), where the Batman encountered undead avenger Deadman, O'Neil and Adams re-invented the Caped Crusader. By *Batman* #217 (December 1969), there was no Wayne Manor or Batcave, and Bruce Wayne had relocated to a Gotham City penthouse. O'Neil – who had been born in the same month and the same year as Batman began – returned the character to his dark roots, paving the way for the Eighties interpretations by Frank Miller and Alan Moore. His and Adams' most enduring creation was the villainous Ra's al Ghul (*Batman* #232,

June 1971), who went on to be one of the DC Universe's most explored super-villains. Even after Adams moved on and Archie Goodwin took over as editor, O'Neil continued to write innovative Batman stories through to 1976, including his revitalization of the Joker in *Batman* #251 (September 1973).

Julius Schwartz had reluctantly taken on editing *Superman* following Weisinger's retirement, and he'd quickly turned to *Batman*'s Dennis O'Neil for help in reviving a flagging character. The writer's first thought was to rein in Superman's extraordinary powers. Over the years various writers and artists had expanded his power to cosmic levels, where he could juggle planets and extinguish suns with his breath. 'There's no problem he can't solve,' O'Neil noted. He set about developing '. . . a storyline that would scale him back almost to what Jerry [Siegel] and Joe [Shuster] started with in 1938 – we never got him back quite that far. For example, he never lost his power of flight'. DC even questioned whether there was any need for this all-powerful superhero at all in Elliot Maggin's 'Must There Be Superman?' (*Superman* #247, January 1972). Superman questions his motivations and ponders whether his heroics are holding mankind back. This consideration of the role and purpose of superheroes within their own fiction set the tone that would lead to the deconstruction of both Batman and Superman in the mid-Eighties.

The withdrawal of Wonder Woman's superpowers had been quickly reversed when sales continued to fall. Reinstated as Wonder Woman, Diana Prince was briefly teamed up with her 'sister' Nubia. However, the old 'bondage' cover images were soon back in vogue, such as that of #196 (October 1971) depicting Wonder Woman chained to a wall, her top ripped open and a target painted on her back . . . Even in death, William Moulton Marston's obsessions were still attached to his character. By 1973, Wonder Woman was back in her old star-spangled costume and fighting the same old battles. As the *Wonder Woman* television show had done little to help sales (only *The Incredible Hulk* seemed to benefit from television exposure, with sales increasing by a third), the comics quickly regressed to the status quo, a fate that also befell the reinvented Superman as the decade wore on.

Comic books had largely been a male preserve since their inception, both behind the scenes in terms of creators and on the page in terms of characters. The heroes were male, and they rescued damsels in distress. For all that Lois Lane might be a role model, for a long time she was depicted as an adjunct to Superman, the pivot in a unrealistically maintained love triangle between her, Superman and Clark Kent. Wonder Woman was the only female superhero to catch on, and she never quite fulfilled her potential. Girls generally didn't read comics, at least not superhero comics, and the perception was that boys didn't want to read about female characters.

There had been a few short-lived and usually half-hearted attempts at female superheroes besides Wonder Woman, but none had become household names. The rise of the feminist movement was another of the new social realities that comics had to take into account. The first attempts to redress the balance were creative stumbles: removing Wonder Woman's super-powers was a mistake. Engaging directly with feminism resulted in misfires, like the Avengers story that saw the superheroes confronted by their female counterparts in a bizarre battle of the sexes (*The Avengers* #83, December 1970). The cover features the Valkyrie and her 'Lady Liberators' preparing to 'finish off these male chauvinist pigs'! Other well-intentioned efforts resulted in caricatures like Thundra (*Fantastic Four* #129, December 1972), a female warrior from a woman-dominated future, and Man-Killer (*Marvel Team-Up* #8, April 1973), a militant feminist Olympic skier who battled Spider-Man.

By 1972 Marvel had launched a trio of female-focused comics created by female writers, with only the Cat showing any superhero potential (the others were jungle adventuress *Shanna the She-Devil* by Carole Seuling, and the workplace soap opera *Night Nurse* by Jean Thomas, wife of Roy). Initially a crime fighter without super-powers, Tigra the Cat appeared in *Claws of the Cat* #1 (November 1972), written by Linda Fite with pencilling by Marie Severin (one of the few prolific female comic book creatives, she created Spider-Woman in 1976). The title lasted four issues, with an additional appearance beside Spider-Man in *Marvel Team-Up* #8, April 1973. Tigra was revamped as a super-powered tiger-woman in a bikini in a two-part tale across *Giant-Size Creatures* #1 (July 1974) and *Werewolf by Night* #20 (August 1974), written by Tony Isabella. There were further sporadic appearances between 1975 and 1978, before she turned up in a supporting role in *The Avengers*.

The other angle taken was to simply create female versions of popular characters, resulting in such 'innovations' as Bruce Banner's unfortunate cousin She-Hulk (*Savage She-Hulk* #1, February 1980), who contracted her condition thanks to a blood transfusion from him; Spider-Woman, who featured in her own series from 1978–83 after a one-shot try out in *Marvel Spotlight* #32 (February 1977); warrior woman Red Sonja, drawn from Robert E. Howard's Conan mythos, who first appeared in *Conan the Barbarian* #23 (February 1973); and Ms. Marvel, a revamp of a late-Sixties character reconfigured as a fusion of alien Kree and human genes in *Ms. Marvel* #1 (January 1977, she'd later take over as Captain Marvel). While these characters would all enjoy extended lives throughout the growing Marvel Universe, none of them really became top-flight characters.

One of the more quirky explorers of the new social relevance in superhero comic books was Steve Gerber, a writer who fused the counter-culture of the Sixties underground comix with the mainstream superhero genre to great satiric effect. Gerber's background was in advertising and he apprenticed at Marvel writing short runs on *Daredevil*, *Iron Man*, and *Sub-Mariner*, as well as various monster books. His first signature title was *Man-Thing*, an empathetic swamp monster that pre-dated DC's similar *Swamp Thing* by eighteen months. He scripted the character's solo title which ran for twenty-two issues between January 1974 and October 1975. Gerber created Howard the Duck as a supporting character in a Man-Thing story in *Adventure into Fear* #19 (December 1973), but the parody character caught on winning a back-up strip in *Giant-Size Man-Thing* before debuting in his own title, *Howard the Duck* #1 (January 1976). Gerber would write twenty-seven issues about Howard, an alien fugitive from another planet who lived on Earth. Among the targets satirized was American politics in the post-Watergate era, with Howard representing the All-Night Party in a spoof of the 1976 Presidential election, gaining Gerber's work a cult following.

Gerber then created (with Mary Skrenes) *Omega the Unknown* (ten issues, 1976–7), which looked at a traditional superhero through the eyes of a twelve-year-old boy. Gerber was fired by Marvel in 1978 due – according to editor Jim Shooter – to the writer's poor deadline management. Gerber launched a long-running legal fight to gain control of *Howard the Duck* (going to court in 1980), bringing mainstream attention to the battle for creators' rights in comics. Gerber did some work for DC, then teamed up with Jack Kirby in 1982 to create *Destroyer Duck* (published by independent Eclipse), a spoof title aimed at raising funds for his ongoing legal challenges.

The late-Sixties underground comix movement had seen the arrival of creator-owned titles, but disputes between writers, artists, and publishers over the ownership of characters had raged right from the very beginning, when

Siegel and Shuster signed away Superman to DC for just $130. In 1973 Siegel and Shuster made a new attempt to recover ownership of Superman using the Copyright Act of 1909 that suggested copyrights were assigned for a period of twenty-eight years and had to be renewed. The case was lost, but by 1975 reports hit the press that Siegel and Shuster were living in near poverty. Embarrassed by the bad press, Warner Communications (owners of DC Comics) gave the pair lifetime pensions of $20,000 each per annum and additional healthcare benefits. DC argued that although there was no legal obligation, the company felt a 'moral obligation' to the creators of their most significant character. This deal also resulted in the pair credited as the creators of Superman across all media, including the hugely successful 1978 blockbuster movie.

The new blood introduced to the business in the Seventies didn't simply accept things as they always had been. Artist Neal Adams attempted to unionize the comic book world, and in 1978 formed the Comic Creators Guild to protect their rights. Industry legend Jack Kirby was in conflict with Marvel to gain ownership of his original artwork, and he eventually quit the company (again) in 1979. These arguments would run for many years, but comic creators of the Eighties learned lessons from Kirby and Gerber. As well as being smarter businessmen about retaining control of their creations, they also gave birth to the field of independent publishing (the true heirs to underground comix), causing the veteran comic book companies to make a significant shake-up in their practices. A Creator's Bill of Rights would be drafted in 1988 to aid creators in avoiding exploitation due to work-for-hire agreements, resulting in a more creator-friendly comic book business.

The late-Seventies should have seen DC Comics enjoying boom years. *Superman: The Movie* (1978) was expected to give superhero comics a sales boost not seen since the

Fifties. DC began a major expansion, launching an additional fifty-seven comics between 1975 and 1979, reviving and refreshing older titles and adding new ones. It was hoped the increased editorial page count (from seventeen to twenty-five pages) would make up for the higher prices (increased from 35c to 50c). However, DC's attempt to exploit the movie opportunity almost led to the collapse of the company.

New DC publisher Jenette Kahn was behind the expansion – which was heralded across the comics in ads headlined 'DC Explosion'. Kahn promised 'our comics should be a little easier to find . . . most harder-to-find comics will get better distribution'. She called the project 'An explosion of new ideas, new concepts, new characters, and new formats . . .' A range of 'Dollar Comics' would offer eighty pages of stories in titles such as *Superman Family* and *World's Finest*, all for $1. New superhero books included *Firestorm*, *Black Lightning*, *Shade the Changing Man* and *Steel*. Jack Kirby's *New Gods* and *Mister Miracle* were part of the DC Explosion, as were the new sword and sorcery fantasy titles such as *Beowulf the Dragon Slayer* and *Stalker the Man With the Stolen Soul*.

However, external factors served to doom DC's ambitious plans. Severe winter storms in late-1977 and early-1978 seriously disrupted distribution of magazines and newspapers to news-stands, proving more detrimental to the newest superheroes than any super-villains. Many newly launched comic books simply didn't reach retailers (Marvel also suffered) and so were not purchased by would-be readers, resulting in a stockpile of returned unsold material.

The combination of the fearful weather, the dubious quality of some of the new titles, and the general economic downturn (affecting the direct costs of paper and printing) that hit America in the late-Seventies doomed the DC Explosion. The planned Explosion quickly turned into the

'DC Implosion' (as fans called the result), with DC's corporate owners Warner Bros. urging immediate and drastic action. As the damage became clear in the summer of 1978, well before any benefits might be felt from the release of *Superman: The Movie* (due that December), 40 per cent of the DC titles were cancelled and many staff abruptly laid off. The entire DC comic book line was cut to just twenty-six ongoing titles, and the venerable *Detective Comics* was almost a casualty, with #480 scheduled to be the last until internal dissent saved it. Instead, the bigger-selling *Batman Family* merged with *Detective Comics*, giving the resulting combined title a new life. Following the dropping of sixty-five titles, DC ended 1978 with eight fewer comics than before the 'Explosion'. Additionally, a raft of planned titles – among them *The Vixen*, featuring the first African-American female DC superhero to star in her own series – didn't see the light of day. Many storylines and characters from these unpublished works would resurface in later DC comics, including Vixen (in *Action Comics* #521 in July 1981 – she later joined the Justice League of America). Despite her role in the rapid expansion and contraction of DC Comics in the late-Seventies, Kahn – along with deputy Paul Levitz – would go on to become a key figure in the evolution of the company across the next twenty-five years.

Growing out of the disaster was a new concept in superhero comics: the limited series that ran for a specified number of issues. In 1979 DC premiered *The World of Krypton*, written by Paul Kupperberg with art by Howard Chaykin and Murphy Anderson. The title was deliberately planned as a three-issue limited run, published between July and September 1979, and it retold (once again) the final days of life on Superman's home world.

More important to the future of superheroes was the new business model *The World of Krypton* represented, with 'limited series' an idea Jack Kirby had long championed.

As the Eighties dawned, there would be a distinct shift in comic book distribution, from news-stands (mass market) to the growing field of specialist comic book stores (a dedicated niche market). The combination of limited-run series and this new distribution model would give publishers more flexibility in the titles they could publish, and would give rise to two dramatic changes for the world of superheroes: the 'graphic novel', and the growth of smaller independent publishers serving a more dedicated fan audience.

10

SUPERHEROES DECONSTRUCTED

At the beginning of the Eighties a new generation of comic book writers and artists felt their work could aspire to more than mere entertainment, and that it might even verge on literary graphic art. They were working towards the fulfilment of novelist John Updike's 1960 prediction that there might in future be 'a doubly talented artist' who could create 'a comic-strip novel masterpiece'. Prime among them were Frank Miller and Alan Moore – both at DC Comics, now the underdog to Marvel's triumphant soap opera superheroes.

Miller and Moore would be the prime beneficiaries of the Seventies creators' rights struggles, reaping the rewards of battles fought by others. A series of independent publishers became established, known for their wider editorial interests and their focus on publishing creator-owned comics. Among the first was Eclipse, active from 1977

until 1993, which published one of the first graphic novels
– *Saber: Slow Fade of an Endangered Species* – aimed at the
newly emerging speciality comic book stores. Will Eisner
pioneered the 'graphic novel' format with *A Contract With
God* (1978), while Jack Kirby's *Captain Victory and the
Galactic Rangers* (Pacific Comics, 1981) was one of the earliest titles published for sale to the direct speciality comic
book store market. Eclipse was a champion of creators'
rights before it became standard practice at Marvel and
DC. Slowly, the independents had an effect on the big two.
Both would introduce imprints to publish 'mature' material, Marvel through Epic and DC through Vertigo. They
also saw independent publishers as creative nurseries where
new creators were discovered, then selectively picked up by
the mainstream. Art Spiegleman's *Maus* (1986) had shown
graphic novels could be a legitimate literary form, but it
was self-consciously personal and politically important.
Could the same be achieved for superheroes?

Miller had begun working for Marvel at the end of the
Seventies on non-superhero books, but by 1979 he was
working on *Peter Parker, The Spectacular Spider-Man*
#27–8 (February–March 1979), which guest starred Dare-
devil. Miller was taken with the blind superhero and asked
to work on the regular title, then in decline. He made his
debut with *Daredevil* #158 (May 1979), which wrapped up
an ongoing story. Miller brought film noir style to Daredevil's world of urban crime, making Marvel's New York
a more realistic environment than that usually seen in
the more fantasy-oriented *Spider-Man*. *Daredevil*'s sales
decline continued unabated. Newly installed as an editor
at Marvel, Dennis O'Neil put Miller on scripting as well as
art duties from #168 (January 1981). Miller introduced ninja
mercenary Elektra and developed Daredevil's martial arts.
He also revised Daredevil's backstory, introducing previously unseen allies and enemies who'd played a major part
in his youth. Darker themes pervaded Miller's Daredevil,

with unexpected story developments (such as the apparent death of Elektra, killed by assassin Bullseye, in *Daredevil* #181, April 1982) making the Marvel world suddenly a more dangerous place. By the time Miller finished his run with #191 (February 1983), he'd turned things around, and 'The Man Without Fear' was one of Marvel's most popular characters.

In 1982 Miller provided the art for a Chris Claremont Wolverine mini-series (which took Logan to Japan and formed the basis for the 2013 movie *The Wolverine*) before launching a creator-owned series through DC. *Ronin* (July 1983–August 1984, later a graphic novel, the format for which it was intended) was a six-issue mini-series that ran across 1983 and 1984, and the writer-artist brought Japanese and European influences to his work. Set in a near-future New York, Ronin told of a masterless samurai (a 'ronin') killed during a battle with the demon Agat, with both their souls trapped within his samurai sword. Released eight centuries later in a desolated wasteland called New York, the ronin inhabits the body of disabled Billy Challas and continues his fight with Agat (there's a lot of Marvel's *Thor* in Ronin). Mixing ancient Japanese legends with near-future bio-technology, Ronin was a cutting-edge superhero.

In 1980, Miller had worked on a Batman Christmas one-shot for DC called 'Wanted: Santa Claus Dead or Alive' (in *DC Special Series* #21, Spring 1980), but his other proposals to relaunch the character (one of them teaming him up with Superman and Wonder Woman in a book to be called *Metropolis*) all failed to interest the publisher. It was only after the success of *Ronin* that Miller had the clout to secure a chance to tackle Batman – the result would be the ground-breaking *Batman: The Dark Knight Returns* (1986).

The four-issue mini-series (February–June 1986) was presented in DC's new prestige format, a perfect-bound comic book printed on heavier paper stock, intended as a more durable artefact. The story picks up a retired Batman, aged fifty-five, who has withdrawn from crime fighting following the death of the second Robin, Jason Todd. After saving a thirteen-year-old girl from a gang, Batman is back in action with a new, female Robin by his side – Carrie Kelley, the teen girl he rescued. Batman's return reawakens the Joker, but the newly re-energized Batman soon defeats the villain. Despite Superman's involvement in deflecting a Russian nuclear warhead from reaching America, the country is soon a lawless post-apocalyptic wasteland following an electro-magnetic pulse that wipes out all power. Batman and his vigilante army ensure that Gotham is the safest place in the United States, embarrassing the remains of the US Government that sends in Superman to eliminate Batman. Their confrontation (during which Superman is weakened by a kryptonite-tipped arrow fired by Green Arrow) results in the apparent death of Batman. However, a coda reveals he is still alive and planning to continue his war on crime.

It may have featured a unique take on Batman and a reactionary Superman who is little more than a tool of the US Government (something Batman takes great relish in pointing out), but *The Dark Knight Returns* was a groundbreaking new way of presenting superhero comics to an older, more literary audience, as well as bringing the medium commercial and critical success and respect. The title sold well (better in the collected graphic novel format, following mainstream hype), and became an incredible influence on the future format of comic books. It also affected the kinds of stories that could be told using the almost fifty-year-old original superheroes, Superman and Batman – in particular it influenced their depiction on film from 1989 well into the twenty-first century. Miller would go on to refresh Batman's origin story in issues #404–7 of *Batman* (February–May 1987), collected as the graphic novel *Batman: Year One*, retelling Batman's origins within his own continuity.

Similarly, Alan Moore's simultaneous re-imagining and deconstruction of the superhero genre would have an equivalent seismic effect. Moore had cut his teeth in underground British comix of the Seventies, before moving on to work on UK titles such as *2000AD* (home of anti-hero Judge Dredd) and *Warrior* (26 issues, from March 1982 to January 1985, where Moore's *V For Vendetta* and *Marvelman* debuted), as well as work for Marvel UK on *Captain Britain*, the UK's equivalent to Captain America. Dedicated to upholding the ancient laws of Britain, this Captain obtained his powers through the Arthurian sorcerer Merlyn. Although created by *The X-Men* writer Chris Claremont, he was given an idiosyncratic, uniquely British makeover by Moore.

Moore became increasingly concerned about creators' rights as he toiled for a variety of American companies, giving characters his own unique stamp. Despite these concerns, Moore accepted an invitation from DC Comics' editor Len Wein to revamp the poorly selling monster comic *Swamp Thing* in 1983. Moore, working with artists Stephen R. Bissette, Rick Veitch, and John Totleben, broke down and rebuilt the character addressing a series of environmental and social issues within a neo-Gothic fantasy/horror context. As part of his project to revise the superhero, Moore began to resurrect a series of long-forgotten DC characters within the pages of *Swamp Thing*, including the Spectre, Deadman, and the Phantom Stranger. Moore worked on *Swamp Thing* for three years, from #20 (January 1984) to #64 (September 1987), excluding #59 and #62. Moore's success opened the doors to the 'British Invasion' of American comics (after the Sixties pop music 'British Invasion' that brought The Beatles and The Rolling Stones to America). Among the British writers that developed careers on US superhero comics through the Eighties and

Nineties were Neil Gaiman (*Sandman*), Grant Morrison (*Animal Man, Doom Patrol, The Invisibles The New X-Men*), Mark Millar (*Ultimate X-Men, The Ultimates, Superman: Red Son* – a Russian-set retelling of the Man of Steel's origin), and Jamie Delano (*Hellblazer*). There was also Northern Irish Garth Ennis (*Hellblazer, Preacher*), and Warren Ellis (*Transmetropolitan, Stormwatch, The Authority*). The majority learned their craft on the UK's *2000 AD*, before their recruitment by DC Comics. Artists included Dave McKean, Brian Bolland, Dave Gibbons, Steve Dillon, and Brendan McCarthy, among others.

Inevitably, working for DC it was only a matter of time before Moore was given the chance to work on a Superman story. The result was 1985's 'For the Man Who Has Everything' (*Superman Annual* #11, 1985), with art by Dave Gibbons and commissioned by veteran DC editor Julius Schwartz (he retired aged seventy-one in 1986, one of the last connections back to Siegel and Shuster, and died in 2004, aged eighty-eight). A quirky tale, it saw Wonder Woman, Batman and Robin visiting Superman in the Fortress of Solitude on his birthday, only to discover the Man of Steel possessed by a plant-like alien that has induced him to hallucinate a dreamworld based upon his 'heart's desire'. This is an excuse on Moore's part to present a darker take on Superman's origins and life. This was followed by a second revisionist tale, 'Whatever Happened to the Man of Tomorrow?' (in *Superman* #423 and *Action Comics* #583, both published in September 1986), drawn by veteran Superman artist Curt Swan. Another sidestep 'imaginary tale', Moore depicted the history of the Silver Age Superman, exploring the character and aiming to provide him with a satisfactory conclusion that sees his secret identity as Clark Kent become public knowledge. It essentially conclusively wrapped up the character's history since 1938.

Moore had shown a tendency to re-imagine and revive traditional superheroes in new ways, whether such legacy figures as Superman or some of the more obscure DC characters he featured in *Swamp Thing*. In this spirit, he followed Frank Miller in further reinventing Batman in 1986's *Batman: The Killing Joke*, in which the Joker escapes Arkham Asylum, embarks on a killing spree, and is eventually stopped by Batman. Although the book offered an insight into the psychopathy of both characters, it nonetheless didn't fulfil Moore's true project when it came to reinventing superheroes.

Brewing in Moore's mind was an idea for an exploration of the superhero as a real-world character, an attempt to depict the consequences for the world if superheroes had really existed since the Forties. The result was *Watchmen* (twelve issues 1986, graphic novel 1987), in which Moore initially set out to repurpose a handful of long-forgotten superheroes published by Charlton Comics, of which DC had obtained ownership in 1985. His original plan was to build a mystery around the death of the Second World War patriotic superhero the Shield, and to feature other members of the Mighty Crusaders (created by Jerry Siegel in 1965, and including characters such as the Fly, the Jaguar, the Comet, and Flygirl). DC thwarted Moore's plan, as editor Dick Giordano, in charge of the project, wanted him to develop an all-new set of heroes, concerned what he might do with pre-established characters.

Moore created a new group of superheroes who would seem familiar by riffing on well-established archetypes, even though they were fresh inventions. He subverted and deconstructed superheroes in an attempt to analyse their mythic basis and examine their cultural effects. Artist Dave Gibbons drew the series, although he became more deeply involved in the creation of the characters and the story with Moore. In creating the backstory, Moore would write insanely detailed scripts for Gibbons. Issues that advanced the story alternated with those that explored the history of the main characters. Set in an alternate Eighties,

Watchmen depicts a world on the brink of nuclear war. This world's point of divergence from history was 1938, the year of the first Superman comic. Although his characters are identified as superheroes, they are really costumed crime-fighters in the style of Batman, with the single exception of Doctor Manhattan, whose super-powers threaten to tip the balance of power between America and Russia. The unpopularity of superheroes sees them banned by law in 1977 (an idea picked up by Marvel's 2006–7 post-9/11 mini-series *Civil War*), and while most retire, a few lonely figures continue their costume-clad battle against miscreants. The story opens with the murder of Edward Blake, previously known as the Comedian, a right-wing military vigilante. His death is investigated by Rorschach, who has continued to maintain his secret identity, and that leads to the reformation of the Forties superhero group the Minutemen, made up of Nite Owl, Doctor Manhattan, Silk Spectre, and her mother, a previous holder of the title, and Ozymandias. Rorschach believes someone is eliminating the remaining costumed heroes, but a larger problem looms in a bizarre attack on New York.

When creating *Watchmen*, Moore noted that it was his deliberate intention to 'explore areas that comics succeed in where no other media is capable of operating', designing the books to be read repeatedly and attempting to make them different from movies (comic books had often been referred to as pre-made movie storyboards, rather than an art form in their own right). Gibbons gave his page layouts a form of authority by adopting a strict nine-panel grid, so when it was deviated from it made an impact. To the artist, *Watchmen* was a 'comic about comics' in which he and Moore set out to explore the potential implications for society if superheroes really existed, while also drawing on the elaborate history of comic book characters as their source material. Alongside the comic book pages, Moore included a variety of prose material in each issue (except

#12), including letters, reports, and newspaper articles that explored various aspects of the world.

As well as exploring 'the idea of the superman manifest within society' Moore and Gibbons looked at people's attitudes to heroes, as well as the effect society might have on such people. Rorschach is an anti-hero, while Ozymandias has both cashed in on the superhero craze (he markets action figures of himself), but also considers the super-powered to be the only people able to manage society (making him the 'villain'). The title draws upon the quote from Roman satirist Juvenal – 'Who watches the watchmen?' – to suggest that no one can police such people. It was an idea that other creators would build upon – notably in Mark Gruenwald's *Squadron Supreme* (1985), and Warren Ellis and Bryan Hitch's *The Authority* (1999).

In taking apart and rebuilding the superhero, Moore wanted to see what made him tick. He analysed the role of the hero in society, whether super-powered or not, and his takedown was equally applicable to politicians (Moore claimed he was writing in reaction to the patrician regimes of Thatcher and Reagan) as to the modern-day obsession with unearned celebrity. Although an avowedly Cold War story, *Watchmen* remains relevant, with little serious comparable development of the superhero since. Moore's nihilistic superheroes would become the template for a new, gritty take on comic book characters that would dominate the Nineties, from Spider-Man villain the Punisher (who'd get his own gun-toting series), to a stripped-down version of Green Arrow as an urban vigilante, and a toughening up of the X-Men – especially Wolverine – under the final years of Claremont's reign. Frank Miller said of his and Moore's work that 'When it comes to superheroes, Alan Moore provided the autopsy and I provided the brass band funeral.' Much of the subsequent development of superheroes was to the dismay of Moore who later lamented that 'the gritty, de-constructivist post-modern superhero comic, as exemplified by *Watchmen* . . . became a genre'.

Both *Watchmen* and *The Dark Knight Returns* put comics in the sphere of legitimate literature, with *Watchmen* listed in *Time* magazine's 2005 survey of the 'Top 100 Best Novels'. The sales of *Watchmen* put DC Comics ahead of Marvel for a brief time. The new graphic novel format that both comics had popularized proved to be a successful way to repackage comics, and quickly became a standard, with most major comic book series collecting recent issues together (both Marvel and DC would also adopt the format for pulpy reprints of their Bronze and Silver Age titles, making them available again to modern collectors in various 'Essential', 'Archive', 'Omnibus', and 'Masterworks' editions). Book stores and libraries began to devote shelf space to graphic novels, rivalling speciality comic stores as an outlet for lead titles.

The comic book industry was changing dramatically, with developments such as specialist stores and new independent publishers being both the beneficiaries and the driving forces behind works like *Watchmen* and *The Dark Knight Returns*. Superhero creators – whether writers or artists – were being far more widely recognized (suggesting a star system with 'big name' creators), and the idea of creators' rights was rapidly becoming an established part of the business. Those who created new superheroes had learned from Siegel and Shuster and kept control of their characters, or entered into carefully worded agreements with DC, Marvel, and others.

As well as the debuts of *Watchmen* and *The Dark Knight Returns*, 1986 also saw the establishment of Dark Horse Comics, one of the few comic book publishers to seriously challenge the big two. Comic book store owner Mike Richardson established Dark Horse as a sympathetic outlet for creators whose work did not fit the mainstream. However, the company quickly moved into television and movie licensing, publishing comic book series connected to such shows and movie franchises as *Buffy the Vampire Slayer*, *Aliens* and *Star Wars* (eventually making their own movies). The company published several significant creator-owned titles, such as Frank Miller's *Sin City* and *300*, and Mike Mignola's offbeat *Hellboy* (all would later become movies).

In the mid-Nineties Dark Horse explored the nature of superheroes in *Comic's Greatest World* (1993–6), set in a urban environment where 'meta-humans' had been created thanks to heretical scientific experimentation in the Thirties. This gave rise to such superhero characters as Ghost (a female reporter who comes back from the dead to solve her own murder and other crimes), Barb Wire (a female bar owner and bounty hunter, played by Pamela Anderson in the 1996 movie), and X (a dark, anti-hero vigilante). Perhaps their most unusual 'superhero' was Paul Chadwick's *Concrete* (1986), in which a normal man's brain was transplanted into a large stone body by aliens – the story follows his attempts to live as normal a life as possible, given the circumstances (a modernist riff on Marvel's the Thing or the Hulk).

Although Dark Horse was the largest, most successful and longest lasting of the new independent publishers, there were a handful of other significant stand-alones or imprints within larger publishers. Marvel's editor-in-chief Jim Shooter departed in 1987 (replaced by Tom DeFalco) and set up Valiant Comics in 1989 to revive older Gold Key characters such as Magnus, Robot Fighter (created in 1963 by Russ Manning), and Solar Man of the Atom (from 1962), before introducing original characters Shadowman (a voodoo empowered musician), Harbinger (teen superheroes), and X-O Manowar (a Visigoth battles aliens using sentient armour). Shooter then established his own self-contained Valiant Universe.

Other prominent independent publishers who arose

during this decade included Malibu Comics (1986–97), which revived characters from Golden Age publisher Centaur, including Amazing Man, Mighty Man and the Protectors, as well as several licensed properties (*Star Trek*, *Tarzan*, *Planet of the Apes*) and some creator-owned characters. The company was purchased by Marvel in 1994, but little has been done with the Malibu characters since. Malibu helped Image Comics (from 1992) become established through access to its distribution network. Image had been formed by a group of eight disaffected creators who'd quit Marvel in a dispute over creators' rights and character ownership. Todd McFarlane (*Spider-Man*), Jim Lee (*The X-Men*), Rob Liefeld (*X-Force*), Marc Silvestri (*Wolverine*), Erik Larsen (*The Amazing Spider-Man*), Jim Valentino (*Guardians of the Galaxy*), and Whilce Portacio (*Uncanny X-Men*) formed Image in a bid to advance the cause of creator-owned publishing. This was dubbed the 'X-odus' as many had worked on Marvel's X-Men comics.

Each of the partners in Image would have free rein when it came to their own work, and they pledged not to interfere in each other's. Each of the main partners established their own studio (patterned after the Golden Age art shops) and published their work through Image. Early successes were McFarlane's Spawn (a Faustian anti-hero reborn from Hell, and the subject of a dire 1997 movie), and Lee's WildC.A.T.s. (a superhero team). Selling millions of copies of their own comics meant that the creators rather than a corporation benefited. One criticism of Image was that, as it was largely run by artists, their comics emphasized the visual content above the storytelling. By the mid-Nineties there were strains in the partnership, with several artists publishing work outside Image. McFarlane went on to even greater success in merchandising while Jim Lee would become co-publisher of DC in 2010 (replacing Paul Levitz). Even into the first decade of the twenty-first century Image was still producing new hits, such as Robert Kirkman's

The Walking Dead (also a popular television series). The company was in a battle for the third spot behind DC and Marvel with Dark Horse and another independent newcomer, IDW Publishing. IDW had been founded in 1999 and quickly established itself in the field of licensed comic book properties (*Star Trek*, *Doctor Who* and *G.I. Joe*). Its first big original hit was Steve Niles' vampire comic book *30 Days of Night* (2002, also a film), although they produced little in the way of original superheroes.

The comic book business had boomed since the mid-Eighties. The interest in superhero history meant old comics in scarce supply became collectors' items. Those disposable, disreputable entertainments of the Forties were suddenly worth thousands if not hundreds of thousands of dollars, and as many had been tossed away or pulped during the wartime paper drives, they were in very short supply. Nostalgic interest apart, early issues of comics featuring major superheroes like Superman and Batman, or issues that featured particularly important events (such as the debut of Wolverine in *The Incredible Hulk* #181) fetched astonishing prices at auction.

While the mainstream popularity of comics, and in particular superhero titles, reached new heights (the launch of Marvel's newest take on *The X-Men* in 1991 sold eight million copies, an all-time sales record), the flood of comics served to undermine the collecting field. Variant covers, limited-run titles, exclusive issues, collectible cards and other innovations were aimed at this collectors' market, but were often produced in such large quantities that their value would fall rather than increase. The comic book speculator boom collapsed around 1993, while only books from the Golden Age (and some select Silver Age titles) could ever be expected to match the going rate for a copy of *Action Comics* #1 of over $1.5 million in 2011. *Detective Comics* #27 – featuring the first appearance of Batman

– sold for just over $1 million in 2010. While a handful of Thirties and Forties DC comics (and a few Marvel titles from the innovative Sixties) became ever more valuable, very few of those published during the Nineties would retain their worth.

With an over-saturated market leading to over-extended retailers, around a third of the speciality comic book stores closed in the mid-Nineties. Several new independent publishers ran into trouble: Valiant was purchased by computer games firm Acclaim, while Image regularly failed to meet release deadlines. Even the two giants of comic book publishing had a tough time. Marvel, which had enthusiastically surfed the wave of the new-found comic book popularity, was publishing close to 100 individual titles at the height of the boom and collapsed into bankruptcy (partly as a result of corporate in-fighting and an attempted move into distribution) in 1996. However, the company was successfully reorganized and returned to its market dominance over DC, becoming in the process ideally positioned for the superhero movie boom of the new millennium.

During all this Eighties innovation, the legacy superheroes – Superman, Batman, Wonder Woman, and their Sixties counterparts Spider-Man, The X-Men and Iron Man – were soldiering on. By 1985, DC Comics had built up a fifty-year rich continuity that was complicated and convoluted. Across comics and characters continuity problems abounded, with many characters having multiple, often inconsistent, backstories or origins that had been retooled, embellished, re-imagined, and reconceptualized by a variety of creators, writers, editors, and artists. With a now well-established and vocal fandom collecting comics and offering feedback to publishers, it became apparent there was an audience newly concerned about such things.

Attempts to write around some of these problems

resulted in the DC Multiverse, which allowed for variants of Earth within the DC Universe so conflicting versions of characters could exist independently of each other (and meet in crossover stories). The return of Golden Age characters in their Silver Age guises was the initial cause of this problem, including revivals of the Flash, Green Lantern, the Atom and Hawkman. A parallel universe featured in *Wonder Woman* #59 (May 1953) allowed Wonder Woman to meet her other universe twin. The same gimmick reoccurred in *Wonder Woman* #89 (April 1957), where an alternate version of Earth was dominated by crime, and in *Justice League of America* #2 (January 1961), in which yet another Earth ('Magic Land') where magic was used instead of science was explored. It was in *The Flash* #123 (September 1961) and the story 'Flash of Two Worlds' (see chapter 6) that the concept of the DC Multiverse was properly established. In *Justice League of America* #22 (September 1963, 'Crisis on Earth-Two'), the villainous Fiddler (a hypnotist who uses music to warp men's minds) establishes that if there is an Earth-1 and an Earth-2, there must also be an Earth-3. (DC's use of words and numerals to designate the various Earths was notoriously inconsistent, so numerals will be used except in story titles, which appear as originally published.)

During the Sixties and Seventies, the basic designations were Earth-1 for the Silver Age heroes, Earth-2 for the older Golden Age heroes, and Earth-3 (*Justice League of America* #29, August 1964), where the Crime Syndicate of America – evil versions of Earth-1's heroes – reign, including Superman's enemy Lex Luthor. Other Earths popped up, including Earth-5 where the original Batman inspires a Bruce Wayne whose parents weren't killed to take up the Bat-cowl (*Detective Comics* #500, March 1981); Earth-12, where the comedic Inferior Five live (*Showcase* #62, June 1966); Earth-14, a Jack Kirby world (*First Issue Special* #13, April 1976); Earth-32, inhabited by another Green Lantern

(*Green Lantern* #32, October 1964); and Earth-154, where the sons of Superman and Batman struggle to live up to their superhero heritage (*World's Finest Comics* #154, December 1966). There were many, many others . . .

The sprawling nature of the DC Multiverse and the conflicting continuity it created formed the basis for a major celebratory event that would take in almost all the DC titles during the company's fiftieth anniversary in 1985. The core of this epic undertaking was a twelve-issue series called *Crisis on Infinite Earths*. Almost every DC superhero turned up during this cosmic existential battle that allowed DC to 'reboot' its comic book universe, clearing the slate for all new stories featuring the company's oldest characters without the baggage of fifty years of continuity. It paved the way for *The Dark Knight Returns*.

The story featured uber-villain the Anti-Monitor who, like some demented DC editor driven insane by the inconsistencies in the company's storytelling, set about eliminating the alternate universes having escaped from his own universe of anti-matter. The heroes of the final five universes remaining (Earth-1, Earth-2, Earth-4, Earth-S that featured Fawcett Publications characters like Shazam and Captain Marvel, and Earth-X where the Nazis won the Second World War), and a group of refugees from other already destroyed universes combine to defeat the Anti-Monitor. Along the way, several pre-Crisis superheroes were spectacularly killed off, including Supergirl and the Barry Allen Flash. The result was a single DC Universe (cleverly combining any bits of the previous universes that DC editors felt they wanted to hang on to – such as the two versions of the Flash, but only one, definitive Superman).

The twelve-instalment *Crisis on Infinite Earths* limited series was written by Marv Wolfman with art by George Pérez, but it spilled beyond that to encompass forty issues of various comics pre-Crisis and a further fifty-nine issues in crossover connected events. The intention by editor Len Wein was to reset DC's character continuity as it was thought that the complicated backstories and high issue numbers were preventing a new generation of readers getting into the habit of reading superhero comics. While intended to draw a line under the confused continuity of the DC Multiverse, the 'Crisis' storyline inspired several other big publishing events for DC including *Zero Hour: Crisis in Time!* (1994, aimed at tidying up future timelines it actually created additional problems), *Identity Crisis* (2004, written by best-selling author Brad Meltzer), *Infinite Crisis* (2005–6, a Crisis sequel written by Geoff Johns that contrasted the older, more positive heroes with the modern, angst-ridden versions) and (the woefully inaccurately named) *Final Crisis* (2008, a contribution from Grant Morrison that sees reality assailed by Darkseid).

As a marketing gimmick, the Crisis concept worked, re-igniting mainstream interest in superhero comics and attracting readers enticed by its epic nature. Fans were well served with in-depth storylines ranging across many comics, allowing them to engage with the crossover celebration as much or as little as they wished. The advertising promised 'The DC Universe will never be the same', and unlike subsequent 'events' more driven by marketing than editorial, it was a promise that was kept. The DC Universe was split in two, with stories designated as having taken place 'pre-Crisis' or 'post-Crisis'.

The result of the Crisis was that DC relaunched some of their core superheroes. Superman was first in 1986, with John Byrne (who had written acclaimed runs on *The X-Men* and *Fantastic Four* for Marvel) re-introducing the character in the six-issue mini-series *The Man of Steel* (July–September 1986), before continuing in *Action Comics* and in *Superman*, which began its numbering from #1 again. Other titles were cancelled or rebooted: *The Flash* ended with #350, *Superman* with #423, and *Wonder*

Woman with #329. Batman was reinvented in the *Batman: Year One* storyline, written by Frank Miller and drawn by David Mazzucchelli. Wonder Woman (eliminated from time during the Crisis) was reintroduced in a new book from February 1987, written by Greg Potter and with art by the Crisis-master, George Pérez.

As the Eighties shaded into the Nineties, it appeared that *Crisis on Infinite Earths* had achieved its aims, but, just as had happened over the previous fifty years, this new DC Universe also built up a brand new equally tangled continuity at a seemingly increased rate, resulting in the company rebooting their reboot in 2011 with DC Comics' poorly received 'New 52'.

Superhero reboots were all the rage from the late-Eighties into the Nineties, referred to as the 'Modern Age' of comic books. Marvel's twelve-issue *Secret Wars* event ended just before DC's *Crisis on Infinite Earths* launched, but their publishing event wasn't driven by an anniversary so much as the possibility of a tie-in toy deal (it built on their 1982 three-issue series *Contest of Champions*). After *Star Wars* action figure manufacturer Kenner licensed the DC super-heroes for their Super Powers Collection (1984–6), Mattel expressed interest in doing the same with the Marvel heroes, but only if the company produced a high-profile event upon which they could hook a toy line. The only stipulation Mattel gave to Marvel editor-in-chief Jim Shooter was that apparently 'kids responded well to the word "Secret"'.

The toy tie-in became the inciting excuse for a massive updating of the Marvel Universe, revising not only the look of many of the heroes (Spider-Man in an all-black ensemble – later revealed to be an alien symbiote – while Iron Man's armour was updated), but revisit the villains, too (Dr Doom's look was less 'medieval'). In *Secret Wars*, an all-powerful cosmic entity called the Beyonder becomes fascinated by Earth's superheroes. He kidnaps a group of heroes and their villainous opposite numbers, transporting them to Battleworld, an arena in a distant galaxy stocked with alien weaponry and technology. There, the Marvel heroes and villains must slug it out . . .

It was a basic concept, much less complex than DC's subsequent *Crisis on Infinite Earths*' storyline (yet fitting to promote toys). Among the heroes captured were the Avengers, the male members of the Fantastic Four, Spider-Man, the Hulk and a handful of X-Men. Magneto was originally on the side of the heroes, but he quickly moved to a 'non-aligned' status after the Avengers turned on him. Among their opponents were Dr Doom, Doctor Octopus, the Lizard, Ultron, and the Enchantress. There were as many soap opera developments, with relationships made and broken, as there was superhero action. *Secret Wars* was weakened as it removed the Marvel characters from their regular environments and pitched them together on an alien world. Most were barely two decades old, so while they had built up back stories they were not quite as convoluted as those of DC. Sequels and spin-offs to the central concept would follow, including *Secret Wars II* (1985–6), a nine-issue series (plus several crossover tie-ins) that saw the Beyonder attempt to conquer Earth (bringing the enemy to a recognizable environment), and 2010's *Spider-Man and the Secret Wars*, which retold events from Spidey's perspective and included several never before revealed elements of the core storyline.

Changes instigated during *Secret Wars* spread throughout the Marvel Universe. As well as Spider-Man's all-black look, Iron Man's new armour appeared from *Iron Man* #200 (November 1985), while Captain America was rebranded simply as the Captain (in a new, all-black outfit) from *Captain America* #337 (January 1988). Issue #300 (March 1991) of *The Avengers* saw a new line-up, including Mister Fantastic and the Invisible Girl from the Fantastic Four, while Wolverine's costume was revised, Thunderstrike replaced Thor, and the X-Men faced a new nemesis in Archangel.

Many of these innovations would be unceremoniously undone in the early-Nineties.

All these dramatic events, especially *Crisis on Infinite Earths*, caused some comic book creators to begin to think the unthinkable: what better way to shake up the world of superheroes than by killing off one of the major names? DC Comics would embrace the concept, leading to 'the Death of Superman' . . .

11

SUPERHEROES
RECONSTRUCTED

The death of Superman – one of the biggest events in superhero history – only happened because the wedding of Clark Kent and Lois Lane was unexpectedly postponed. DC Comics' big plan for the early Nineties was to finally see the Man of Steel married off to his longtime admirer (they'd once been married in the newspaper strip, but that was later dismissed as 'a dream'). However, as the television series *Lois and Clark: The New Adventures of Superman* was in development, the decision was taken to postpone the wedding in the comics to tie in with the new show. That left an empty slot in DC's planning for the year. In meetings to discuss alternatives, *Adventures of Superman* writer Jerry Orway jokingly said: 'If we can't get Superman married, we ought to just kill him'. Crazy as it seemed, the idea rapidly caught on among DC's editors.

'The Death of Superman' (October 1992–October 1993)

was one of the main legacies of DC's 1985 event, *Crisis on Infinite Earths*. John Byrne's subsequent *Man of Steel* Superman reboot had not been the success that DC had anticipated, with Byrne quitting the book and sales falling. In an attempt to engage more female readers the romance angle was played up and, in a switch from the original formula, Lois Lane was in love with Clark Kent rather than Superman, resulting in the proposal of marriage. With the romance also central to the *Lois and Clark* television show, the wedding planned for the comic was off, at least for the time being. The initially jokey idea of killing off the ultimate superhero was taken more seriously, as – according to *Superman* group editor Mike Carlin – '. . . the world was taking Superman for granted, so we literally said "Let's show what the world would be like without Superman".'

Heavily trailed in a series of enigmatic ads featuring a gloved fist punching a steel wall promising 'Doomsday is coming!', the Death of Superman became the most-hyped and most successful special event in the history of comic book publishing – a field not short of an outlandish gimmick. Preliminary teasers in several other comics built up to the reveal of a brand new, and ultimately fatal, adversary for Superman as alien destroyer Doomsday appeared in *Superman* #75 (January 1993). Superman and the Justice League tackle the newly-arrived menace, but find him a formidable adversary thwarting their every effort to contain or destroy him. The climax is a one-on-one battle between Superman and Doomsday (whose only motive is chaos and destruction) throughout Metropolis. Issue #75 (one of the alternate available covers was black with an all-red 'S'-shield logo dripping blood) depicted the final struggle in a series of 22 panels, each taking up an entire page. The final battle outside the *Daily Planet* building sees Doomsday destroyed, but Superman also dies of his wounds in the arms of Lois Lane.

The shocking storyline was picked up in the second

story arc, 'Funeral for a Friend' (spread throughout various titles, January–June 1993), in which other superheroes and friends of the Man of Steel pay tribute at the mausoleum built in his honour in Metropolis, many of them sporting a black armband with a distinctive 'S'-shield logo. Sinister forces abduct Superman's body, but it is soon recovered by Lois Lane and Supergirl (a non-Kryptonian version), who speculate that someone may have planned to produce a Superman clone. 'Funeral for a Friend' not only explored the impact of the death of Superman, but also how it affected the wider world (US President Bill Clinton was among those at the funeral). Crime soars, while other costumed superheroes of Metropolis attempt to fill the Superman-shaped hole. DC wound up all the Superman comics for a three-month hiatus.

After countless adventures since 1938, the prospect of the Man of Steel finally meeting his end sparked huge main-stream media interest. It also provoked a sales uplift in all the associated comic books, including *Action Comics*, *Superman*, *Superman: The Man of Steel*, and *Adventures of Superman*. This was an unintended consequence of the need to concoct a rapid replacement story for the aborted wedding, not the contrived marketing gimmick critics pre-sumed (although DC's marketing departments were not slow to see the possibilities). Many of the issues, including that apparently 'final' one of *Superman* were snapped up as potential collectors' items. Almost three million copies of *Superman* #75 were shipped to stores, with most selling out on the day of release. The first five issues of the concluding sequel series, 'Reign of the Supermen', were the top five sell-ing comics for the month. While it was largely celebrated at the time, there were some – such as Mile High Comics owner Chuck Rozanski – who would blame the later Nine-ties downturn in sales upon the Death of Superman event.

Following three months when no new Superman comics were published, DC relaunched the line (adding to the cynicism) with 'Reign of the Supermen', that saw four new superheroes put forward as potential Superman replacements (each claimed to be carrying the mantle of the original). *The Adventures of Superman* #500 saw Jonathan Kent, who died of a heart attack following his adoptive Superson's death, visit the afterlife where he persuades Superman's 'soul' to return. Then the four contenders to the title of Superman emerged.

Superman: The Man of Steel #22 saw John Henry Irons claim to represent the spirit of Superman in his military-sourced armour under the title Man of Steel, while *Superman* #78 introduced The Man of Tomorrow, a cyborg 'Superman'. *The Adventures of Superman* #501 featured The Metropolis Kid, a teenage clone of Superman who rejected the nickname 'Superboy'. Finally, there was The Last Son of Krypton, an energy-powered alien masquerading as Superman in *Action Comics* #687. All four candidates were plausible replacements, with two revealing genuine memories to Lois Lane that only Superman would know. The Man of Steel and The Metropolis Kid were quickly eliminated, but it took longer for the cyborg Man of Tomorrow and the alien Last Son of Krypton to be equally discounted. The solution was revealed to be that The Eradicator (as this reformed super-villain would be known) posing as The Last Son of Krypton had secured Superman's body in a 'regeneration matrix' within the Fortress of Solitude, recreating the original Superman, albeit in a temporarily weakened state. This new (and genuine) Superman contender sealed the deal when he confirms to Lois that Clark Kent's favourite movie was *To Kill a Mockingbird* (1962). Recovering his strength, Superman battles and eliminates the remaining cyborg pretender. The new Superman would retain his longer, unkempt hair for much of the Nineties.

This wasn't the first time Superman had been seen to die, just the most high profile; the world's first superhero had been killed off by his own creator as far back as 1961. Jerry Siegel had Lex Luthor use Element Z to cure cancer, earning him a reprieve from jail. Luthor then proceeded to kill Superman (also witnessed by the staff of the *Daily Planet*) with a Kryptonite ray developed from Element Z. A funeral is held, with Batman in attendance in full costume. So worried by the implications of Siegel's enthusiasm (no doubt partly driven by his long-standing enmity for DC) for killing their cash-cow, the story was heavily billed as 'An exciting three-part imaginary novel . . . full of astounding surprises!' and closed with an epilogue that claimed: '. . . this was only an imaginary story . . . and the chances are a million to one it will never happen!'

It would take until 1992's Death of Superman before this tale was told 'for real'. Even Siegel was caught up in the media madness when he visited DC to meet with editor Mike Carlin, reportedly telling him that he was 'very impressed' with Carlin's version. Superman's co-creator Joe Shuster had died earlier in the year, aged seventy-eight. Enthusiasm for killing off the Man of Steel in 'imaginary' ways blossomed following the Death of Superman. He died repeatedly at the hands of Gog in 1999's *The Kingdom*, written by Mark Waid (who introduced 'hypertime' to explain away his 'imaginary' story). Grant Morrison had his turn in 2008's *All-Star Superman*, where Lex Luthor contrives for Superman to get too close to the sun and so begin the long, slow process of dying from a radiation overdose. This gives the declining Superman the opportunity to put his earthly affairs in order, which also provided Morrison the chance to revisit a variety of classic Superman icons including the bottle city of Kandor, the *Daily Planet* newspaper, and Otto Binder's villainous anti-Superman Bizarro from 1958. Morrison's aim was to 'make a big definitive statement about superheroes and life, all that . . . featuring the first and greatest superhero of them all'. *SupemanHomepage* editor Steve Younis noted of The Death of Superman that while '. . . characters dying in comic books is not the big shock it once was', readers 'know that characters can always come back somehow. Death in comic books is rarely permanent, so to do a "death of" story it really needs to have a great hook and an even better reason to attempt it.'

It had long been a problem for superhero comics that the escalation of powers in both heroes and villains never seemed to reach a conclusion. The heroes always had to win, but each time they had to be matched against a 'worthy' opponent. What both the Death of Superman and the following Batman KnightSaga dared to do was play out the consequences if the villains were to win. This required new villains (Doomsday for Superman, Bane for Batman) capable of defeating the superheroes. The implications of such a move were that subsequent books would have to 'realistically' follow through on the after-effects, otherwise they'd prove as pointless and affectless as the many battles of the past. The closure of the Superman line for a while was the logical result of the removal of the main character. The Death of Superman had been a risk, but DC editors knew that something significant was required to shake up superhero comics. The problem thereafter was that killing off a superhero became a crutch for floundering books, and readers now knew it was unlikely to last. However, the effect of Bane on Batman would not be quite the same, as the story would have major implications for the future of both the Caped Crusader and Bruce Wayne.

Batman: Knightfall was the Dark Knight's equivalent to the Death of Superman, a year-long, editorially driven, impactful event that also served as a publicity hook. Running from April 1993 through to August 1994, the Knightfall saga comprised three story arcs threaded through all the Batman books. Individually they were known as Knightfall, Knightquest and KnightsEnd, but collectively became the KnightSaga.

Over a long working weekend, DC's Batman editor Dennis O'Neil gathered his current writers, including Chuck Dixon and Alan Grant, to develop the epic. At the time (it was claimed) they had no idea that the Superman editorial team was also working on a major, character-changing storyline. As the Superman story was first to print, it may have appeared the Batman team had simply followed suit, but their equivalent was in development simultaneously. In fact, the KnightSaga had grown out of a two-part storyline first considered in 1991. As had by now become standard practice at DC, the seeds of the story were sown in earlier comic books that built up to the first instalment of Knightfall, including the *Sword of Azrael* (October 1992) mini-series and the *Vengeance of Bane* (January 1993) one-shot that put in place the two main antagonists.

The character of Azrael started out as Jean-Paul Valley, a young student at Gotham University who becomes a stand-in Batman when Bruce Wayne is put out of action by Bane, and who was an orphan raised in an isolated and seemingly forgotten Central American prison. As the subject of a super-soldier experiment, Bane developed super-strength before breaking out of his prison and vowing to storm Gotham City and depose its 'king': Batman.

For the first time since *Crisis on Infinite Earths*, the various Batman titles shared an ongoing storyline, with Knightfall running across *Batman* #492–500 and issues #659–66 of *Detective Comics*, published between April and October 1993. Events in the Batman books saw Bruce Wayne ruminating on his position as Batman, feeling that recent run-ins with villains such as Black Mask, Metalhead, and a sharp-shooter assassin who targets Commissioner Gordon, had shown he was losing his edge. While trying to guide Valley in the ways of the superhero, Wayne undergoes psychological treatment to overcome his fatigue and ennui. It is in this condition that Batman becomes aware of Bane. He is not ready to confront such a relentless threat, and Bane's taunting is followed by a breakout of villains from Arkham Asylum.

Bane's plan was to weaken Batman by freeing the inmates, creating a narrative structure for a variety of hero-villain encounters (including Poison Ivy, the Joker and the Scarecrow), before building to the ultimate face-off between Batman and Bane. *Batman* #497 (July 1993) featured a now-iconic cover showing Bane breaking Batman's back, an event that occurs within the Batcave under Wayne Manor. Symbolically, this was a villain finally 'breaking' the Batman, leaving Bruce Wayne a paraplegic dependent upon a wheelchair. The humiliation Bane piles upon Batman is worse, displaying his broken body to the population of Gotham, signifying Bane's consolidation of power.

DC fans were having a turbulent time of it, as 1992 became 1993. With the 'Funeral for a Friend' storyline just dealing with the death of Superman, they were confronted with the invaliding of Batman (while attempting to quell the breakout at Arkham Asylum, both Batman and Robin wear black armbands with the 'S'-shield symbol). As the rest of the saga would demonstrate, Batman's fate wasn't as simple as the 'death' that befell Superman. Wayne's spirit was broken at the same time as his body, allowing for rumination on the role of the costumed superhero in society. While Valley initially makes an adequate temporary stand-in as Batman, an encounter with the Scarecrow and exposure to fear gas causes the already fragile would-be hero to tip over the edge into insanity, allowing dormant 'programming' to turn him into the villainous Azrael. Using an augmented mechanically assisted Batman supersuit, Valley holds it together long enough to defeat Bane.

Knightquest would follow Valley's tenure as Batman, while Wayne underwent physical rehabilitation and then searched for his vanished therapist, Shondra Kinsolving. Caught up in a telekinetic battle between her and Benedict Asp, her villainous brother-by-adoption, Wayne's back is miraculously healed. KnightsEnd sees Wayne out of retirement and retraining as Batman so he can replace the increasingly crazy Valley. Their confrontations result in the destruction of the Batmobile and lead to Valley's (partial) rehabilitation. Batman then has to rebuild the trust of the people of Gotham and Commissioner Gordon, while contemplating his own frailties, both physical and mental. This darker turn in the Batman saga was taken, according to O'Neil, due to the increasing popularity of anti-hero figures during the early-Nineties, specifically movie characters like the Terminator (Arnold Schwarzenegger) and James Bond (played in a gritty style by Timothy Dalton). While the Death of Superman arc would form the basis for several failed attempts to relaunch the Superman movie franchise in the Nineties and early twenty-first century [see chapter 14], this big Batman comic book event did find its way into the movies, eventually. As well as affecting the ongoing Batman storylines for much of the decade, the introduction of Bane to the pantheon of Batman supervillains would result in an audio and animated version of Knightfall.

Ten years on from DC's 1985 *Crisis on Infinite Earths*, comic book fans were becoming increasingly fed-up with big event-driven storylines and crossovers. They were seen as commercial exploitation, a lure to make readers buy complete sets of many comics to experience the entire storyline, rather than editorially driven stories in their own right (as the first two had been). These doubts didn't seem to concern the big comic book companies, with DC embarking on yet another company-wide crossover event dubbed *Zero Hour*, a five-issue limited series (starting in September 1994) focused on Green Lantern Hal Jordan. Subtitled Crisis in Time, *Zero Hour* was a deliberate follow-up to *Crisis on Infinite Earths*, but it failed to replicate its impact.

The next step was the return of inter-company crossovers, with Marvel and DC characters appearing in each other's comics. The 1997 Marvel vs DC event saw two 'brothers' who personified the two biggest superhero universes challenge each other to a series of duels (echoing Marvel's earlier *Secret Wars*). Running across four issues and scripted by the Death of Superman's Dan Jurgens, the outcome of the various battles between Marvel and DC superheroes were determined through reader ballots. The process clearly showed Marvel to be more popular than DC, with Spider-Man, Storm and Wolverine winning their respective battles, and only Superman and Batman triumphing for DC. In a much-hyped finale, Batman defeated Captain America. Although DC had the more high-profile events in terms of mainstream publicity, with the Death of Superman in particular (although Batman's crippling became well known), Marvel was not to be left out of the 'event' game, joining the fray with the Spider-Clone Saga and *Marvels*.

Published between 1994 and 1996, the Spider-Clone Saga was intended to last under a year, but buoyant sales persuaded Marvel to extend its run, resulting in changes to Spider-Man that fans grew to dislike. Writer Terry Kavanagh originated the idea of a series dealing with Spider-Man clones as a way to depict different versions of Marvel's core character, without impacting on the main comic book. Along with Howard Mackie and Gerry Conway, Kavanagh was riffing on an original 1973 storyline of Conway's that followed the death of Gwen Stacy. The Jackal – actually Peter Parker's biology professor – clones both Parker and Stacy, then forces the original Spider-Man to fight his clone.

Picking up on these story threads from two decades before, the new storyline revealed that the clone Spider-Man – now going by the name of Ben – had not been destroyed, but was actually the original Peter Parker, while the survivor who all these years had thought he was Peter was the clone (this proved unpopular with long-standing Spider-Man fans and with some of the book's creative staff). While Peter retires from being Spider-Man, Ben takes over, until the returning Green Goblin (another unpopular choice, given his key role in the iconic Death of Gwen Stacy) reveals that he has manipulated events and Peter is the original after all (in reality, a quick creative fix following the outcry). Ben dies saving Peter and his clone body disintegrates, proving the Goblin was telling the truth.

Running through all the Spider-Man titles between October 1994 to December 1996, the Spider-Clone Saga was an often-confusing and convoluted tale. The result was a reboot of Spider-Man, but behind-the-scenes confusion, seemingly random story developments, artificially extended story arcs, and repeated reversals as to the truth made the Spider-Clone Saga a creative failure. In *Amazing Spider-Man* #400, the writers even had the temerity to kill off Peter Parker's Aunt May, a mainstay of the Spider-Man titles since 1962.

When it was all over, *Spider-Man* editor Mark Bernardo admitted '. . . the story arc was initially planned to be short, but rapidly spun out of control and ended as a fiasco. Ironically, the whole storyline which was supposed to simplify Spider-Man's mythos and ultimately bring him "back to basics" ended up complicating everything beyond what anyone imagined.' The Spider-Clone Saga revealed that unless there was a clearly agreed single plot throughline (something simple like killing Superman or crippling Batman) then multi-title events could end up damaging the reputation of a much-cherished superhero.

Alternatively, with the *Marvels* series (four issues, January to April 1994), Marvel proved they could do superhero nostalgia right. Written by Kurt Busiek and featuring painted art by Alex Ross, *Marvels* spanned the period from 1939 (when Marvel itself began) to 1974. It depicted superheroes from a 'street level' view through photographer Phil Sheldon. Through his eyes, the major events of the Marvel Universe unfolded, including the public revelation of the original Human Torch, Namor the Sub-Mariner and Captain America. Sheldon experiences the Second World War and the Sixties counter-culture, all the while aware of the 'Marvels', costumed superheroes who seem to be as much a threat as a benevolence. In the Sixties, he sees New York become home to two costumed superhero teams, the Fantastic Four and the Avengers, before the emergence of the X-Men troubles him about what the existence of these 'superheroes' means for mankind. By the Seventies, Sheldon has chronicled his experiences and explored his ambivalent feelings about superheroes in his book, *Marvels*. Other characters included Spider-Man, Doctor Octopus and Ghost Rider. A retelling of the 'Death of Gwen Stacy' storyline was built in.

Winner of the Will Eisner Comic Industry Award for Best Finite Series, *Marvels* showed how an 'event' could be done well, briefly retelling the origins of selected characters (a vogue in superhero comics throughout the Eighties and Nineties), while filtering the entire superhero phenomenon through the eyes of an ordinary observer whose life parallels the creation and evolution of most of the main (Marvel) heroes. Ross would go on to do something similar in DC's 1996 limited four-issue series *Kingdom Come* (May–August 1996) that had 'traditional' superheroes like Superman and Batman confront truly amoral vigilantes in another self-aware exploration of the meaning of the superhero. These reconstructions were a gentler response to the Eighties' takedown of superheroes in *Watchmen* and *Batman: The Dark Knight Returns*. Infused with reverential nostalgia, both *Marvels* and *Kingdom Come* proved that the comic book event was still viable if properly conceived.

* * *

The patriotic superheroes of the Second World War made a sudden return to comics in the wake of the 11 September 2001 attack on the United States. As with the battles against Hitler and Mussolini, the assembled superheroes including Batman, Superman, Spider-Man and the Hulk could not be seen to triumph over America's newest enemies. In the real world, the 'war on terror' declared by President George W. Bush would prove to be all but unwinnable. Regardless, the creatives overseeing the exploits of the superheroes in the offices of Marvel and DC knew they couldn't ignore such a seismic event. While DC's heroes inhabited Metropolis and Gotham – both stand-ins for New York – Marvel's superheroes proudly lived in the real place. Spider-Man was as much a symbol of New York as the World Trade Center towers, demolished by the impact of those planes on that September day.

Marvel produced their response in two comics sold as fundraisers for the 'first responders', police, firemen, and medics, many of whom had lost their lives rescuing those caught up in the carnage. *Heroes* was first on shelves in December 2001, and it depicted Marvel's fictional heroes such as Spider-Man, the Silver Surfer and Captain America (a particularly apt choice, given his pedigree) standing – depicted literally, but meant metaphorically – shoulder-to-shoulder with the real-life heroes of 9/11. The cover showed a fireman carrying an injured figure out of the wreckage of the Twin Towers. The issue included images of the Hulk kneeling by an upturned fireman's helmet, pages in which Marvel heroes aided rescue workers (but where the focus was always on the regular people, rather than the costumed heroes), and accounts of the reactions of citizens and superheroes alike to the attacks.

Heroes set the tone for other works. *A Moment of Silence* presented four wordless tales offering a variety of perspectives on 9/11, with a cover by Joe Quesada and Alex Ross. The absence of text in these art-driven tales was one way of recognizing the failure of words alone to deal with the trauma from both the attacks and the heroic responses of ordinary people. The book featured a foreword from then-Mayor of New York, Rudy Giuliani. In February 2002 Marvel published *The Amazing Spider-Man* #36 (with an all-black cover) in which writer J. Michael Strazynski explored how Spider-Man and other Marvel figures such as Captain America, Dr Doom, Magneto, and Daredevil reacted to the attacks. Marvel's editor-in-chief Joe Quesada recalled: 'The line between those guys [first responders] and a guy who puts on a costume was really thin. Spider-Man is our everyman, he is New York. The whole thing was a metaphor about the line between the real-world heroes and superheroes. Marvel is at its best when telling stories related to the real world – *Civil War* was an off-shoot of that. It's about today in America, the split in the country.'

The books came about quickly, although a lot of thought was put into how exactly these fictional heroes should be used in response to such a devastating real-world tragedy. In the end, Marvel president Bill James felt it was enough for their characters to show solidarity with those who suffered. 'This just felt like the right thing to do,' he said, 'so we did it'. Between them, this trio of Marvel superhero comic books raised a net profit of over $1 million for charities supporting the families of victims, the most successful fundraising project in the history of the art form.

DC also produced fundraising issues, but its first response to the event was accidental and weirdly predictive. On sale in stores from 12 September 2001, *The Adventures of Superman* #596 (cover dated November) featured the Man of Steel pulling open his shirt-and-tie to reveal the red 'S'-shield on a black background (rather than the traditional yellow), with the words above reading: 'This is NOT a job for Superman'. The first panel of the second page showed a view looking up at the smoking Lexcorp Twin Towers of Metropolis. Considering this was created months before, it's an intriguing coincidence that this comic was published the day after 9/11. DC produced two other volumes, the first – *9–11 Artists Respond* – in association with Dark Horse, Chaos!, and Image, and the rather grandly titled second – *9–11 The World's Finest Comic Book Writers & Artists Tell Stories to Remember* – through DC itself.

Beyond the direct responses, the subject of 9/11 and the aftermath did seed itself through superhero stories for years to come. In *The Boys* #19–22 (Dynamite, 2008), Garth Ennis rewrites 9/11 so three of the four planes are shot down, while the fourth is brought down by superheroes, but still results in considerable loss of life when the plane hits the Brooklyn Bridge. Marvel produced a short-run series called *The Call of Duty* (2002–3) in which emergency workers dealt with the paranormal in the wake of the 9/11 attacks. Brian K. Vaughn's *Ex Machina* (DC/Wildstorm, 2004–10) was set in an alternate world after 9/11 in which the world's single superhero, Mitchell Hundred (aka The Great Machine), becomes the Mayor of New York. Instalments of *Human Target* (#2–3, DC/Vertigo, 2003), by Peter Milligan, featured a man who faked his death in the attacks to escape embezzlement charges, but is given a chance at redemption. Marvel's *Civil War* (2006–7), written by Mark Millar, saw superheroes split over the need to be registered by the Government or face being outlawed. Like the last 'just' war in the Forties, the events of September 2001 left superheroes largely impotent, unable to respond except in offering support and sympathy. It was in superhero cinema that the most graphic responses to 9/11 would be seen [see chapter 14].

By 2004 DC was in the reboot business again, laying the groundwork throughout their comic books for a major reshuffling of their continuity. Once again they'd be revamping characters, retelling origin stories, and carefully trying to ignore the events of 1994's misguided *Zero Hour*. The *Infinite Crisis* storyline was based on a seven-issue limited series that ran from December 2005 to June 2006, but was carefully built around the core superhero characters of Superman (present in two versions, Kal-El and Kal-L, capitalizing on the early spelling revision), Batman and Wonder Woman.

A direct sequel to 1985's *Crisis on Infinite Earths*, DC pulled the same trick in the hope of revitalizing their core characters. The parallel Earths were key, featuring the alternate Superman Kal-L from Earth-2. The theme was the nature of heroism, a key question surrounding superheroes. The heroes of the modern age were perceived as darker than their equivalents from the Golden or Silver Ages. *Infinite Crisis* would compare and contrast these heroes.

It started well, as these revamps often did, with pre-order sales of close to 250,000 copies for *Infinite Crisis* #1 (December 2005). Geoff Johns, a regular writer on DC's *The Flash* and *The Avengers*, was behind *Infinite Crisis* that began with Superman, Batman and Wonder Woman at odds with each other. When the alternate Superman from Earth-2 appears, he tries to persuade Batman that Earth-1 was flawed (following *Crisis on Infinite Earths*), and that Earth-2 would make for a better replacement. The various storylines follow this quest for a perfect world among the alternate Earths, with many casualties along the way. Various heroes and villains are involved in the saga, including the Flash, Nightwing, Wonder Girl, and Firestorm. A huge number of Green Lanterns alone are wiped out by Superboy-Prime, who attempts to reboot the universe with himself as the only remaining superhero. It takes two Supermen to drag Superboy-Prime to the ruins of Krypton, where the older Kal-L dies. In the end Superboy-Prime is imprisoned by the Green Lantern Corps (the elimination of Superboy was partly down to Jerry Siegel's heirs contesting ownership – the Superman co-creator died in 1996, aged eighty-one).

This kind of open-ended conclusion repeatedly devalued attempts at resetting the DC Universe, as nothing ever seemed to be final and everything was open to being revisited again in another sequel. DC did just that, launching *One Year Later* (in which the core trinity of heroes were followed up twelve months afterwards) and *52* (which filled in the missing year and saw Grant Morrison, Greg Rucka and Mark Waid join Johns as writers), alongside various Crisis Aftermath books that dealt with the fallout from *Infinite Crisis*. *One Year Later* follows a depowered Superman as Clark Kent uses his journalistic skills to fight crime in Metropolis, saw Batman return to a crime-ridden Gotham and begin again his battle with wrongdoers, and had Wonder Woman working for the US Department of Metahuman Affairs. Other superheroes were rewritten or revised at the same time. In an unusual move, *52* (May 2006 to May 2007) was a weekly (rather than monthly) book filling in the missing year, across fifty-two individual issues, one for each week. It dealt with the absence of Superman, Batman and Wonder Woman, and chronicled the actions of many other superheroes of the DC Universe during this time.

In some ways this was all mere prelude to *Final Crisis* (seven issues, 2008), Grant Morrison's mini-series that saw Darkseid cause the removal of various superheroes throughout time and unleash the Anti-Life Equation upon Earth. Amid the metaphysical mash-up Batman is apparently killed (he's not, only sent back in time, although Bob Kane – his creator – had died in 1998, aged eighty-three), and only Superman is left alive at the end of creation, where he faces the remains of Darkseid's 'essence' in a final battle. Even that's not the end, as the true power behind the throne emerges: Mandrakk, the Dark Monitor. Summoning an army of Supermen from across the Multiverse (one clearly modelled on incoming US President Barack Obama), Superman restores the Earth. Meanwhile, Bruce Wayne is trapped in prehistory, drawing bat symbols on cave walls . . .

DC had often looked back on its own history. Titles like *The Golden Age* (four issues, 1993–4) had Golden Age heroes involved in the post-war McCarthy-era debates of the Fifties, while *Silver Age* (twelve issues, 2000) was a series of one-shots celebrating and satirizing Silver Age heroes. Between 2005 and 2008 DC devoted an entire imprint to looking backwards with their *All Star* line. This was intended as a rival to Marvel's similar *Ultimate* line that featured updated twenty-first-century versions of Spider-Man, the X-Men, the Avengers and the Fantastic Four, each with their own revised origin, running from 2000. The aim was to revive the *All Star* titles of the past and match them with the best creators, writers and artists of the twenty-first century. The hope was to present characters unburdened by decades of continuity, partly in preparation for anticipated superhero movies. However, only Batman and Superman, under writers Frank Miller and Grant Morrison respectively, were given the *All Star* treatment, and other planned titles were quietly abandoned. While both *All-Star Batman* and *All-Star Superman* sold well initially, the Miller story came in for sustained criticism just at a time when his star was waning in the comic book world, while Morrison's version of Superman won the Eisner Award for Best New Series in 2006. This mixed reception may have shown DC more clearly the dangers inherent in endless relaunches and reboots, and contributed to the 'big bang' restart of *The New 52* (from 2011).

The various reboots and crossovers, far from simplifying the DC Universe had instead added complicated layers of bizarre continuity and even more Multiverse alternatives for fans and collectors to obsess about. In a brave move, DC decided it was time to start everything from scratch.

This would allow some editorial freedom, as well as giving a new range of titles a welcome marketing boost. The initiative became known as *The New 52* – named after the fifty-two alternative universes within DC continuity.

It started with the crossover story *Flashpoint* in 2011 (five issues, May to September 2011) that spilled into a variety of one-shots and mini-series that saw only Barry Allen (the Flash), his grandson Bart Allen (Kid Flash) and Booster Gold (a self-obsessed Justice League member from the future) aware of significant alternations to the world. Superman is held in government detention, the world's best-known superhero is Cyborg (a Teen Titan, now a founder of the Justice League) and 'Thomas' Wayne is a peculiar Batman and casino magnate. The villain is Eobard Thawne, but the Flash saves the day by merging all the existing universes and alternate timelines, wittily including the DC imprints Vertigo and Wildstorm, into a single, brand new DC Universe.

With *Flashpoint* concluded, all the existing DC titles were cancelled and then relaunched with brand new #1 issues both in print and as new digital titles. It was a moment of historic change for the company (with DC Comics now part of Warner Bros. DC Entertainment subsidiary) and for readers. Over a five-week period there were fifty-two brand new issue #1s for all the major DC superheroes, many with new costumes and revised backstories. It had taken almost seventy-five years, but finally the DC Universe was enjoying a genuine fresh start. First out was *Justice League* #1 (September 2011), written by Geoff Johns and drawn by Jim Lee. There soon followed new starts for Batman, Superman, Wonder Woman, Green Lantern, the Flash, and Aquaman.

'We really want to inject new life in our characters,' Dan DiDio, co-publisher of DC with Jim Lee, told *USA Today*. 'This was a chance to start, not at the beginning, but at a point where our characters are younger and the stories

are being told for today's audience.' As with the legends
and myths that originally inspired them, the original DC
superheroes of the Thirties and Forties were born again
for a new audience, using new technology, but at their core
still stories of heroes and villains, monsters and myths.

With the movie versions of DC's superhero characters
now more important than ever before and bringing in
much more money, the comic book side of the empire could
afford to experiment a little. The digital launch of *The New
52* was intended to open up DC's comic books to a younger
audience who had been attracted through the big-screen
superheroes. For years the fan-focused, continuity-rich
superheroes had only been accessible to those willing to
put the time and effort to find a way into the stories. With
The New 52, the aim was to keep things simple, clear, and
– above all – accessible.

Writers were able to pick which elements of past continuity to retain and which to dump. The set-up of *The New 52*
was that superheroes had only appeared in the world over
the previous five years, and are viewed with great ambiva-
lence by the population. Superman was given a makeover,
with two new looks, one featuring jeans and a T-shirt with
an 'S'-logo and a cape, the other made-up of Kryptonian battle armour that looked like the classic Superman
costume. His alien nature was played up, effectively dis-
tancing him from humanity. Batman had a rebooted, but
very familiar, continuity, as did Green Lantern. Many of
the superheroes were subject to government interference
and control (echoing Marvel's *Civil War* and the ongoing
fallout from 9/11).

Gimmicks were still used to promote the comics. The
first anniversary of the relaunch in September 2012 was
dubbed 'Zero Month', with every title gaining a collectible #0 featuring stand-alone stories, often origin tales. By
September 2013, the focus of *The New 52* had turned to the
villains of the DC Universe, with all the comics devoted

to various evil characters, while Geoff Johns and David Finch's limited series *Forever Evil* highlighted bad guys.

From the beginning, *The New 52* was an equivocal success, with the new titles selling around 200,000 copies, while *Justice League* #1 was the top-selling comic book of 2011, although critical reaction to the relaunch was mixed. For the first time in many years, DC surpassed Marvel as the biggest-selling comic book publisher – for a short while at least. By the end of the year, Marvel was back on top, but *The New 52* had given DC a new lease of life.

The perennial issue of a lack of female creators and a lack of female characters was raised once more in connection with *The New 52*, with the relaunch significantly reducing the number of women involved in DC Comics behind the scenes as writers and artists (only Gail Simone and Amy Reeder remained). DC promised to redress the balance in future. New versions of some female characters were criticized as exploitative, especially Catwoman and Red Hood. Many books built around female characters had been cancelled but not replaced, and many of the new characters were seen as over-sexualized, a long-standing fault in the comic book depictions of female superheroes.

There were several behind-the-scenes ructions during the first few years of *The New 52*, with writers, artists and others in conflict with DC management over the direction certain books should take. Writer/artist George Pérez (a creative force on *Crisis on Infinite Earths* and the *Wonder Woman* reboot) quit *Superman* after just six issues over editorial oversight and last-minute rewriting. Rob Liefeld (a controversial founder of Image Comics), hired to handle *Deathstroke*, also quit over rewriting. By December 2012, Gail Simone was no longer writing *Batgirl* (she'd been working on versions of the Barbara Gordon character for a decade) claiming to have been fired via email, although she was quickly rehired and picked up the title two issues later.

In September 2013, the writer and artist of *Batwoman*

both walked out amid a controversy surrounding the depiction of a gay wedding (DC claimed they didn't want any of their new characters married, gay or otherwise). Comics had featured gay superheroes since at least 1992 when Marvel's Northstar came out in *Alpha Flight* #106 (March 1992). It would take until 2012 for either DC or Marvel comics to feature their first gay wedding, and again it featured Northstar who married his non-super-powered partner Kyle in *Astonishing X-Men* #51 (August 2012). It is true to say that most superheroes who have declared themselves gay tend to be obscure or little known, including the Young Avengers' Hulkling and Wiccan (which provoked a debate in the letters page), X-Men Rictor and Shatter-star (who shared the first gay kiss in superhero comics in *X-Factor* #45, August 2009, written by GLAAD award-winner Peter David, a development that upset their creator, Rob Liefeld), and original Green Lantern Alan Scott in *The New 52*. Superman and Batman avatars Apollo and Mid-nighter in *The Authority* were depicted in a relationship, as well as working together as a superhero team. They'd be married in 2006 in comics' first gay wedding. The most mainstream yet is Batwoman. That fuss had come shortly after a controversy surrounding author Orson Scott Card's guest run on *Adventures of Superman* where his anti-gay views caused artist Chris Sprouse to quit the title and a petition to be raised calling for Card's removal as his views conflicted with Superman's all-inclusive ideals. Card's story was shelved. This all suggested a high degree of tur-moil behind the scenes of *The New 52*, with editorial direc-tion cited as too restrictive and too vague (at the same time) by those exiting the company. All relaunches are fraught with problems, and especially in the world of comics, a revamp as large and all-encompassing as *The New 52* was not going to please every reader or creator, but the turmoil at DC suggested a troubled creative time.

Marvel Comics (who were now part of the Disney

empire from 2009) launched Marvel NOW! in 2012, aiming to similarly revitalize their core titles and introduce new ones. The aim was the same: accessibility. All comics had to be welcoming to new readers and as free as possible of long, complicated backstories. The first wave was launched in October 2012 as 'the next chapter in the ongoing saga of the Marvel Universe,' according to editor-in-chief Axel Alonso. Each new issue #1 was designed as a jumping-on point for readers to get involved in the adventures of the Avengers, the X-Men, Captain America, the Fantastic Four, the Hulk and Iron Man, among others.

The rebranding was seen as a 'renewal' following the conclusion of the Avengers vs. X-Men cross-company event (April–October 2012), that Marvel saw as the capstone to a decade of complex and not always successful storytelling. The titles were relaunched with new creative teams, revised character designs and new start stories, all part of something called the 'Marvel ReEvolution Initiative'. Alonso saw the Initiative as kicking off 'our next decade worth of stories'. Partly that would involve moving writers and artists away from characters they had become comfortable with onto new ones that might present them with a new challenge. It wasn't the full reboot of DC's *The New 52*, as Marvel wanted to both carry their core readers with them and provide potential new readers (attracted to the comics through the success of the recent movies) with a clear starting point. Instead, the creators at Marvel regarded Marvel NOW! as a new 'season' of stories within the larger Marvel Universe. As the creators rediscovered the characters from first principles, it was hoped that readers would rediscover the comics.

The use of digital 'apps' (applications used on tablet computers such as an iPad) would help drive uptake of the new line among younger, tech-savvy readers. As with DC, Marvel were having to adapt to changes affecting the wider publishing world, from books and newspapers, to magazines and comics as everything moved to the digital realm. The widespread use of smartphones and tablets gave Marvel and DC a new way of reaching readers, as print circulations threatened to nosedive once more. Innovations proliferated, like DC's 'DC2: Multiverse' dynamic interactive artwork that allowed readers to determine the end of the story, offering multiple potential outcomes. Marvel's Infinite Comics promised similar 'augmented reality' comic book developments.

Inevitably at some point, as so often in comic books – whether it was Jerry Siegel and Joe Shuster, Bob Kane, Stan Lee, Jack Kirby, or Steve Ditko – some driven writer or artist will come along able to harness the new media now available in the service of great stories featuring a new breed of great superheroes, giving comic books, whether in print or in digital form, a whole new lease of life.

PART 5: DOMINATION!

12

SUPERHEROES BEYOND THE PAGE: UP, UP AND AWAY!

Bringing superheroes to life on screen has been a constant challenge as moviemakers fought with technology in their attempts to make audiences believe a man could fly or swing across the city hanging from spiderwebs. The story of live action superhero movies and television shows is the story of the changes in technology, from the practical chemical film of the Forties to the all-digital productions of the twenty-first century. However, the first superhero – Superman – was initially dramatized in sound only.

The first non-comic book version of Superman was not a movie or a serial but a long-running radio drama that began in 1940, airing for eleven years until 1951 (when it made way for the George Reeves television series). The radio show was part of a merchandising boom that saw Superman's image plastered over everything from puzzles and games, greeting cards to bubblegum. Bob Maxwell, a former pulp writer put in charge of the DC merchandising subsidiary Superman Inc., was charged with ruthlessly exploiting the Superman brand beyond comics and newspaper strips. Before television, radio was the dominant domestic medium for home entertainment.

Maxwell created the series with Allen Duchovny, DC's publicity head and later a producer on animated superhero television shows. They produced sample shows displaying the potential of Superman on radio to prospective sponsors (the vast majority of radio output depended upon sponsors – often soap manufacturers, hence the term 'soaps' and 'soap operas' for daily domestic dramas). These never-broadcast pilots attracted Hecker's Oat Cereal and the show was on the air as a syndicated series from 12 February 1940, starring on WOR in New York City and another ten stations. The fifteen-minute dramas, titled *The Adventures of Superman*, starred experienced radio announcer and actor Clayton 'Bud' Collyer as Superman and Clark Kent, vocally distinguishing between the Man of Steel and the 'mild mannered reporter'. Collyer remained uncredited at his own request. Joan Alexander regularly played Lois Lane, first appearing in the seventh episode, after Rollie Bester, wife of *Green Lantern* writer and science fiction author Alfred Bester, originated the role.

It was the radio series' opening narration, first delivered by George Lowther, and later by Jackson Beck and heard in several variants, that delivered one of the more unforgettable aspects of the Superman phenomenon. It was a short summation of his abilities: 'Faster than a speeding bullet! More powerful than a locomotive! Able to leap tall buildings at a single bound! Look, up in the sky! It's a bird. It's a plane. It's Superman!' Key aspects of the Superman mythos would originate from radio not comics, although many would later be adopted and adapted. The deadly element Kryptonite came from the radio series in 1943. A particularly memorable set of episodes saw the Scarlet

Widow divide stolen Kryptonite among a group of villains – including the Vulture (not the Marvel super-villain) and the Laugher – so they could eliminate Superman. The iconic phrases 'Up, up, and away!' and 'This looks like a job for Superman' were frequently used on the show. Characters invented for radio included newspaper editor Perry White (Julian Noa) and junior copy boy (later cub reporter and photographer) Jimmy Olsen (played by Jackie Kelt, and later Jack Grimes). The radio show also suggested that Superman could fly, when in the comics all he could then do was 'leap tall buildings'. The judicious application of dynamic sound effects was enough . . . The first superhero team-up between Superman and Batman (most often played by Matt Crowley) happened on radio (from 1945, they would feature in thirteen serials together).

The first episode, 'The Baby from Krypton' written by George Ludlam, retold Superman's origin, with Orson Welles' *Mercury Theatre on the Air* star Agnes Moorhead playing Kal-El's mother, Lara. This presented additional background of life on Krypton, while the second instalment (aired two days later, as the show went out three times a week) 'Clark Kent, Reporter' avoided complications by having Kal-El grow to adulthood during his voyage to Earth. A series of pulp adventures followed, and by March 1940 the show had adopted multi-episode stories complete with thrilling cliffhangers. Just ten weeks into the series' original run, it had achieved a 5.6 rating, the highest of any show aimed at junior listeners – and 35 per cent of listeners were adults. From August 1942, the series aired on the Mutual Broadcasting System (MBS) as a live, fifteen-minute-per-episode children's serial, starting again with an origin story, until February 1949 when it was expanded to thirty minutes. The American Broadcasting Company (ABC) took on the show from October 1949, again in thirty-minute episodes, but pitched it as a drama with appeal to adults. By the end of the syndicated run, *The Adventures of Superman* was airing in eighty-five markets across the US.

Memorable stories saw Superman go up against Atom Man, the creation of a Nazi scientist out to gain revenge for Germany's defeat in the war. A 1946 story, 'Clan of the Fiery Cross', saw Superman take on the Ku Klux Klan as part of a wider campaign for racial and religious tolerance, which also saw Collyer publicly confirm his role as Superman. Collyer left the show after more than 2,000 instalments, just under a year before it finished in 1951, and was replaced by Michael Fitzmaurice. Collyer went on to voice Superman not only in the Fleischer/Famous animated shorts that ran concurrently, but also in the animated television shows *The New Adventures of Superman* (1966–7), *Superman-Aquaman Hour of Adventure* (1967–8) and *Batman-Superman Hour of Adventure* (1968–9). By the time of Collyer's departure, Bob Maxwell was already working on a new Superman for the new medium of television.

Seventeen short animated cartoons saw Superman fly high on the big screen between 1941 and 1943, and brought the character one step closer to live action. Fleischer Studios, best known for Betty Boop and Popeye animated shorts produced the first nine. Paramount's Famous Studios produced the second batch of eight. Paramount had won the rights to make Superman cartoons, and they sub-contracted the job to brothers Max and Dave Fleischer who – in an attempt to get out of the deal – claimed each cartoon would cost $100,000, four times the standard budget for an animated short. Paramount offered $50,000 per short (still twice the standard), allowing the Fleischers to produce films of extreme high quality that have stood the test of time. The first, simply titled 'Superman', was released on 26 September 1941 (others followed almost monthly) and was nominated for the 1941 Oscar for Best Short Subject: Cartoons.

Using much of the cast from the radio serial and

employing the famous 'Faster than a speeding bullet!' narration, the Superman shorts quickly retold the Man of Steel's familiar origins before pitching him into eight more episodes in which he'd battle against a mad scientist, a flying robot army, bullion train robbers, a resurrected prehistoric dinosaur that terrifies Metropolis, a criminal gang who fly around in a bullet-shaped rocket, a comet that threatens Earth, escaped circus animals, an earthquake and a deadly volcanic eruption!

The dynamic, shadowy film noir atmosphere of the Fleischer shorts would later influence Bruce Timm in creating *Batman: The Animated Series* (1992–5) and *Superman: The Animated Series* (1996–2000), as both lifted much of the Fleischer style, according to Timm. Superman comic book artist Alex Ross (*Kingdom Come*) also cited the Fleischer animations as an influence on his illustrations of Superman. The music of Sammy Timberg helped propel the shorts to their exciting, tightly edited conclusions.

When the Fleischer Studio was re-organized by Paramount as Famous Studios (without the Fleischers), the animation was simplified and the high concept science fiction and fantasy-driven plots replaced by jingoistic and patriotic tales, beginning with the 18 September 1942 release 'Japoteurs' in which Superman prevents Japanese saboteurs from stealing an American bomber. Later instalments saw the Man of Steel travel to Japan to sabotage the enemy's war effort in 'Eleventh Hour', while an angry Adolf Hitler featured in 'Jungle Drums', upset when Superman thwarts a Nazi plot. The series concluded with 'Secret Agent', released on 30 July 1943, in which Superman helps a Federal agent capture a ring of gangsters. The high cost (now $30,000 per episode) was one reason for its cancellation, along with waning interest from exhibitors. The Forties animated Superman cartoons have since enjoyed a healthy afterlife on television, video and DVD, and are rated among the finest short animated films ever made, with the first instalment ranked at #33 in *The Fifty Greatest Cartoons*, as voted on by animation professionals. Another satisfied viewer of the Superman cartoons was Jerry Siegel, who noted: 'They were great. That was full animation, and the early cartoons adhered very closely to what we were doing in the comics.'

Following radio and animation, Superman came rather late to live action, beaten to the punch by other superheroes, not least of which was his DC stablemate Batman. That wasn't due to lack of interest: almost as soon as Superman hit the comic book page, Republic Studios expressed their desire to bring his super-exploits to the big screen in live action. Chapterplay serials were big business in the Forties, playing to packed movie houses, unreeling one roughly-twenty-minute episode each week running for between twelve and fifteen instalments. Each exciting chapter of the larger story would end in a near-impossible cliffhanger, with the hero and his friends in some mortal danger, which they would quickly escape 'with one bound' at the start of the following instalment. They were the precursors of later episodic, formulaic television drama and soap operas, but enjoyed by enthusiastic audiences.

Republic Pictures was a specialist in Westerns, serials and cheap B-movies. They had been in negotiation with DC Comics about bringing Superman to the movies in early-1940, but the exclusive deal to make the Fleischer shorts meant that no other Superman film could be produced, animated or live action. Republic quickly reworked their planned Superman script into the fifteen-chapter serial *Mysterious Doctor Satan* (1940), turning Superman into the invented-for-the-movies masked superhero the Copper-head, whose methods were more like Batman's. The Copperhead's love interest remained named Lois, though.

Republic moved onto Fawcett Comics, signing a deal to bring Captain Marvel to the screen. The result was the twelve-chapter *Adventures of Captain Marvel* released to theatres from 28 March 1941, the first-ever live action screen superhero who'd originated in comics. Western star Tom Tyler was Captain Marvel, while Frank Coghlan played his youthful alter ego, Billy Batson. Serial veterans John English and William Witney directed, although Witney was concerned they'd have trouble producing convincing flying effects. Special effects experts Theodore and Howard Lydecker solved the problem, flying a human dummy on near-invisible wires, cleverly intercut with footage of Tyler or stuntman Dave Sharpe. The story had Captain Marvel up against masked villain the Scorpion, out to control a deadly weapon. As with the comic book, DC attempted to legally block the release of the serial. They failed, but *Adventures of Captain Marvel* proved it was possible to bring a superhero to the screen in live action.

Its success opened the floodgates, with pulp hero the Phantom (based on Lee Falk's newspaper strip and starring Tom Tyler) following in a fifteen-instalment chapterplay from Columbia in 1943, and Captain America (the first Marvel superhero on screen, and the only one for the next three decades) coming to the screen in fifteen chapters in 1944. This was Republic's final superhero serial and its most expensive. As with most of the serials, significant changes were made from the comic books. District Attorney Grant Gardner (Dick Purcell) is Captain America, quite different from soldier Steve Rogers. Captain America is out to unmask the Scarab, another of the many wartime serial villains searching for super-weapons such as the 'Dynamic Vibrator' and the 'Electronic Firebolt'. Unusually, the secret identity of the Scarab was revealed to the viewer early on as museum curator Dr Cyrus Maldor (Lionel Atwill), although it still takes Captain America many instalments to figure it out . . .

The live action film rights to Superman finally went to low-budget producer Sam Katzman in 1947, and he brought the serial to Columbia Studios after both Universal and Republic declined. Columbia had previously produced a Batman serial in 1943. Katzman was a notorious penny-pincher when it came to budgets, and the *Superman* serial suffered. Instead of the inventive methods for the flying scenes in Republic's *Adventures of Captain Marvel*, Katzman employed cheap poorly animated sequences to depict the Man of Steel taking to the skies. These cartoons were not as polished as the earlier Fleischer versions and integrated badly with the live action. The low budget also saw repeated re-use of the same scenes of Superman flying over countryside in almost every instalment. The story of Superman's origins was retold, then he came into conflict with the Spider Lady (Carol Forman) over the control of a 'Reducer Ray'. Kryptonite was used frequently to incapacitate the Man of Steel (and to string the threadbare plot out). The serial was released to theatres from 5 January 1948.

Early publicity for *Superman* (officially adapted from the radio show), claimed that Columbia and Katzman had failed to find anyone to play Superman, so they'd hired the real deal! Kirk Alyn, an actor and former dancer was only playing Clark Kent, it was claimed. Noel Neill played the thankless role of Lois Lane, and the rapid pace of filming took its toll on the actors (it was shot in less than four weeks), and rarely allowed for more than one take of each scene. Despite this – and more thanks to the wide appeal of Superman – it rapidly became the most successful serial ever produced. It had cost $350,000 for four hours of screen time, but took over $1 million at the box office.

A sequel was inevitable, and it arrived in the form of *Atom Man vs. Superman* (note the billing order) in 1950. Lex Luthor (Lyle Talbot, wearing an ill-fitting bald cap) appeared, adopting the unlikely villainous disguise of 'Atom Man', who blackmails the inhabitants of Metropolis with atomic destruction. Also featured are Lois Lane

(Noel Neill again), *Daily Planet* editor Perry White (Pierre Watkin), and Jimmy Olsen (Tommy Bond). Luthor attempts to create synthetic Kryptonite (also a plot point in 1983's *Superman III*), and manages to banish Superman to 'the empty doom', reminiscent of the comics' Phantom Zone (seen in the 1978 *Superman*). More cheap animated flying effects were used, while shots of Kirk Alyn in flight were improved by turning the camera on its side. In the climax, a squadron of animated flying saucers controlled by Luthor attack Metropolis. *Atom Man vs. Superman* had ambition, but it was badly let down by poor special effects.

That wouldn't stop Superman, though, and he was back on screen the following year in the film *Superman and the Mole Men* (1951). This provided the first outing for George Reeves as Superman/Clark Kent and was the basis for the long-running *Adventures of Superman* television series. Shot in black and white in less than two weeks, the fifty-eight-minute movie was a try-out for the television series (it was later re-edited to provide the closing two instalments of the first season under the title 'The Unknown People'). The script was by Bob Maxwell and DC's editor Whitney Ellsworth (under the pen name Richard Fielding), and was directed by quickie serial expert Lee 'Roll 'Em' Sholem.

Television saw the end of much radio drama and, eventually, the movie serials. It was the obvious next place for Superman to land, and DC's Jack Liebowitz was keen to exercise stronger control. As a proof of concept, *Superman and the Mole Men* worked well enough, although it was a little unambitious. The underground dwelling 'mole men' are midgets wearing more ill-fitting bald caps, whose lives have been disrupted due to oil drilling. Their most fearsome weapon is apparently a vacuum cleaner with some sci-fi tubing attached, and some of Superman's flying scenes were still shown using animation lifted from the serials. However, there was a more grown-up tone to this

Superman, with some of the juvenile elements of the radio show and serials jettisoned.

Kellogg's were signed up as sponsors (they'd also been involved heavily with the later radio shows) and the television series began filming in 1951. It would be on air between 1952 and 1958 for six seasons, 104 half-hour episodes, with the final four seasons filmed in colour. George Reeves was an inspired choice as a tougher Clark Kent and a folksy Superman. He'd played minor roles in Hollywood, but had never hit the big time. Coming up on forty after a stint in the army, he was grateful for the opportunity and set out to make the role his own. He committed seriously to a part that some other actors regarded as rather silly, and became a morale-boosting cheerleader on set and an affable ambassador for the show in public. He put up with the often-uncomfortable wire system used to produce the tele-visual illusion of flight, and threw himself wholeheartedly into the stunt work the part required.

Cast alongside him was Phyllis Coates as Lois Lane, a character more developed than she had been in most pre-vious appearances. She was much more of an enterpris-ing reporter. Noel Neill returned from the second season onwards. Jimmy Olsen also featured, played by Jack Larson as comic relief, as did Perry White, played by John Ham-ilton. Early on, the film noir-like plots concerned gang-sters and racketeers (as had the earliest *Superman* comics), but later stories became more science fiction-like with the series becoming more light-hearted. Villains became cari-catured, and the violence of early episodes was lessened following pressure from sponsors. Reeves directed some of the final episodes, and appeared on the popular *I Love Lucy* as Superman.

Plans were in place for at least two more years of *Adventures of Superman* episodes but had to be abandoned following the mysterious death of George Reeves in June 1959. Although his death from a gunshot wound was officially ruled suicide, those who knew Reeves felt it was unlikely, as professionally and personally he had so much going on. Reeves' story formed the basis for the movie *Hollywoodland* (2006), starring Ben Affleck (who got to wear the Superman costume in that, as well as playing both Daredevil and Batman in other superhero movies).

The loss of his star didn't slow down Whitney Ellsworth, who attempted to produce two spin-offs. The first, *Super-pup*, had been filmed in colour on the show's sets in 1958. This terrible pilot episode featured actors bizarrely dressed in dog costumes playing canine versions of Superman and others. Never aired, it has some resemblance to the later *The Banana Splits Adventure Hour* (1968–70). *Super-pup* remains a weird footnote in the history of live action superheroes and can be viewed on YouTube. The second was a pilot for *The Adventures of Superboy*, made in 1961. Johnny Rockwell played a young Clark Kent/Superboy in a light-hearted drama set in Smallville. Bunny Henning played Lara Lang. Thirteen scripts were written, but only the twenty-five-minute pilot entitled 'Rajah's Ransom' was made, and it can also be seen on YouTube.

Of these initial live action attempts to portray Superman, the television series was clearly the most successful. It made the biggest impact through frequent re-runs, and the decision to film the later episodes in colour proved prescient as it helped give the show a longer life. Reeves' portrayal of both Superman and Clark Kent would go on to heavily inform the definitive version from his near-namesake Christopher Reeve in 1978's big screen movie.

Superman was the original comic book superhero, but Batman had been the first of the pair to hit celluloid, although the resulting serials were not impressive. The less-than-dynamic Lewis Wilson was first to portray Batman in the 1943 fifteen-chapter serial from Columbia. More wartime propaganda than a genuine attempt to reflect the comics on film, the serial dispensed with the comic book villains, instead opting to invent a new one, Japanese agent Dr Daka (J. Carrol Naish). Douglas Croft enthusiastically portrayed Robin. At least Bruce Wayne's loyal butler Alfred (William Austin) put in an appearance, and his look in the comics changed as a result. Despite the departures from established Batman lore, the serial did contribute to the growing Bat-mythos. The secret entrance to the Batcave through a grandfather clock was first seen here and later used in the comic, in the same way that Clark Kent transforming into Superman in a phone booth had come from the cartoons. However, the Batmobile was nothing more than a black Cadillac.

Dr Daka – who operates out of a base hidden in a funhouse – has a device that turns people into mind-controlled zombies, while Batman operates as a government agent out to thwart his plans. At the climax Daka falls into his own trap, a pit filled with crocodiles. Censors prevented Batman acting as the vigilante he was intended to be, and the low-budget single-take regime at Columbia meant that the serial looked cheap and included a fair number of continuity errors and poorly realized fight scenes. The ears on Batman's costume looked more like devil's horns, while the costume appeared baggy and shapeless, just like Wilson's physique. It being wartime and this being propaganda, a fair number of racist comments (Batman refers to Daka as 'a Jap') are made and non-Americans are particularly poorly depicted.

Despite this, *Batman* was a success, enough to lead to a 1949 sequel, entitled *Batman and Robin*. This second batch of fifteen chapters saw Robert Lowry replace Wilson as Batman, with the addition of Johnny Duncan as Robin. The budget strains showed on screen again, with little improvement in the costumes, and the Bat-Cadillac was replaced with a 1949 Mercury convertible. Joining the Dynamic Duo for this outing were Jane Adams as Vicki

Vale and Lyle Talbot as Commissioner Gordon. The Bat-Signal made its movie debut, too.

As with the first serial, the opponent was invented for the screen. The Wizard is a villain whose face is hidden by a hood. He has a device that controls vehicles and sets about playing havoc with the lives of Batman and Robin. As with *Adventures of Captain Marvel* almost a decade before, the identity of the Wizard is a secret until the reveal in the final chapter, thus making the entire serial a guessing game for the audience. The problem with both the *Batman* and *Superman* serials (and most of the other serial adventures featuring superheroes) is that they were not superhero movies as such but just another version of the long-established serial format with masked figures, some of whom happened to have super-powers. There was little accommodation in these films for the superheroes as depicted in comics.

In 1965, the 1943 *Batman* serial was re-released in a marathon showing entitled *An Evening with Batman and Robin*. This venture was so successful, especially at theatres near college campuses, that it inspired the creation of the less-than-serious 1966 *Batman* television show. For three seasons between January 1966 and March 1968 the colourful twice-weekly (for the first two seasons) series attempted to recapture the thrills of the serials, with a dash of the comics and knowing humour thrown in. Between the first two seasons, the same cast and crew made a *Batman* (1966) movie in the same style.

Produced by 20th Century Fox and William Dozier's Greenway Productions for ABC Television, *Batman* starred Adam West as a camp Caped Crusader and Burt Ward as his punning sidekick, Robin. Part Sixties 'pop art' explosion, part high camp comedy, the Sixties *Batman* played to the widest possible audience (just when the comics were adopting a new seriousness), rapidly becoming the most popular show on air. The 'pow' and 'zap' graphics of the comics were used on screen to great effect, and the series deliberately focused on the outré villains, bringing in star names to play the guest villain of the week.

West and Ward played their roles with a contagious enthusiasm, with West in particular relishing the dialogue given to Batman, a role he claimed later to have played seriously. Frank Gorshin played the Riddler in the opening two-part episode, and stars who followed in his footsteps of villainy (some from the comics, others created for the series) included Burgess Meredith (as the Penguin); Cesar Romero (the Joker); Julie Newmar, Eartha Kitt, and Lee Meriwether (all as Catwoman); Vincent Price (Egghead); Tallulah Bankhead (Black Widow); Joan Collins (Siren); Ida Lupino (Dr Spellcraft); and Zsa Zsa Gabor (Minerva).

The unforgettable Neal Hefti theme tune, the brilliant Batmobile (the most popular version), the Bat-Signal, and the depiction of Gotham all became iconic, becoming many young viewers' first contact with Batman. Initially, *Batman* enjoyed wild popularity, capturing the swinging Sixties zeitgeist in its mix of humour, hi-jinks and comic capers. For those who took comics seriously, though, this version would have a long-lasting negative impact, making the character a no-go zone until the 1989 Tim Burton movie.

As quickly as it had become a hit, *Batman* became yesterday's news as the ratings suffered a huge drop during the 1968 third and final season. ABC pulled the plug on new episodes, but the 120 made continued to run on local stations in re-runs for many years, making them very familiar to generations of viewers. An animated follow-up, *The New Adventures of Batman* (1977), featured the voices of West and Ward, while West's Batman appeared in the animated *Super Friends* (1973–86, based on Justice League of America). Ward and West's Batman and Robin even made two guest appearances on Seventies' *Scooby-Doo* episodes.

The 1966 show made a star of Adam West (he continues

to trade on the part well into the twenty-first century), and his version of Batman (which in the popular imagination easily surpassed that seen in the comics) was finally allowed into the hallowed halls of DC itself with the *Batman '66* (2013) comic book that adapted the West and Ward versions of Batman and Robin to the comic page (only possible after years of legal confusion had been resolved).

Superman also jumped on the camp bandwagon in 1966, this time live on stage in 'It's a Bird . . . It's a Plane . . . It's Superman' which ran for 129 performances on Broadway. Popular with younger matinee audiences, the humorous spectacle of Superman (Bob Holiday) swinging from a flying rig across stage while warbling unmemorable tunes failed to amuse adult audiences. David Newman and Robert Benton wrote the book, and they'd be further involved in the Seventies Superman movies. The show was adapted for television in 1975, and was briefly revived twice in 1967, and again in 1992, 2002, 2007, 2010, and 2013.

Indeed, superheroes have generally not soared on stage, with the rock musical *Spider-Man: Turn off the Dark* (from 2011) suffering a troubled history of delays and accidents and a critical drubbing. The 2012 spoof production *Holy Musical, Batman!* played briefly in Chicago and is viewable in its entirety on YouTube, while in 2008 the generic superhero piece *Save the World* played in New York, following the success of the television series *Heroes*. Perhaps the most successful live action stage versions of superheroes have been the stunt spectacular arena shows, such as *Marvel Universe LIVE!* and *Batman Live!*, where the show is more like circus than theatre.

The initial success of *Batman* on TV in 1966 spawned at least one serial superhero-influenced spin off in *The Green Hornet*. George W. Trendle created the Green Hornet as the hero of a radio serial in 1936, following the adventures of masked crime-fighter Britt Reid, who is aided by his Japanese (later Filipino, due to the Second World War) sidekick Kato. Like Batman, the Green Hornet featured in two Forties film serials (*The Green Hornet*, 1940, and *The Green Hornet Strikes Again!*, 1941) from Universal Pictures, directed by Ford Beebe. Following *Batman*'s television success, the Hornet also came to ABC for a single season of crime-fighting adventures starring Van Williams as Reid/the Hornet, and Bruce Lee as Kato. The characters even enjoyed a two-episodes crossover with Batman, appearing in 'A Piece of the Action' and 'Batman's Satisfaction', during the show's second season in early March 1967. The Green Hornet also featured in comics (1940–9, 1967 and 1989–95) and as the focus of an unsuccessful spoof feature film in 2011.

Batman and Superman had proved popular as live action cinema and television superheroes, but none of the various interpretations had been fully realized to true fans' satisfaction. New attempts would be made in the Seventies to bring superheroes to television, but budgets and technology would ultimately let them down. It would only be with Christopher Reeve's big screen *Superman* in 1978 that mainstream audiences would finally be convinced that a man could, indeed, fly.

13

SUPERHEROES BEYOND THE PAGE: BELIEVING A MAN CAN FLY

Following Batman's popular Sixties outing, the Seventies were to prove the first truly successful era for superheroes on television. *Batman* producer William Dozier had made an unsuccessful attempt at a *Wonder Woman* series in 1967, producing a five-minute pilot, while there was a 1974 TV movie that featured Cathy Lee Crosby as a non-super-powered Wonder Woman. The follow-up 1975 television movie featured the comic book wartime setting as well as Lynda Carter in the iconic outfit and led to a first season of regular episodes on ABC (1975–9). Although a ratings success, the show was expensive. Dropped by ABC after a year, it was picked up by CBS but retooled into a contemporary-set series still featuring Carter, the show's major asset.

The series introduced the idea of Diana Prince turning into Wonder Woman by spinning on the spot, later incorporated into the comics and animated shows such as *Justice League Unlimited* (2004–6). Initially true to the comic origin of the character (from animated titles featuring comic book panels, through to the use of animated starbursts for scene transitions, and the appearance of comic book-style text on screen), the series drifted away from its four-colour roots. The first season featured Debra Winger (*Terms of Endearment*) in two stories as Wonder Girl, Diana's younger sister Drusilla.

Diana's slow ageing, due to her Amazon nature, saw the same character appear in the Seventies-set episodes of the second and third seasons. She became an agent of a crime-fighting organization receiving orders from an unseen boss (in *Charlie's Angels* style). While early episodes saw Wonder Woman use her super-powers to vanquish criminal gangs, later instalments featured robots, a clone of Adolf Hitler, and invading aliens. The third season's attempts to remain 'hip' resulted in episodes featuring skateboarding and disco. Diana also developed the power to communicate telepathically with animals. The series was cancelled in favour of *The Dukes of Hazzard*. Several non-comic book superhero adventure television series also aired in the Seventies, including *The Six Million Dollar Man* (1974–8), *The Bionic Woman* (1976–8) and *Man from Atlantis* (1977–8, a combined knock-off of Sub-Mariner and Aquaman, starring Patrick Duffy).

There was a more direct, if not entirely successful, superhero television adaptation in Marvel's *The Amazing Spider-Man* (1977), first of the new wave of Marvel superheroes to come to the small screen. This followed the warmly remembered (and often psychedelic) animated *Spider-Man* (1967–70) ABC series (featuring work by Ralph Bakshi) and the 'Spidey Super Stories' segments of educational show *The Electric Company* that used on-screen speech balloons to teach children to read. *The Amazing Spider-Man* (1977–9) starred Nicholas Hammond in a run of only thirteen episodes aired over almost three years. A two-hour pilot movie (released theatrically in Europe) retold Spider-Man's origins. Hammond's Spider-Man suffered from the same baggy suit problems as the original Batman back in 1943. Stan Lee dismissed the show as 'too juvenile', and it was cancelled, considered a failure by most fans.

More successful was *The Incredible Hulk*, which ran for five years from 1977, clocking up eighty-two episodes. Developed by Kenneth Johnson, who also created *The Bionic Woman*, the series deviated from the comic book but became the version of the Hulk most recalled by mainstream audiences. Bill Bixby turned in an affecting performance as the tortured David Banner, while bodybuilder Lou Ferrigno made a solid effort in bringing the big green fella to life. Pursued by newspaper reporter Jack McGee (Jack Colvin), Banner is on the run after an accident dosed him with gamma rays, resulting in his anger-driven transformations into the Hulk. Banner's warning catchphrase 'Don't make me angry, you wouldn't like me when I'm angry' caught on, and the series was a great example of episodic superhero adventures on television (mainly thanks to Johnson's production). A trio of follow-up television movies (*The Incredible Hulk Returns*, 1988; *The Trial of the Incredible Hulk*, 1989; and *The Death of the Incredible Hulk*, 1990) continued the story, with the characters of Thor (Eric Allen Kramer) and Daredevil (Rex Smith) featuring in the hope of spinning-off additional standalone series (it didn't work). The death of Bill Bixby in 1993 put an end to the ongoing show.

Two notable Marvel characters appeared in dedicated television movies as the Seventies drew to a close. The first was *Doctor Strange* (1978), with Stan Lee as a consultant and intended as the pilot for a full, never made series. Peter Hooten starred in the CBS movie, written and directed by Phillip DeGuere. Strange finds himself in conflict with sorceress Morgana Le Fey. John Mills brought some class to the otherwise feeble production as Strange's father, Thomas Lindmer. This and the other CBS Marvel shows (including *The Incredible Hulk*) were the result of an exclusive development deal between the publisher and the broadcaster. Lee was involved in all the projects, but felt he had the most input into *Doctor Strange*.

There were also two Captain America television movies that starred Red Brown and featured a completely revamped origin and back story. In *Captain America* (1979) and *Captain America II: Death Too Soon* (1979), his wartime origins were abandoned, replaced with a chemical accident that results in Steve Rogers (Brown) injected with a 'super steroid', giving him enhanced strength and reflexes. This Captain America is a US special agent with a rocket-powered motorbike (he wears a blue bike helmet) with a hang-glider attachment. The bike's windshield is detachable and doubles up as Cap's round shield. The sequel sees Captain America up against a revolutionary terrorist general (Christopher Lee) who threatens Portland with an age-accelerating chemical. When the general throws a vial of the chemical at Captain America, it rebounds off the hero's shield and causes his own ageing to death.

One of the most unusual television outings for superheroes in the Seventies has to be *Legends of the Superheroes* (1979). This mixture of variety show and drama brought back Adam West as Batman and Burt Ward as Robin (along with that iconic Batmobile), teaming them with Captain Marvel (Garrett Craig), Green Lantern (Howard Murphy), the Flash (Rod Haase), and the Atom (Alfie Wise), among others. The first of the two hours sees the heroes unite to celebrate the birthday of elderly hero Scarlet Cyclone, only for the Legion of Doom (including Frank Gorshin reprising the Riddler) to crash the party, causing the heroes to search out a hidden bomb. Falling into a trap, they are exposed to a potion that removes their super-powers. The second hour was patterned after a 'celebrity roast', hosted by Ed McMahon, in which each of the superheroes' shortcomings were exposed. Even more bizarrely, this includes a musical number. *Legends of the Superheroes* was an odd, but unforgettable final fling for the television comic book superheroes of the Sixties and Seventies that can now be seen on DVD.

The road to 1978's phenomenally successful and influential *Superman: The Movie* was long. Developed from 1973, several writers and directors made attempts at adapting the Superman story to modern cinema, before Tom Mankiewicz succeeded in both cutting down Mario (*The Godfather*) Puzo's gargantuan original screenplay, and giving the film a more serious sheen. Producers Ilya and Alexander Salkind (who'd taken a year to persuade DC they'd do justice to the property) felt secure enough that a new, big-budget *Superman* blockbuster would be a success that they shot the movie and much of its sequel, *Superman II*, together.

Their biggest initial problem was finding a new Superman, a selection process subject to the veto of DC Comics. A list of agreed names was worked up, including bizarre suggestions such as Muhammad Ali, Steve McQueen and Clint Eastwood. Pre-production began in 1976 without a leading man, although Marlon Brando had been signed as Superman's father Jor-El and Gene Hackman was cast as Lex Luthor, who plans to destroy California as part of a real estate development plan. Director Richard Donner was committed to making both films.

The casting search for Superman continued, with figures such as Robert Redford, Burt Reynolds, and Sylvester Stallone under consideration. The hunt widened to take in unknown actors, with a rumoured 200 considered. The movie's casting director had suggested Christopher Reeve, but Donner and his producers were not initially convinced, fearing he was too young and not athletic enough. Reeve, then aged twenty-five, was screen tested in February 1977, and prepared for the role by undergoing a diet and exercise regime supervised by Darth Vader actor Dave Prowse. He won over Donner, and shooting began the following month at Pinewood Studios where Krypton was constructed. The two films shot for over eighteen months, finally wrapping in October 1978, with Richard Lester completing *Superman II* after Donner fell out with the Salkinds and left the project (Donner's cut was later reconstructed and released on DVD in 2006).

The promotional material for the first movie promised 'You'll believe a man can fly', but the production team originally had little idea how to achieve the effect. The previous options of animation or someone simply jumping in and out of scenes would not be credible in a production of this ambition. The main effect was a combination of wire suspension, blue-screen shooting, back projection, and the new Zoptic front projection system created by Zoran Perisic, with Reeve sometimes held aloft on a specially built body cast. It was enough to give the movie a unique gimmick: genuinely convincing flying effects that no live action superhero movie had previously achieved.

Although aiming for release in June 1978, the fortieth anniversary of *Action Comics* #1, delays in filming and post-production resulted in a December 1978 opening. The film grossed just over $300 million worldwide, just behind *Grease*, the biggest movie of the year. Critic Roger Ebert summed up the opinions of many in the *Chicago Sun-Times*: '*Superman* is a pure delight, a wondrous combination of all the old-fashioned things we never really get tired of: adventure and romance, heroes and villains, earthshaking special effects and wit. Reeve is perfectly cast in the role. Any poor choice would have ruined the film.' The combination of the charismatic Reeve as Superman and his distinctly different, diffident performance as Clark Kent, the music of John Williams, and director Richard Donner's skill in combining the awe of Superman's abilities (especially the exuberant flying scenes) with some down-to-earth characters, not least of which was Margot Kidder's sharp-witted Lois Lane, established a high water mark that no *Superman* film has yet matched.

The sequels proved to be a series of diminishing returns, with *Superman II* (1980) matching Reeve's Man of Steel against a trio of Kryptonian criminals led by General Zod (Terence Stamp), modelled after those seen in 'The Three Supermen from Krypton' (*Superman* #65, July 1950). Lois Lane discovers Superman's secret identity as Clark Kent (although her knowledge is wiped by the film's conclusion), and Lex Luthor returns having escaped prison. The troubled production combined with a creeping increase in humour meant that the second movie was not as good as the first, but many fans take both films together as telling one complete Superman saga.

The rot really set in with Richard Lester's *Superman III* (1983). Having been so reverent of their source material in the first two films, from the sepia-tinted opening of *Superman* in which a kid is seen flicking through the pages of *Action Comics* #1, through to the replacement of the American flag on the White House at the end of *Superman II*, the Salkinds dropped the ball. The comedy overwhelmed the super-heroics, with flavour-of-the-moment comic Richard Pryor as the clueless Gus Gorman. The only saving grace was Reeve's performance, especially in conflict with an evil version of himself. Annette O'Toole was a fine addition as Lana Lang, but the rest was a let down after the near-perfect way the first two movies had both captured the essence of Superman held in the popular imagination. The first three films included almost every Superman story that's worth telling, from his origins, to battling Lex Luthor, losing and regaining his powers, revealing his identity to Lois Lane, and coming into conflict with himself.

Spin-off movie *Supergirl* (1984) and the final Christopher Reeve Superman instalment *Superman IV: The Quest for Peace* (1987) were surplus to requirements, and saw the most successful (to that point) superhero film franchise die in an ignominious fashion. Comedy was again to the fore in Jeannot Szwarc's *Supergirl*, and although Helen Slater made for a light, fresh-faced Supergirl, she was surrounded by figures (Peter Cook, Peter O'Toole, and Faye Dunaway) who clearly thought a superhero movie was an excuse to camp it up. The fourth *Superman*, directed by Sydney J. Furie, was a misbegotten mess, despite star Christopher Reeve's attempt to control the project. It was his idea to feature Nuclear Man (Mark Pillow), reflecting his strong anti-nuclear views, but extreme cost cutting by Cannon Films ruined the movie, resulting in an incoherent mess.

The film's failure critically and at the box office (it only took $15 million in the US) damaged star Christopher Reeve, who'd become disillusioned during production fearing the film would be 'terrible'. Despite this, Reeve remained (and to many still remains) the movies' best live action version of Superman. Paralysed in 1995 after falling from a horse, Reeve continued acting and appeared in a couple of *Smallville* episodes. He always regarded the role of Superman as a boon, noting: 'Siegel and Shuster created a piece of American mythology. It was my privilege to be the on-screen custodian of the character in the Seventies and Eighties. There will be many interpretations of Superman, but the original character created by two teenagers in the Thirties will last forever.' Christopher Reeve died of cardiac arrest in 2004, aged just fifty-two.

Television in the Eighties and Nineties made several attempts to followup Reeve's triumphant turn as the screen's greatest Superman. *The Greatest American Hero* (1981–3) starred William Katt as a teacher gifted by aliens with super-abilities and a red superhero outfit. The family comedy show enjoyed a following, but *Superboy* (1988–92) did more to properly represent the superhero cause on television. Produced by the Salkinds (just as Superman reached his fiftieth anniversary) as a spin-off from the first trio of Superman movies, the show starred John Haymes Newton as the younger Clark Kent/Superboy. Several DC writers contributed scripts, and the show developed across four seasons (with Gerard Christopher starring from season two). Having begun as a light-hearted romp, the series took on darker, more serious tones, perhaps reflecting the concurrent big-screen *Batman* movies. The fourth season finale originally showed Superboy dead at the hands of Lex Luthor, but had to be reworked to explain he'd faked his death as the series was then cancelled. The ongoing legal battle over *Superboy* saw the show vanish from the air and remain unavailable for many years before a 2005 resolution allowed for the complete series to be released on DVD.

For over a decade Christopher Reeve's Superman held the crown as the best live action realization of the superhero on film. As a long-in-gestation big-budget Batman movie neared production at the end of the Eighties, a casting controversy would show just how difficult it was to find a suitable actor to embody iconic four-colour superheroes on screen.

Batman (1989) would be the biggest film of its year, and it would set the template for many superhero movies of the Nineties and beyond, but the route to Gotham City success wasn't easy. Producer Jon Peters had struggled for several years to mount a production that would get as far away from the camp of the 1966 television series as possible, but the vision did not come into focus until director Tim Burton was attached. Burton's dark fairytale sensibilities had come to the fore in *Beetlejuice* (1988), so he was charged with bringing something of the graphic novels *The Dark Knight Returns* and *The Killing Joke* to the screen. An initial script by comic book writer Steve Englehart was reworked by Sam Hamm to include flashbacks to cover the origin story, rather than build the film around a chronological re-telling as had been done in 1978's *Superman*. Burton worked with production designer Anton Furst to create a distinctive Gotham City, making the city a character in the film in the way that Metropolis had never really been in any of the Superman films. Burton felt the darkness of the city reflected the dark heart of Batman.

The biggest problem was finding leading actors to take on the roles of Batman and his nemesis, the Joker. Among the names suggested as a possible Batman were Mel Gibson, Pierce Brosnan (later James Bond), *Magnum PI* star Tom Selleck, and comic actor Bill Murray. Burton settled on Michael Keaton (the star of *Beetlejuice*), an actor largely known for his light, comedic roles. This unleashed a controversy in comic book fandom (over 50,000 letters of protest were received by Warner Bros.), who rebelled against the choice and campaigned against the film. Batman creator Bob Kane was hired as 'creative consultant' largely as a sop to Batman fans (he also has a brief cameo). Only after seeing the film did fans accept the seriousness with which Keaton approached the role. Equally known for larger-than-life performances, Jack Nicholson became the Joker, thanks to an epic payday ($6 million up front, plus a large percentage of the box office gross, said to have netted the actor around $60 million) that put him on a par with Marlon Brando in *Superman*. He beat Tim Curry, John Lithgow and even David Bowie to the role.

The film was shot in the UK at Pinewood Studios between October 1988 and January 1989, and featured Kim Basinger as Vicki Vale and Michael Gough as Alfred. Batman's sidekick Robin was originally in the script, with Kiefer Sutherland under consideration, but the character was dropped in rewrites, as Burton wanted the focus solely on Batman. He saw the film as a 'duel of the freaks', matching Batman and the Joker as equal, but opposite forces. The film was aided on its way to blockbuster status thanks to a smart marketing campaign that popularized a streamlined Bat logo. The film grossed $411 million globally, becoming the first film to earn over $100 million in just ten days. It remained the highest-grossing comic book superhero film until Christopher Nolan's Batman reinvention *The Dark Knight* surpassed it in 2008.

Burton's *Batman* provided an origin story for the Joker that saw him responsible for the death of Bruce Wayne's parents before a chemical accident transformed him from a petty criminal into a super-villain. While the film was a huge success, it did attract criticism for putting style before substance, and for focusing on design over plot. One of the results of the movie was Bruce Timm's *Batman: The Animated Series* (1992–5), an acclaimed animated television show modelled after the Fleischer Superman shorts of the Forties. It, in turn, gave rise to the theatrically released animated movie *Batman: Mask of the Phantasm* (1993), and *Superman: The Animated Series* (1996–2000) in the same distinctive neo-noir art deco style.

The success of *Batman* led to *Batman Returns* (1992), which many considered superior. Burton again directed, with Keaton's Batman matched by Michelle Pfeiffer's Catwoman. Her origin story saw her transform from a put-upon secretary into a female avenger clad in PVC. The film was a social satire, with businessman Max Shreck (Christopher Walken) planning a Gotham power plant, and the Penguin's (Danny DeVito) ill-fated run for mayor in revenge on those responsible for his life in the city's sewers. Robin was again in the script (with Marlon Wayans set to play him as a teenage tearaway), but was dropped again. Perhaps due to its darker feel, *Batman Returns* took less at the worldwide box office, totalling $283 million, despite largely positive reviews. This was enough to make the movie the third-highest grossing of 1992.

Keen to produce more audience-friendly Batman films, Warner Bros. enlisted Joel Schumacher as the director of both *Batman Forever* (1995) and *Batman & Robin* (1997). Val Kilmer replaced Keaton for *Batman Forever*, with Nicole Kidman as Dr Chase Meridian, Tommy Lee Jones as Two-Face and Jim Carrey as the Riddler. Robin finally made his debut, played by Chris O'Donnell. Schumacher attempted a return to the original *Batman* comics, avoiding the dark fairytale that had infused Burton's version. Unfortunately, his two Batman films were more comparable to the camp goofiness of the Adam West series than to anything that ever appeared between comic book covers. Mixed reviews met this more colourful instalment, but an increased worldwide box office take of $336 in 1995 guaranteed a fourth film.

Kilmer was replaced by *E.R.* star George Clooney, matched with a larger role for O'Donnell's Robin, who made it into the title in *Batman & Robin* (1997). Arnold Schwarzenegger took top billing as a campy Mr Freeze, while the stars' rubber costumes were redesigned to sport prominent nipples. Also included was Poison Ivy (Uma Thurman) and Alicia Silverstone as the niece of Alfred who becomes Batgirl. In an ill-advised shift in tone, the film played the Batman concepts for laughs, but failed to find a receptive audience, with comic book fans denigrating it for its attitude towards Batman, and general audiences turned off by the tongue-in-cheek approach. It crashed and burned at the box office, garnering just $238 worldwide, and became a byword for disastrous movie making. *Los Angeles Times'* film critic Kenneth Turan blamed the movie for killing off the Batman film franchise.

In the Nineties, as Batman took flight on the big screen, superheroes got darker on the small screen. Highly regarded was *The Flash* (1990–1), a film noir-infused take on super-speedy Barry Allen, starring John Wesley Shipp as Allen and Amanda Pays as scientist Tina McGee, who supplies his technology and serves as a love interest. Taking comic book super-heroics seriously, rather than playing them for laughs, *The Flash* won a legion of fans in its single season. Guest star villains, such as *Star Wars'* Mark Hamill as the Trickster, may have recalled the Sixties *Batman* show, but however outlandish the characters or the situation, this Flash always took itself seriously. As an expensive, special effects-driven show, *The Flash* failed to secure enough viewers to continue beyond one season, but it did mark the territory later occupied by such shows as *The Cape* (2011), among others.

The biggest superhero show of the Nineties was far more light and positive – *Lois and Clark: The New Adventures of Superman* (1993–7) focused on romance as much as on super-heroics. Dean Cain succeeded in filling Christopher Reeve's large cape as a younger, more innocent Superman and more dynamic Clark Kent, with Teri Hatcher modelling her Lois Lane after that of Margot Kidder. The key word on *Lois and Clark* was 'fun' as it largely dispensed with the darkness of the big-screen Batman and joyously reflected the feelgood nature of the Superman mythos.

The origin story is retold, set in the mid-Sixties (so making Clark/Superman contemporary to the Nineties), with the Kents christening their son 'Clark Jerome Kent' (a nod to Jerry Siegel). Clark's mother fashions his Superman suit, before he makes his way to Metropolis, secures a job at the *Daily Planet*, and rescues co-worker Lois Lane, causing her to develop an infatuation with Superman. All the elements of the core story are replayed as romantic comedy, and the episodic format allowed for variety, with some episodes more serious in nature than others, but lots of character comedy suffused the show.

Lex Luthor (John Shea) is depicted as a corrupt Metropolis businessman who frequently clashes with Superman and Clark, while other villains such as Mister Mxyzptlk, the Prankster, Metallo and the Toyman were drawn from the DC comics. The show became more action focused as it developed, while playing up the romantic angle between Lois and Clark. By its third year on air the series was attracting fifteen million viewers, as it ran various episodes teasing the impending wedding of the main characters. The marriage eventually occurred in a fourth season episode entitled 'Swear to God, This Time We're Not Kidding', and the series eventually ended on an unresolved cliffhanger.

Lois and Clark proved a weekly superhero television show was possible, even before digital technology made effects easier and cheaper. Riding on the coat-tails of the Superman movies, Dean Cain was both close enough to and yet different enough from Christopher Reeve's portrayal for the series to succeed. It was also an amusing, enjoyable take on the superhero concept that had become somewhat darker in concurrent big-screen movies, so providing a welcome contrast. Cain would also later appear in an episode of *Smallville*.

A variety of superhero films in the Nineties took their cue from the first two dark Batman movies. The *Darkman* trilogy (1990–6) was Sam Raimi's attempt at his own movie superhero after failing to secure the rights to either Batman or pulp hero the Shadow. Liam Neeson starred as a scientist attacked and left for dead by a mobster, but who comes back to gain revenge thanks to his synthetic skin. It's a colourful, dynamic tribute to the Universal monster movies of the Thirties and Forties that spawned two direct-to-video sequels, *The Return of Durant* (1995) and *Die, Darkman, Die* (1996) that recast the central role and built up supporting character Durant, played by Larry Drake.

The Nineties finally saw movie screens featuring a variety of black superheroes. Todd McFarlane's *Spawn* (1997) starred Michael Jai White as the back-from-Hell avenger in a very ropey movie directed by former ILM animator Mark Dippé, although it can claim to be the first movie to feature an African-American actor to play an actual comic book superhero. Shaquille O'Neal followed as the DC character John Henry Irons in *Steel* (1997), from the 1993 publishing event Reign of the Supermen. Easily the best of this run of movies was *Blade* (1998), starring Wesley Snipes as Marvel's vampire hunter. A stylish movie directed by Stephen Norrington, *Blade* was not only a black super-hero, but part-vampire anti-hero. *Blade*'s success led to two sequels (*Blade II*, 2002; *Blade: Trinity*, 2004) and a short-lived *Blade* television series (2006).

James O'Barr's grim gothic comic book hero the Crow became an ill-fated film directed by Alex Proyas in 1994, more remembered for the on-set shooting death of Bran-don Lee (son of *The Green Hornet*'s Bruce Lee) than for its stylish visuals and seductive gothic atmosphere. Lee's Eric Draven returns from the dead to avenge the killing of him-self and his fiancée. Three movie sequels – *The Crow: City of Angels* (1995), *The Crow: Salvation* (2000), *The Crow: Wicked Prayer* (2005) – and a television series (*The Crow: Stairway to Heaven*, 1998) explored various resurrected 'Crow' characters, to diminishing effect. A twenty-first-century reboot remains trapped in development hell.

Female superheroes continued to be notable due to their absence. Perhaps the most visible was the *Black Scorpion* series. Joan Severance starred in the Roger Corman-produced 1995 television movie as the Batman-like cos-tumed vigilante. Sequel *Black Scorpion II: Aftershock* (1996) followed, again with Severance. Michelle Lintel took the part for the 2001 television series. Beyond 1984's *Super-girl* there was little to celebrate, though 1995's *Tank Girl* had its moments, with Lori Petty as Tank Girl and Naomi Watts as Jet Girl. Both the Dark Horse comic book-inspired *Barb Wire* (1996, starring Pamela Anderson) and the long-in-gestation *Catwoman* (2004, with Halle Berry, with no connection to *Batman Returns*) have little to recommend them. Better was *Elektra* (2005), a *Daredevil* spin-off fea-turing Jennifer Garner (who later married *Daredevil* – and future *Batman* – actor Ben Affleck). The only hope for female superheroes lay in the explosion of twenty-first-century superhero filmmaking to eventually find room for Wonder Woman or Ms. Marvel on the big screen.

The biggest character from Britain's *2000AD* has been brought to the movie screen twice, first by Sylvester Stallone in the critically panned *Judge Dredd* (1995) and then by Karl Urban in the more widely appreciated *Dredd* (2012). The first played to Stallone's vanity by having Dredd remove his iconic helmet (never done in the comics). Lessons were learned for the second, in which Urban stays masked throughout. The first film leaned toward comedy (in sidekick Rob Schneider), while the second movie upped the violence to match that depicted in the comics, garnering an adult rating in the process. Made as a British project (shot in South Africa), *Dredd* was truer to the character and settings created by John Wagner and Carlos Ezquerra than the previous version. Although a box office failure, fans hoped for a sequel.

Another notable trend in superhero movies in the Nineties was the revival of pulp heroes, such as *The Rocketeer* (1991, based on Dave Stevens comics), *The Shadow* (1994, based on Walter B. Gibson's radio serial character from 1931) and *The Phantom* (1996, based on Lee Falk's newspaper strip), a trend revived in the twenty-first century with films like *The Spirit* (2008, based on Will Eisner's idiosyncratic newspaper strips) and *The Green Hornet* (2011, played as a comedy spoof starring Seth Rogen).

Following the Seventies' hugely successful reinvention of Superman with the charismatic Christopher Reeve, and the darker Batman in Michael Keaton's performance – as well as all the spin-offs and movies inspired by their success – the superhero movie might have been thought to be in robust health through the Nineties. However, this was nothing compared to what was to come as the Marvel Age of superhero movies dawned.

14

SUPERHEROES BEYOND THE PAGE: THE MARVEL AGE OF MOVIES

The first Marvel age of superhero movies was launched somewhat ignominiously with the George Lucas-produced *Howard the Duck* (1986). Poorly received, it was followed by *The Punisher* (1989), a lame action movie in which musclebound Dolph Lungren played Frank Castle, the 'one man weapon against crime' driven by revenge over his slain family. There were two later follow-ups in *The Punisher* (2004), with Thomas Jane, and *Punisher: War Zone* (2008), with Ray Stevenson. All these films proved was that Punisher was never going to be core material to support the Marvel Universe on film.

Classic superheroes were tackled in *Captain America* (1990) and *The Fantastic Four* (1994), but both films failed to do justice to their respective characters. Matt Salinger (son of reclusive writer J. D. Salinger) played Steve Rogers, with Scott Paulin as his nemesis, the Red Skull. The wartime setting was retained, with Captain America frozen and revived in the present day. Unfortunately, the film was simply cheap, lacking the effects technology to do superheroes justice. *The Fantastic Four* suffered a similar low-budget fate. Made on behalf of German producer Bernd Eichinger by B-movie specialist Roger Corman for $1 million simply to extend a rights option, it remained unreleased (before escaping as a bootleg, initially on VHS). The film put Eichinger in prime position to exploit the post *X-Men* (2000) superhero movie boom with *Fantastic Four* (2005) and *Fantastic 4* [sic]: *Rise of the Silver Surfer* (2007). This time the origin story had a $90 million budget and a star-name cast with Ioan Gruffudd as Reed Richards, Jessica Alba as Sue Storm, Chris Evans as Johnny Storm, Michael Chicklis as Ben Grimm/the Thing, and Julian McMahon as Dr Doom. A big-budget success, it led to the $130 million sequel *Fantastic 4: Rise of the Silver Surfer*, which added Jack Kirby's 'herald of Galactus', with Doug Jones playing the Surfer, voiced by Laurence Fishburne. A star-driven reboot of the series – back to the original title of *The Fantastic Four* – was scheduled for release in 2015 from *Chronicle* (2012) director Josh Trank.

These early Marvel movies, along with *Blade* (1998), paved the way for the far more successful second Marvel age launched by 20th Century Fox's *X-Men* (2000). Bryan Singer's movie was the first since the Donner *Superman* and Burton's *Batman* to do superheroes on screen properly. With heavyweights like Patrick Stewart as Professor X and Ian McKellen as Magneto, the tone was set early for this serious version of the comics. A starry name cast played the super-powered mutants, but the breakout (as he'd been in the comics) was Wolverine, brought to life by Hugh Jackman (cast after first choices Russell Crowe and Dougray Scott dropped out). The ensemble nature of the movie meant there was space for female characters (Halle Berry as Storm, Anna Paquin as Rogue and Famke Janssen as Jean Grey) to take their place alongside the more traditional male superheroes. Arguably, *X-Men* was the first superhero movie to break through to a mainstream audience that didn't feature the 'big two', Superman or Batman. Jackman's charismatic Wolverine laid the groundwork for a franchise that looks set to span decades.

Singer once again helmed the direct sequel *X2: X-Men United* (2003), but dropped out of *X-Men: The Last Stand* (2006), which saw war break out between the X-Men and the Brotherhood of Mutants, to take on *Superman Returns* (2006). Instead, Brett Ratner wrapped up the trilogy, but the third film – in which a 'cure' for mutation is discovered and Magneto resurrects Jean Grey as Phoenix – was the poor relation in critical response. Jackman was rewarded with two solo films, *X-Men Origins: Wolverine* (2009) and *The Wolverine* (2013), both of which met with mixed receptions. The fading franchise was given a new lease of life with the Sixties-set *X-Men: First Class* (2011), that saw James McAvoy play the younger Professor X and Michael Fassbender take on the role of young Magneto. The sequel, *X-Men: Days of Future Past* (2014), brought both X-casts together in a time-jumping epic based on a much-loved comic book story, altered to put the focus on Jackman's Wolverine once again.

This new seriousness in superhero cinema spilled over into the next hugely successful Marvel-originated franchise, Columbia Pictures' exuberant *Spider-Man* series starring Tobey Maguire as Peter Parker. The path from the 1977 Nicholas Hammond television series to the record-breaking *Spider-Man* (2002) involved Roger Corman, Cannon Films (for five years between 1985 and 1990), Cannon's successor Carolco, and *Avatar* director James Cameron. In the meantime, Marvel Comics had declared bankruptcy in 1996 (as did Carolco), and was reorganized by 1998, when (after years of legal delays) the Spider-Man movie rights ended up with Columbia.

Sam Raimi (*The Evil Dead*, 1981) was a surprise choice for this blockbuster production. His recent successes had been mid-budget movies, but as a life-long fan of comics he'd already created *Darkman* (1990) and brought a comic book sensibility to *Army of Darkness* (1992). Raimi toned down his frenetic camerawork for *Spider-Man*, although he made the most of the scenes where Spidey was seen to swing across the city skyline. The movie enjoyed a huge record-breaking opening weekend, eventually taking $822 million worldwide. Raimi and Maguire made the next two films, *Spider-Man 2* (2004), featuring Alfred Molina as Doctor Octopus, and *Spider-Man 3* (2007), in which a trio of villains – Venom, Sandman, and a new Green Goblin – almost overwhelmed the story. The Spider-Man franchise would be rebooted within five years.

In the meantime, by 2005 Marvel had got its act together when it came to exploiting its superheroes on the big screen, via Marvel Studios. The only restriction was that due to pre-existing agreements the rights to The Fantastic Four, Silver Surfer, Daredevil (and Elektra), and The X-Men were held by 20th Century Fox, while Spider-Man and Ghost Rider were with Columbia (Sony Pictures). The unlikely-to-be-exploited Namor the Sub-Mariner rights were at Universal, while Lionsgate Cinema had control of Man-Thing and the Punisher, and Blade remained with New Line Cinema. Otherwise, Marvel was free to use any of its other characters, and studio boss Kevin Feige set out to develop a slate of productions (distributed through Paramount) that would feature the same interconnected stories and character crossovers that were a key signature of the Marvel Universe comics since the Sixties. This potential attracted Disney to Marvel, who bought the company for $4 billion in 2009.

* * *

Before 'The Avengers Initiative' (as the grand Marvel plan became known), Marvel's long-term rival DC brought Batman back to the big screen, drawing on the newly serious approach to cinematic superheroes of *X-Men*. The failure of the camp *Batman & Robin* in 1997 had put the Bat-franchise out to pasture, but there were always creative writers and directors interested in bringing the Caped Crusader back. One was screenwriter David S. Goyer, who developed a more realistic take on the Dark Knight with Christopher Nolan.

Goyer wrote the *JSA* (1999) for DC Comics, before co-creating television series *FlashForward* (2009). He previously scripted *The Crow: City of Angels* (1996), and wrote the screenplays for the trilogy of *Blade* (1998–2004) movies, before working on *Batman Begins* (2005). Nolan launched his career with the London-set low-budget urban thriller *Following* (1998), before making the narratively scrambled *Memento* (2000) and *Insomnia* (2002, remade from a 1997 Norwegian film). He teamed with Goyer to approach Warner Bros. in 2003 about making a more 'human' Batman film, grounded in reality and a 'relatable' world, drawing upon the strictures of classical drama rather than the excesses of comic book fantasy – the result was *Batman Begins*.

The film presented a more elaborate cinematic origin story for Batman, with Bruce Wayne not donning the Bat-suit for over an hour. Christian Bale was cast, a choice that did not provoke the fan outcry that had initially accompanied Michael Keaton, Val Kilmer, and George Clooney. Michael Caine took the role of Alfred, while Morgan Freeman played Wayne's business and technology facilitator Lucius Fox (featured in DC comics since 1979). Liam Neeson played Ra's al Ghul, leader of the ancient League of Shadows, who disguised as Henri Ducard acts as a mentor to Bruce Wayne, teaching him the martial arts he later puts to use as Batman. Cillian Murphy was Jonathan Crane, better known as the Scarecrow, who uses poison fear gas to disrupt Gotham City. Gary Oldman won a new legion of fans as the stoic Gotham City police officer James Gordon.

Bale's Bruce Wayne and Batman were the most grounded versions seen on film. Drawing on Keaton's approach, Bale eschewed the silliness of the portrayals by Adam West and Clooney. To Goyer, Bale was the only actor whom he felt could bring a distinctive character to each of Wayne and Batman, however Bale was subject to some ridicule for his choice to deepen his voice to gravelly effect when in Batman mode (something Keaton had also done to a lesser degree). Nolan noted that Bale had 'exactly the balance of darkness and light that we were looking for'.

The movie dropped the fantasy aspects of Tim Burton and Joel Schumacher, instead placing its Bruce Wayne and Batman in a more recognizably real film noir-style world, where Chicago (in *Batman Begins* and *The Dark Knight*, 2008) and Pittsburgh (in *The Dark Knight Rises*, 2012) doubled for Gotham City. Goyer deliberately looked towards Donner's 1978 *Superman* as a way to depict the growth of Bruce Wayne as a contemporary twenty-first-century character and his eventual transformation into Batman. *X-Men* had prepared the way for *Batman Begins*, resulting in a very receptive audience for a serious superhero movie that gave the film a worldwide box office take of $373 million (less than Tim Burton's *Batman* took in 1989). However, it dramatically set the stage for the two sequels in Nolan's epic Batman saga, *The Dark Knight* (2008) and *The Dark Knight Rises* (2012), which both grossed more than $1 billion each.

Nolan and Goyer's take on Batman would unleash a host of new superhero movies, many of which kicked off with darker, more realistic origin stories for their central characters (including Iron Man, The Incredible Hulk and such non-superhero franchises as *Star Trek*, *Terminator*, Sherlock Holmes, and James Bond). Critics felt that Nolan displayed more clearly than Burton what motivates Bruce Wayne to become Batman, and presented the choice as a burden he had to bear, physically and psychologically. Nolan was clear on one thing about his Batman universe: other costumed superheroes did not exist, as otherwise he felt that Wayne's choices would be very different. This version was nothing like the eventual Marvel Cinematic Universe, or the succeeding version of the Caped Crusader that would put him cape-to-cape with the Man of Steel.

The deconstruction of superheroes that had dominated comics in the mid-Eighties had partly inspired the new take on Batman, and it was evident in several other distinctive superhero movies of the early twenty-first century. Both *Hancock* (2008) and *Watchmen* (2009) took a different view of the superhero. In *Hancock*, Will Smith played an alcoholic, reckless, uncaring hero who has to learn how to use his powers to people's benefit (a topic tackled in *The Return of Captain Invincible*, 1983), while *Watchmen* was an all-too-faithful retelling of the comic (albeit with an altered climax), directed by Zack Snyder (*The Man of Steel*).

A host of comic book movies presented characters who were unusual or had powers, but were not necessarily straight-forwardly heroic. Nicolas Cage starred in *Ghost Rider* (2007) and *Ghost Rider: Spirit of Vengeance* (2012) as supernatural superhero Johnny Blaze, a stunt motorcyclist recruited by the Devil to wreak vengeance on Earth. Ron Perlman was Mike Mignola's Hellboy in Guillermo del Toro's films *Hellboy* (2004) and *Hellboy II: The Golden Army* (2008), a demonic creature conjured up by Nazis but raised to act in defence of humanity. Keanu Reeves was exorcist John Constantine in *Constantine* (2005), based on the *Hellblazer* comics, battling demons and angels alike (with a television spin-off in development). Also blurring the lines was action movie *Wanted* (2008), in which James

McAvoy's ordinary accountant discovers he has superhuman abilities and is part of a secret assassins guild.

Perhaps one of the best superhero movies (not always recognized as such) was M. Night Shyamalan's *Unbreakable* (2000), starring Bruce Willis and Samuel L. Jackson (later to play Marvel's Nick Fury across multiple films). Willis is David Dunn, sole survivor of a train wreck, who slowly discovers he's indestructible. Jackson's Elijah Price was born with a rare disease that make his bones break easily, resulting in the nickname Mr Glass. A superhero and super-villain origin story, *Unbreakable* places Dunn and Glass at the opposite ends of a spectrum, where one is an unwilling hero and the other an unwitting villain. It's a clever perspective on the superhero, subtly applying the idea of comic book panels to shots and giving each character a distinctive colour scheme. Director Quentin Tarantino hailed the movie as 'a brilliant retelling of the Superman mythology'.

Television got in on the superhero deconstruction, too, with series such as *Heroes* and *Misfits*. In its first season, *Heroes* (2006–10) was a razor-sharp dissection of the superhero genre, presenting a group of people worldwide who develop super-powers. The show lost its way in later seasons, but it was notable for taking the *Unbreakable* approach to the villain Sylar (Zachary Quinto), a watchmaker who targets other superheroes to steal their powers. It also echoes *Watchmen* as the heroes gather to avert a nuclear blast foretold for New York City. Similarly, the British-set *Misfits* (2009–13) saw a group of young people all serving community service sentences caught up in a lightning storm that gives them diverse super-powers. Packed with irreverence, the show also got tangled in its own mythology, but the second series built around a future-version of Simon (Iwan Rheon) helping his friends was well done.

The biggest superhero television show was *Smallville* (2001–11), a revised retelling of Kal-El's early years. Tom Welling played Clark Kent in a long-running series whose defining motto was 'No flights, no tights'. Drawing widely on DC Comics' back catalogue for inspiration and freely remixing or reinventing elements, the show had young Clark Kent become friends with the slightly older Lex Luthor, while the 'meteor rocks' that had fallen to Earth with Kal-El's spaceship are responsible for a variety of characters developing super-powers, some becoming heroes while others turn to villainy. The longer the show ran, the harder it became to delay the moment when Clark Kent would have to become Superman. It was a popular and – thanks in large part to advancement in special effects technology – a convincing expansion of the Superman mythos. It spawned a short-lived associated series in *Birds of Prey* (2002–3) that failed to adequately draw on the Batman back story in the same successful way. There was also an unsuccessful pilot made for *Aquaman* (2006), starring Justin Hartley (later featured in *Smallville* as Oliver Queen/Green Arrow). A long-mooted young Bruce Wayne series has yet to make it to air, although the planned *Gotham* (2014) set in a pre-Batman Gotham City is promising.

Somewhat less successful was *Mutant X* (2001–4), which resembled a low-budget television version of the X-Men, the conceptually similar *Alphas* (2011–12), and the US remake of the British Seventies show *The Tomorrow People* (2013–). It took the rise of the Marvel movies and DC Comic's twenty-first-century attempts to get its cinematic house in order to kickstart a new breed of television superheroes. First up was *Arrow* (2012–), a reinvention of the Oliver Queen story for the youth audience of The CW, spearheading a new wave of superhero television shows.

A decade after emerging from bankruptcy Marvel finally got its act together in its cinematic universe, so much so that it largely outclassed the DC films released during the same period. Dubbed 'phase one' by Marvel, the first batch of movies built to the release of *The Avengers* (2012), the one significant superhero team where the movie rights remained with Marvel itself.

The plan kicked off with the 2008 *Iron Man*, a movie in development for over fifteen years at other studios (Nicolas Cage and Tom Cruise were considered for the lead role, with Tarantino and Joss Whedon as directors) before the rights reverted to Marvel in 2006. Director Jon Favreau (who'd acted in *Daredevil*) took a risk on Robert Downey, Jr to play Tony Stark, an actor with a troubled past and a difficult reputation. Despite the complaints of naysayers, it was an inspired choice, putting his character at the heart of the Marvel movie project. With Iron Man suits made by the Stan Winston company, and state-of-the-art special effects, *Iron Man* followed the highly effective *Spider-Man* trilogy in proving that digital filmmaking processes had finally caught up with the imagery regularly depicted in four-colour comic books.

Retelling Iron Man's origin story, the movie updated events to the contemporary conflict in Afghanistan where Stark constructs his first primitive Iron Man suit while held by terrorists. Pepper Potts (Gwyneth Paltrow) and James Rhodes (Terence Howard) appear, alongside Agent Coulson (Clark Gregg) from SHIELD, a character created for the movie who proved so popular he eventually featured in a spin-off television series. The story climaxed with Stark in an armour-suited battle with his father's business partner Obadiah Stane (*Iron Man* #163, October 1982, played by Jeff Bridges) for control of the technology. A post-credits scene (a feature of each Marvel movie) sees Stark visited by Nick Fury (Samuel L. Jackson) recruiting for 'the Avengers initiative'. Since *X-Men*, Stan Lee had enjoyed a cameo appearance in most movies based on Marvel properties, and *Iron Man* continued the tradition.

The highly anticipated movie proved to be a huge hit, grossing $585 million worldwide within a year of release. The humour and lightness of touch of Downey, Jr combined with the spy and adventure movie trappings that Favreau deliberately evoked turned a niche comic book property into a mass-audience mainstream breakout hit that set the stage for the next instalments.

Unfortunately, *Iron Man 2* (2010, quickly produced by the same team) was a disappointment, with Stark in conflict with the US Government, Russian terrorist Ivan Vanko (Mickey Rourke) and his pal Colonel Rhodes. It introduced Scarlett Johansson as 'Black Widow' Natasha Romanov (later a member of the Avengers) and featured a post-credits appearance from Agent Coulson reporting the discovery of a huge hammer in the New Mexico desert. With a complicated and diffuse storyline, the film was a critical failure. According to *The Hollywood Reporter* '. . . everything fun and terrific about *Iron Man*, a mere two years ago, has vanished with its sequel. In its place, *Iron Man 2* has substituted noise, confusion, multiple villains, irrelevant stunts and misguided storylines'. Nonetheless, the film was the seventh-highest grossing of the year in the US, taking almost $624 million worldwide, beating the previous movie.

Iron Man 3 (2013) – following *The Avengers* – redeemed the franchise, dealing with Stark's post-Avengers trauma, and refocusing on the man not the armour. The film cleverly repurposed one of the comic's more tricky-to-handle villains in the Mandarin (Ben Kingsley), and built on the success of *The Avengers* with an astonishing $1.2 billion at the global box office, making it the fifth-highest grossing film of all time (as of 2013). The post-credits appearance of Bruce Banner hinted at a future Hulk movie. The best of the three films, *Iron Man 3*'s success saw Robert Downey, Jr sign up for two *Avengers* sequels.

The second plank of Marvel's launch came that same summer as *Iron Man* with *The Incredible Hulk* (2008). This followed Ang Lee's 2003 *Hulk*, a sometimes bizarre superhero art movie mix that featured Eric Bana as Bruce

Banner and director Lee himself performing motion capture for the CGI Hulk, seen bounding through the desert in one of the film's best scenes. Produced under the previous Marvel regime, that film was a disappointment, taking $245 million at the worldwide box office. Marvel needed to reboot the Hulk as part of its wider plans, so 2008's _The Incredible Hulk_ started over, with Edward Norton as Banner and action specialist Louis Leterrier behind the camera. Cleverly opening with a riff on the old television series title sequence that retells the character's origins, the film pitted Banner/Hulk against Tim Roth's Russian Emil Blonsky who is transformed into a creature known as the Abomination. A scene where the Hulk faces off against army tanks was closest to capturing the comics. The customary post-credits sequence saw Banner visited by Stark, who recruits him for the growing Avengers team. Widely praised in comparison with the previous movie, this lighter, more humorous take on the character grossed $263.5 million worldwide, well short of _Iron Man_'s takings two months earlier. It was enough to secure Hulk a place in _The Avengers_, although Edward Norton, who had heavy input into the script, would not return.

It would be two years before _Thor_ (2011) and _Captain America: The First Avenger_ (2011) picked up the threads. Faithful to the Sixties originals, but realized through modern digital effects, these two films couldn't have been more different. _Thor_ – surprisingly directed by acclaimed Shakespearean actor Kenneth Branagh – was a fantasy epic, linking the mythological world of Asgard to contemporary America. Chris Hemsworth personified the 'god' fallen to Earth, while Natalie Portman played astrophysicist Jane Foster. The hammer discovered by SHIELD is Mjolnir, Thor's weapon. Thor's brother Loki (Tom Hiddleston) claims the throne on Asgard, motivating Thor's return where he must make amends with his father, Odin (Anthony Hopkins). With the high-flown fantasy played straight (as if by Shakespeare), *Thor* showed mainstream audiences a different side to the Marvel Universe, partly preparing for the far-out space opera of *Guardians of the Galaxy* (2014). Surprisingly popular, *Thor* scored almost $450 million at the worldwide box office.

Captain America: The First Avenger (2011) was a period piece set during the Second World War. In 1942, Steve Rogers' (Chris Evans) is transformed into Captain America (initially as a character touting for war bond sales), before he tangles with the Red Skull, Nazi officer Johann Schmidt, who used an earlier version of the 'super soldier' serum on himself. Aided by 'Bucky' Barnes (Sebastian Stan) and girlfriend British agent Carter (Hayley Atwell), Cap and a team of specialists raid Red Skull's HYDRA base, liberating the mysterious Tesseract. Crashing to his death, Rogers is assumed lost – until a coda shows him revived in the present day. After the credits, Captain America is added to the Avengers line-up by Nick Fury. The film grossed just over $368 million worldwide, and was the final puzzle piece in the elaborate cinematic set-up for the main course of Marvel phase one, *The Avengers*.

The main Marvel superheroes and super-villains featured in the previous five films (including *Iron Man 2*) – Tony Stark, Black Widow, Hulk, Thor, Loki, Captain America, and Nick Fury – were brought together for *The Avengers* (2012), which quickly became the third-highest grossing film of all time with $1.5 billion worldwide (behind James Cameron's double-whammy of *Avatar* and *Titanic*, and just ahead of Christopher Nolan's *The Dark Knight*), and broke any number of international box office records. The original actors all returned, except for Edward Norton who was replaced by Mark Ruffalo as the Hulk. Clark Gregg returned as Agent Coulson, joined by Jeremy Renner as Hawkeye. Their combined talents were required to defeat an invasion of New York by the alien Chitauri, masterminded by Loki using the Tesseract. While the team work together to retrieve the Tesseract and capture Loki, true to the comics (and their natures) they squabble and bicker over what exactly should be done and who should do it – this element of Marvel's approach to superheroes is one of the major factors that made these outlandish characters accessible to moviegoers. The comic sequence in which the Hulk subdues Loki was particularly popular. When the battle is won, a post-credit sequence reveals the Chitauri's master to have been Thanos, one of the superhuman Eternals.

Joss Whedon, who directed *The Avengers* and reworked the existing screenplay, was a long-standing fan of Marvel's comics (he wrote for *Astonishing X-Men*, among others) and had previously displayed his lightness of touch with pop culture heroes in television series *Buffy the Vampire Slayer* (1997–2003), co-writing the original *Toy Story* (1995), and the horror film deconstruction *The Cabin in the Woods* (2012). His take on the film's diverse characters (the key to its success) was that '. . . these people shouldn't be in the same room, let alone on the same team, and that's the very definition of family'. The film was a triumphant end to phase one of Marvel's grand cinematic gamble. *Variety* called *The Avengers* 'a superior, state-of-the-art model . . . Joss Whedon's buoyant, witty and robustly entertaining superhero smash-up is escapism of a sophisticated order, boasting a tonal assurance and rich reserves of humor . . .' The spin-off television series, *Agents of SHIELD* (2013–) was overseen by Whedon and provided a follow-up focusing on a group of mismatched SHIELD agents who deal with alien artefacts and rogue superheroes. The show revived Clark Gregg's Agent Coulson (seemingly killed in *The Avengers*), and made his mysterious resurrection an ongoing plot point.

Phase two of Marvel's cinematic superhero domination was kicked off by *Iron Man 3* (2013), whose blockbuster box office takings doubled those of the franchise's previous instalment in the wake of *The Avengers*. It was quickly followed by stand-alone sequels for two of the super-team's main members in *Thor: The Dark World* (2013), in which Thor faced Malekith (Christopher Eccleston) and the 'dark elves', and *Captain America: The Winter Soldier* (2014), in which Rogers teams with the Black Widow and the Falcon to take on a powerful adversary known as 'the Winter Soldier' (based on a 2005 comic book story that had 'Bucky' Barnes programmed as a Russian assassin).

In the run up to 2015's Joss Whedon-directed blockbuster sequel *The Avengers: Age of Ultron*, in which James Spader would voice the artificial intelligence Ultron, Marvel took its biggest risk with the space opera, *Guardians of the Galaxy* (2014). Created by Arnold Drake and Gene Colan in 1969, this unlikely team of spacefarers had been revived in comics in 2008 by Dan Abnett and Andy Lanning. Among the Guardians are Peter Quill (Chris Pratt), a human pilot who left Earth in the Eighties and now goes by the name of Star-Lord; Gamora (Zoe Saldana), adopted daughter of Thanos; alien warrior Drax, the destroyer (Dave Bautista); and Rocket Racoon, a genetically engineered racoon and ace marksman, realized with CGI and voiced by Bradley Cooper. Appearing as the evil Nebula, associate of Thanos, was Karen Gillan, previously *Doctor Who* companion Amy Pond in the BBC fantasy series. Director James Gunn was charged with bringing such an unlikely ensemble to the screen in a populist way, under the creative supervision of Whedon (who as part of his deal on *The Avengers* had oversight on all the other related projects).

Marvel were determined not to shy away from making movies featuring the more obscure superheroes from their back catalogue. With so many potential mainstream figures such as Spider-Man and the X-Men tied up with other studios, they had little choice. Phase three, which would lead up to a third instalment of *The Avengers*, was initiated by *Ant-Man* (2015), the unlikely figure of Henry Pym whose 'super-power' allows him to shrink to microscopic size, directed by Edgar Wright (*Shaun of the Dead*).

The all-encompassing nature of Marvel's unique cinematic universe is a significant part of its success. Combining all the major characters in one joined-up world created a larger whole. As well as television series (several more were planned to follow *Agents of SHIELD*, including shows featuring Daredevil, Luke Cage, Jessica Jones, and Iron Fist), peripheral figures such as Coulson and Carter were developed further in a series of Marvel One-Shot (echoing comics terminology) shorts released on DVDs attached to the main feature films. Possible films in phase three included projects built around Nick Fury (a supporting character so far), the magical Dr Strange, or a new team consisting of Marvel's lesser-known B-level heroes. A sequel to *The Incredible Hulk*, featuring *The Avengers'* Mark Ruffalo, has been mooted, as have films featuring the Inhumans or Ms. Marvel. With a full slate of inter-connected superhero movies stretching into the next decade, Marvel look set to dominate the cinematic environment leaving DC Comics' efforts standing.

The return of the original superhero, Superman, to the big screen was a frustrating process that didn't produce the desired results with both *Superman Returns* (2006) and *Man of Steel* (2013) widely considered disappointing, but in very different ways. After *Superman IV: The Quest for Peace* (1987) brought the Christopher Reeve films to an ignominious end, the movie rights reverted to the Salkinds, who attempted to launch *Superman: The New Movie* in the early Nineties featuring Superman's death (predating DC's own 'Death of Superman') and resurrection within the bottle city of Kandor. The project didn't progress, but studio Warner Bros. would spend the following seventeen years and $50 million in development costs working on new Superman movie proposals, working through nine screenwriters, three directors, and seven different films.

The screen rights to Superman were returned to Warner

Bros. in 1993, who immediately settled on the Death of Superman storyline and handed the project to *Batman* producer Jon Peters. Actively developed between 1994 and 1996, *Superman Reborn* would match the Man of Steel against Doomsday, but had the added twist of Kal-El's 'life essence' being transferred to Lois Lane before he 'dies', resulting in her giving birth to a new Superman. Jonathan Lethem's screenplay was quickly discarded, replaced by Gregory Poirier's attempt. This time Brainiac was responsible for the creation of Doomsday, who kills Superman. Kal-El is resurrected but with weakened powers, so has to use a robotic suit while he recovers.

Filmmaker and comic book writer Kevin Smith was then brought on to the project, with a title change to *Superman Lives*. Producer Peters gave Smith a series of requirements and limitations, including that Superman should not wear the traditional outfit nor fly (two core attributes), which formed the basis for a twenty-minute comedy routine delivered by Smith as part of the DVD *An Evening With Kevin Smith* (2002). Smith worked through several script drafts, based around the death and resurrection of Superman, and suggested eventual Batman Ben Affleck as a possible Clark Kent/Superman. *Batman*'s Tim Burton was signed up to direct, and cast Nicolas Cage with a summer 1998 target release date to mark Superman's sixtieth anniversary. The film got as far as test photographs of Cage in a potential Superman costume before the plug was pulled, but only after Wesley Strick reworked the screenplay to feature Lex Luthor (possibly Kevin Spacey) who merges with Brainiac to produce 'Lexiac'. Deemed too expensive, Warner Bros. hired Dan Gilroy to rewrite the script to bring the budget down to $100 million. Tim Burton moved on to *Sleepy Hollow* (1999), and the Superman project was dead once more.

After the brief involvement of *Terminator 2* writer William Wisher, Paul Attanasio was paid a reported $1.7 million to write a fresh take on the death and rebirth of Superman in April 2001. Peters offered Will Smith the role, with *Charlie's Angels* director McG attached. Early the following year that project was also dropped in favour of a new script by *Mission: Impossible III's* J. J. Abrams. Ignoring the Death of Superman, *Superman: Flyby* was a complete reboot, starting the series from scratch. At the same time, the studio was developing a competing script with the working title of *Batman vs. Superman*, with Wolfgang Peterson attached to direct Andrew Kevin Walker's screenplay. This had a retired Bruce Wayne battling Superman, who he blames for the death of his fiancée at the hands of the Joker. Their conflict has been engineered by Lex Luthor, who the pair unite to defeat. Christian Bale and Josh Hartnett were lined up for the roles of Batman and Superman.

Warner Bros. executives could not decide between *Batman vs. Superman* and Abrams' *Superman: Flyby*, which told of a civil war on Krypton that precedes Kal-El's flight to Earth. Planned as a trilogy, director Brett Ratner was attached in September 2002. Christopher Reeve, a consultant on the project, suggested *Smallville's* Tom Welling should play Superman. Several actors auditioned, including *The Mummy's* Brendan Fraser and *Bones'* David Boreanaz, before McG was rehired. Both films were then dropped in favour of Bryan Singer's *Superman Returns*.

Singer started from scratch, but enthusiastically embraced the first two Richard Donner films, positioning his as a sequel to the Salkinds' *Superman II* (ignoring the following two movies). Abandoning comic book sources, Singer picked up the saga with Superman returning to Earth after a five-year absence during which he'd searched the remains of Krypton for survivors. He finds Lois Lane has a five-year-old child. The film's antagonist was Kevin Spacey's Lex Luthor. Singer cast the unknown Brandon Routh as Superman, citing his likeness to Reeve as key. Using archive footage, Marlon Brando was worked into the film as Jor-El. A $10 million opening 'Return to Krypton' sequence was completed but cut (later included on BluRay). Although too long at 154 minutes, the film grossed $391 million worldwide, but was regarded as a leaden over-reverential tribute to the *Superman* film from 1978.

Between *Superman Returns* and *Man of Steel*, DC (whose distribution is through Warner Bros.) released the two Nolan Batman sequels to great acclaim and box office takings, and the movie of *Watchmen*, as well as two dramatic superhero misfires: *Jonah Hex* (2010) and *Green Lantern* (2011). Starring Josh Brolin, Hex was a little-known occult Western character who made his debut in *All-Star Western* #10 (February–March 1972). Unsure of tone, violent and unfocused, *Jonah Hex* was the kind of film that gave comic book movies a bad name. *Green Lantern*, directed by James Bond veteran Martin Campbell (*GoldenEye*, *Casino Royale*), starred Ryan Reynolds as Hal Jordan in a convoluted narrative overloaded with special effects that grossed a poor $220 million worldwide, well under expectations for a would-be blockbuster intended to launch a franchise. A sequel seemed unlikely and undeserved.

While Marvel was dominating movie screens with their superhero-populated Avengers initiative, DC's characters (apart from Batman) were languishing in desperately poor movies that squandered decades of comic book mythology. The answer appeared to be another new Superman film, this time rebooting the franchise, retelling the origin story updated for the twenty-first century. Various DC writers, including Grant Morrison, Geoff Johns, Mark Waid, and Brad Meltzer, all pitched story ideas before the successful *Batman* team of Nolan and Goyer were brought in, although *Watchmen*'s Zack Snyder would direct. *Man of Steel* was the first step in DC's attempt to widen their filmic universe to match Marvel's. Henry Cavill won the role of Superman, after being considered for both the aborted *Flyby* and *Superman Returns*. A more extravagant Krypton opened the movie, before a fractured narrative chronicled Kal-El's life on Earth, from childhood through to adulthood where he is depicted as a wanderer occasionally helping people out. The arrival of General Zod (Michael Shannon), and his plan to terraform Earth into a new Krypton prompts Clark Kent to explore his Kryptonian heritage, don a revised version of the classic Superman suit, and triumph over evil. The relationship between Lois Lane and Clark Kent is revised, so that by the time he turns up at the *Daily Planet* at the end, she is fully aware of his dual nature. In the destruction of New York (as Metropolis) seen in *Man of Steel*, and equally in *The Avengers*, the post-9/11 superhero movies reached their apotheosis. Criticized for a lack of humour and for failing to capture the ethos of Superman seen in the comic books, *Man of Steel* brought in $663 million worldwide, matching Marvel's *Iron Man 2*, rather than *The Avengers* or *Iron Man 3*'s totals in the billions.

Man of Steel was laced with hints of what was to come, such as a satellite branded 'Wayne Enterprises'. At 2013's San Diego ComiCon, Warner Bros. announced the fast-tracked sequel would take a different tack. With Goyer writing, Snyder directing and Cavill leading the cast, the follow-up movie was represented with just a logo: a combination of the Superman 'S'-shield and the Batman icon. Inspired by the 1985 comic book *The Dark Knight Returns*, *Batman vs. Superman* (the working title) was announced for a 2015 release, with Ben Affleck cast as Batman in August 2013. The inevitable internet outcry that greeted his casting recalled that which welcomed Michael Keaton a quarter of a century previously. The film was expected to be one of DC's building blocks towards an eventual Justice League team movie to match Marvel's Avengers films.

15

THE NEVER-ENDING BATTLE OF THE SUPERHEROES

America, a civilization with a far shorter history than Europe, had to invent its own myths. Superheroes are the American equivalent of the ancient Greek or Roman mythologies. It is no coincidence that they first became popular between the Depression and the Second World War, when America was in need of heroes. They were further developed in times of social and political unrest, primarily in the Sixties and the Eighties. They have endured as mythical characters that rise above day-to-day concerns, delivering messages of what's right and just. These secular saviours are most popular at times of communal stress, so it is no surprise that superheroes had their own role to play in the Second World War and in the aftermath of 9/11. They are infinitely adaptable to fit the times, yet are communal creations with a variety of editors, writers and artists as their temporary caretakers. They provide moral examples and serve as an optimistic statement about the future, showing what humanity can strive to be. Their costumes are not subtle, and their battles are never-ending due to the serial forms – whether comics or movies – that showcase them.

For many, superheroes define comic books, yet for even more people superheroes define modern movies. They have given rise to two pop culture powerhouses in DC Comics and Marvel Comics, companies that are ensuring super-heroes have a future, whether in enhanced digital comics or on the big screen where every year sees new box office records demolished by superhero blockbusters. It was reck-oned that DC and Marvel have in excess of 5,000 unique characters each, so many have yet to be mined for movies, yet those movies still need the humble comic books to develop new characters and new stories for them to be inspired by. 'The comic book is an American invention,' said *The Dark Knight Returns*' Frank Miller. 'It was only a matter of time that cinema could develop to the point where it could start portraying that kind of fantasy.'

Rooted in myths and legends of the ancient past, the never-ending stories of modern superheroes serve the very same function in our technological society as they did in ancient times. Mankind continues to need these myths to make sense of his world. Like in those ancient stories, the lives of superheroes undergo infinite variations and retell-ings, but the individuals themselves always remain true to their core aspects no matter how many different talents rework them to better fit the times.

As Marvel Comics' chief creative officer Joe Quesada said: 'These stories we tell are very much akin to stories of ancient gods and the stories of the Great Hunt, or cave paintings, stories of great heroes. We need them now more than ever as they are representational of us and our hopes and dreams.' The first great modern American mythology was the Western, tales of the frontier and the expansion of civilization westwards. Superheroes have replaced Westerns as a new American myth for a new technological age, from the Thirties to the twenty-first century. Across the past seventy-five years, through comics and movies these uniquely American icons have become heroes for the whole world.

Stan Lee was ninety years old in 2012, so witnessed *The Avengers* triumph at the box office after he'd spent many years striving to launch the Marvel cinematic universe. He was one of the last connections back to the beginning of comic book superheroes almost three-quarters of a century earlier, to Siegel and Shuster who'd started it all. He'd witnessed the rise of the superheroes, from Superman, Batman and Wonder Woman to his own Spider-Man, Iron Man, the X-Men, and the Avengers, from comic book page to screen dominance. At heart he was still at one with that boy who in April 1938 picked up *Action Comics* #1 off the news-stand, little knowing the incredible future that awaited the superhero genre.

ACKNOWLEDGEMENTS

Top of the list to thank is my own personal Wonder Woman, Brigid Cherry, who put up with my months of superhero monomania. Next, Paul Simpson, who read over the manuscript several times, offered suggestions and pointed out when I'd wandered off topic. Finally, James Kerr, who applied his in-depth comic book knowledge to the text and provided some very useful research material. Thanks also to everyone at Constable & Robinson, including Duncan Proudfoot, Clive Hebard and David Lloyd.

BIBLIOGRAPHY

Will Brooker. *Batman Unmasked: Analyzing a Cultural Icon* (New York: Continuum, 2000).

Will Brooker. *Hunting the Dark Knight: Twenty-First Century Batman* (London: I.B. Tauris, 2012).

Peter Coogan. *Superhero: The Secret Origin of a Genre* (Austin: Monkey Bran Books, 2006).

Les Daniels. *Batman: The Complete History* (San Francisco: Chronicle Books, 1999).

Les Daniels. *DC Comics: Sixty Years of the World's Favorite Comic Book Heroes* (London: Virgin Books, 1995).

Les Daniels. *Marvel: Five Fabulous Decades of the World's Greatest Comics* (New York: Harry J. Abrams, Inc., 1991).

Les Daniels. *Superman: The Complete History* (San Francisco: Chronicle Books, 1998).

Les Daniels. *Wonder Woman: The Complete History* (San Francisco: Chronicle Books, 2000).

Charles Hatfield, Jeet Heer, Kent Worcester (Eds). *The Superhero Reader* (Jackson: University Press of Mississippi, 2013).

Tom De Haven. *Our Hero: Superman on Earth* (New Haven: Yale University Press, 2010).

Steve Duin and Mike Richardson. *Comics: Between the Panels* (Milwaukee: Dark Horse Comics, 1998).

Randy Duncan and Matthew J. Smith. *The Power of Comics: History, Form and Culture* (New York: Continuum, 2009).

Jean-Paul Gabilliet. *Of Comics and Men: A Cultural History of American Comic Books* (Jackson: University Press of Mississippi, 2010).

Laura Gilbert, Hannah Dolin (Eds). *DC Comics: Year by Year – A Visual Chronicle* (London: Dorling Kindersley, 2010).

Ian Gordon, Mark Jancovich, Matthew P. McAllister (Eds). *Film and Comic Books* (Jackson: University Press of Mississippi, 2007).

David Hajdu. *The Ten Cent Plague: The Great Comic Book Scare and How it Changed America* (New York: Farrar, Straus and Giroux, 2008).

Sean Howe. *Marvel Comics: The Untold Story* (New York: HarperCollins, 2012).

Gerard Jones. *Men of Tomorrow: Geeks, Gangsters, and the Birth of the Comic Book* (London: William Heinemann, 2005).

Paul Levitz. *75 Years of DC Comics: The Art of Modern Mythmaking* (Los Angeles: Taschen, 2013).

Lawrence Maslon and Michael Kantor. *Superheroes: Capes, Cowls, and the Creation of Comic Book Culture* (New York: Crown Archetype/Random House, 2013).

Grant Morrison. *Supergods* (New York: Siegel & Grau, 2012).

Roberta E. Pearson and William Uricchio (Eds). *The Many Lives of the Batman* (New York: Routledge, 1991).

Jordan Raphael and Tom Spurgeon. *Stan Lee and the Rise and Fall of the American Comic Book* (Chicago: Chicago Review Press, 2003).

Dan Raviv. *Comic Wars: Marvel's Battle for Survival* (New York: Heroes Books, 2004).

David Reynolds. *Superheroes: An Analysis of Popular Culture's Modern Myths* (Newfoundland: Memorial University of Newfoundland, 2011).

Brad Ricca. *Super-Boys: The Amazing Adventures of Jerry Siegel and Joe Shuster – the Creators of Superman* (New York: St Martin's Press, 2013).

Ronin Ro. *Tales to Astonish: Jack Kirby, Stan Lee, and the American Comic Book Revolution* (New York: Bloomsbury, 2004).

Jake Rossen. *Superman vs. Hollywood: How Fiendish Producers, devious Directors and Warring Writers Grounded an American Icon* (Chicago: Chicago Review Press, 2008).

Steve Saffel. *Spider-Man: The Icon* (London: Titan Books, 2007).

Catherine Saunders, Heather Scott, Julia March, Alastair Dougall (Eds). *Marvel Chronicle: A Year by Year History* (London: Dorling Kindersley, 2008).

Michael Schumacher. *Will Eisner: A Dreamer's Life in Comics* (New York: Bloomsbury, 2010).

Bruce Scivally. *Billion Dollar Batman: A History of the Caped Crusader on Film, Radio and Television, From 10¢ Comic Book to Global Icon* (Illinois: Bruce Scivally, 2011).

Jim Steranko. *History of Comics (2 Vols)*, (Reading PA: Supergraphics, 1970–72).

Larry Tye. *Superman: The High-Flying History of America's Most Enduring Hero* (New York: Random House, 2012).

Glen Weldon. *Superman: The Unauthorized Biography* (New Jersey: John Wiley & Sons, 2013).

Bradford W. Wright. *Comic Book Nation: The Transformation of Youth Culture in America* (Baltimore: Johns Hopkins University Press, 2001).

In addition to works cited in the text (individual issues of DC and Marvel comic books and others), back issues of Roy Thomas's prozine *Alter Ego* were also useful.

INDEX